Developing Backbone.js Applications

Addy Osmani

O'REILLY®

Beijing · Cambridge · Farnham · Köln · Sebastopol · Tokyo

Developing Backbone.js Applications

by Addy Osmani

Published by O'Reilly Media, Inc., 1005 Gravenstein Highway North, Sebastopol, CA 95472.

O'Reilly books may be purchased for educational, business, or sales promotional use. Online editions are also available for most titles (*http://my.safaribooksonline.com*). For more information, contact our corporate/institutional sales department: 800-998-9938 or *corporate@oreilly.com*.

Editor: Mary Treseler	**Indexer:** Ellen Troutman Zaig
Production Editor: Melanie Yarbrough	**Cover Designer:** Randy Comer
Copyeditor: Rachel Monaghan	**Interior Designer:** David Futato
Proofreader: Rachel Leach	**Illustrator:** Rebecca Demarest

May 2013:   First Edition

Revision History for the First Edition:

2013-05-08:   First release

See *http://oreilly.com/catalog/errata.csp?isbn=9781449328252* for release details.

ISBN: 978-1-449-32825-2

[LSI]

Table of Contents

Preface

Not so long ago, *data-rich web application* was an oxymoron. Today, these applications are everywhere, and you need to know how to build them.

Traditionally, web applications left the heavy lifting of data to servers that pushed HTML to the browser in complete page loads. The use of client-side JavaScript was limited to improving the user experience. Now this relationship has been inverted—client applications pull raw data from the server and render it into the browser when and where it is needed.

Think of the Ajax shopping cart, which doesn't require a refresh on the page when you add an item to your basket. Initially, jQuery was the go-to library for this paradigm. Its nature was to make Ajax requests, then update text on the page and so on. However, this pattern with jQuery revealed that we have implicit model data on the client side.

The rise of arbitrary code on the client side that can talk to the server however it sees fit has meant an increase in client-side complexity. Good architecture on the client side has gone from an afterthought to essential—you can't just hack together some jQuery code and expect it to scale as your application grows. Most likely, you would end up with a nightmarish tangle of UI callbacks entwined with business logic, destined to be discarded by the poor soul who inherits your code.

Thankfully, there are a growing number of JavaScript libraries that can help improve the structure and maintainability of your code, making it easier for you to build ambitious interfaces without a great deal of effort. Backbone.js (*http://document cloud.github.com/backbone/*) has quickly become one of the most popular open source solutions to these issues, and in this book I will walk you through it in depth.

We'll begin with the fundamentals, work our way through the exercises, and learn how to build an application that is both cleanly organized and maintainable. If you are a developer looking to write code that can be more easily read, structured, and extended, this guide can help you.

Improving developer education is important to me, which is why this book is released under a Creative Commons Attribution-NonCommercial-ShareAlike 3.0 Unported license (*http://creativecommons.org/licenses/by-nc-sa/3.0/*). This means you can purchase or grab a copy of the book for free (*http://addyosmani.github.com/backbone-fundamentals/*) or help to further improve it (*https://github.com/addyosmani/backbone-fundamentals/*). Corrections to existing material are always welcome, and I hope that together we can provide the community with an up-to-date resource that is of help.

My extended thanks go out to Jeremy Ashkenas (*https://github.com/jashkenas*) and DocumentCloud (*https://www.documentcloud.org*) for creating Backbone.js and several members of the community (*https://github.com/addyosmani/backbone-fundamentals/contributors*) for their assistance making this project far better than I could have imagined.

Target Audience

This book is targeted at novice to intermediate developers wishing to learn how to better structure their client-side code. An understanding of JavaScript fundamentals is required to get the most out of it; however, I have tried to provide a basic description of these concepts where possible.

Credits

None of this work would have been possible without the time and effort invested by the other developers and authors in the community who helped contribute to it. I would like to extend my thanks to:

- Marc Friedman (*https://github.com/dcmaf*)
- Derick Bailey (*https://github.com/derickbailey*)
- Ryan Eastridge (*https://github.com/eastridge*)
- Jack Franklin (*https://github.com/jackfranklin*)

- David Amend (*https://github.com/raDiesle*)
- Mike Ball (*https://github.com/mdb*)
- Uģis Ozols (*https://github.com/ugisozols*)
- Björn Ekengren (*https://github.com/Ekengren*)

as well as our other excellent contributors (*http://bit.ly/11KCLYp*) who made this project possible.

Reading

I assume your level of knowledge about JavaScript goes beyond the basics; thus, certain topics, such as object literals, are skipped. If you need to learn more about the language, I am happy to suggest:

- *Eloquent JavaScript*
- *JavaScript: The Definitive Guide* by David Flanagan (O'Reilly)
- *Effective JavaScript* by David Herman (Pearson)
- *JavaScript: The Good Parts* by Douglas Crockford (O'Reilly)
- *Object-Oriented JavaScript* by Stoyan Stefanov (Packt Publishing)

Conventions Used in This Book

The following typographical conventions are used in this book:

Italic
> Indicates new terms, URLs, email addresses, filenames, and file extensions.

`Constant width`
> Used for program listings, as well as within paragraphs to refer to program elements such as variable or function names, databases, data types, environment variables, statements, and keywords.

`Constant width bold`
> Shows commands or other text that should be typed literally by the user.

`Constant width italic`
> Shows text that should be replaced with user-supplied values or by values determined by context.

This icon signifies a tip, suggestion, or general note.

 This icon indicates a warning or caution.

Using Code Examples

This book is here to help you get your job done. In general, if this book includes code examples, you may use the code in your programs and documentation. You do not need to contact us for permission unless you're reproducing a significant portion of the code. For example, writing a program that uses several chunks of code from this book does not require permission. Selling or distributing a CD-ROM of examples from O'Reilly books does require permission. Answering a question by citing this book and quoting example code does not require permission. Incorporating a significant amount of example code from this book into your product's documentation does require permission.

We appreciate, but do not require, attribution. An attribution usually includes the title, author, publisher, and ISBN. For example: "*Developing Backbone.js Applications* by Adnan Osmani (O'Reilly). Copyright 2013 Addy Osmani, 978-1-449-32825-2."

If you feel your use of code examples falls outside fair use or the permission given above, feel free to contact us at *permissions@oreilly.com*.

Safari® Books Online

 Safari Books Online (*www.safaribooksonline.com*) is an on-demand digital library that delivers expert content in both book and video form from the world's leading authors in technology and business.

Technology professionals, software developers, web designers, and business and creative professionals use Safari Books Online as their primary resource for research, problem solving, learning, and certification training.

Safari Books Online offers a range of product mixes and pricing programs for organizations, government agencies, and individuals. Subscribers have access to thousands of books, training videos, and prepublication manuscripts in one fully searchable database from publishers like O'Reilly Media, Prentice Hall Professional, Addison-Wesley Professional, Microsoft Press, Sams, Que, Peachpit Press, Focal Press, Cisco Press, John Wiley & Sons, Syngress, Morgan Kaufmann, IBM Redbooks, Packt, Adobe Press, FT Press, Apress, Manning, New Riders, McGraw-Hill, Jones & Bartlett, Course

Technology, and dozens more. For more information about Safari Books Online, please visit us online.

How to Contact Us

Please address comments and questions concerning this book to the publisher:

> O'Reilly Media, Inc.
> 1005 Gravenstein Highway North
> Sebastopol, CA 95472
> 800-998-9938 (in the United States or Canada)
> 707-829-0515 (international or local)
> 707-829-0104 (fax)

We have a web page for this book, where we list errata, examples, and any additional information. You can access this page at *http://oreil.ly/dev_backbone_js_apps*.

To comment or ask technical questions about this book, send email to *bookquestions@oreilly.com*.

For more information about our books, courses, conferences, and news, see our website at *http://www.oreilly.com*.

Find us on Facebook: *http://facebook.com/oreilly*

Follow us on Twitter: *http://twitter.com/oreillymedia*

Watch us on YouTube: *http://www.youtube.com/oreillymedia*

Acknowledgments

I am indebted to the technical reviewers whose fantastic work helped improve this book. Their knowledge, energy, and passion have helped shape it into a better learning resource, and they continue to serve as a source of inspiration. Thanks go out to:

- Derick and Marc (once again)
- Jeremy Ashkenas (*https://github.com/jashkenas*)
- Samuel Clay (*https://github.com/samuelclay*)
- Mat Scales (*http://github.com/wibblymat*)
- Alex Graul (*https://github.com/alexgraul*)
- Dusan Gledovic (*https://github.com/g6scheme*)
- Sindre Sorhus (*https://github.com/sindresorhus*)

I would also like to thank my loving family for their patience and support while I worked on this book, as well as my brilliant editor, Mary Treseler.

CHAPTER 1

Introduction

Frank Lloyd Wright once said, "You can't make an architect. But you can open the doors and windows toward the light as you see it." In this book, I hope to shed some light on how to improve the structure of your web applications, opening doors to what will hopefully be more maintainable, readable applications in your future.

The goal of all architecture is to build something well—in our case, to craft code that is enduring and delights both us and the developers who will maintain our code long after we are gone. We all want our architecture to be simple, yet beautiful.

Modern JavaScript frameworks and libraries can bring structure and organization to your projects, establishing a maintainable foundation right from the start. They build on the trials and tribulations of developers who have had to work around callback chaos similar to that which you are facing now or may face in the near future.

When you are developing applications using just jQuery, the missing piece is a way to structure and organize your code. It's very easy to create a JavaScript app that ends up a tangled mess of jQuery selectors and callbacks, all desperately trying to keep data in sync between the HTML for your UI, the logic in your JavaScript, and calls to your API for data.

Without something to help tame the mess, you're likely to string together a set of independent plug-ins and libraries to make up the functionality or build everything from scratch and have to maintain it yourself. Backbone solves this problem for you, providing a way to cleanly organize code and separating responsibilities into recognizable pieces that are easy to maintain.

In *Developing Backbone.js Applications*, I and several other experienced authors will show you how to improve your web application structure using version 1.0 of the popular JavaScript library Backbone.js.

What Is MVC?

A number of modern JavaScript frameworks provide developers an easy path to organizing their code using variations of a pattern known as MVC (Model-View-Controller). MVC separates the concerns in an application into three parts:

- Models represent the domain-specific knowledge and data in an application. Think of this as being a type of data you can model—like a user, photo, or todo note. Models can notify observers when their state changes.

- Views typically constitute the user interface in an application (such as markup and templates), but don't have to. They observe models, but don't directly communicate with them.

- Controllers handle input (clicks or user actions) and update models.

Thus, in an MVC application, user input is acted upon by controllers, which update models. Views observe models and update the user interface when changes occur.

JavaScript MVC frameworks don't always strictly follow this pattern, however. Some solutions (including Backbone.js) merge the responsibility of the controller into the view, while other approaches insert additional components into the mix.

For this reason we refer to such frameworks as following the MV* pattern—that is, you're likely to have a model and a view, but a distinct controller might not be present and other components may come into play.

What Is Backbone.js?

Backbone.js (Figure 1-1) is a lightweight JavaScript library that adds structure to your client-side code. It makes it easy to manage and decouple concerns in your application, leaving you with code that is more maintainable in the long term.

Developers commonly use libraries like Backbone.js to create *single-page applications* (SPAs). SPAs are web applications that load into the browser and then react to data changes on the client side without requiring complete page refreshes from the server.

Backbone is mature and popular, sporting both a vibrant developer community and a wealth of available plug-ins and extensions that build upon it. It has been used to create nontrivial applications by companies such as Disqus, Walmart, SoundCloud, and LinkedIn.

Figure 1-1. The Backbone.js home page

Backbone focuses on giving you helpful methods for querying and manipulating your data rather than reinventing the JavaScript object model. It's a library, rather than a framework, that scales well and plays well with others, from embedded widgets to large-scale applications.

And because Backbone is small, there is also less your users have to download on mobile or slower connections. The entire Backbone source can be read and understood in just a few hours.

When Do I Need a JavaScript MVC Framework?

When building a single-page application using JavaScript, whether it involves a complex user interface or simply trying to reduce the number of HTTP requests required for new views, you will likely find yourself inventing many of the pieces that make up an MV* framework.

At the outset, it isn't terribly difficult to write your own application framework that offers some opinionated way to avoid spaghetti code; however, to say that it is equally as trivial to write something as robust as Backbone would be a grossly incorrect assumption.

There's a lot more that goes into structuring an application than tying together a DOM manipulation library, templating, and routing. Mature MV* frameworks typically include not only the pieces you would find yourself writing, but also solutions to problems you'll find yourself running into down the road. This is a time-saver whose value you shouldn't underestimate.

So, where will you likely need an MV* framework and where won't you?

If you're writing an application where much of the heavy lifting for view rendering and data manipulation will be occurring in the browser, you may find a JavaScript MV* framework useful. Examples of applications that fall into this category are Gmail, News-Blur, and the LinkedIn mobile app.

These types of applications typically download a single payload containing all the scripts, stylesheets, and markup users need for common tasks and then perform a lot of additional behavior in the background. For instance, it's trivial to switch between reading an email or document to writing one without sending a new page request to the server.

If, however, you're building an application that still relies on the server for most of the heavy lifting of page/view rendering and you're just using a little JavaScript or jQuery to make things more interactive, an MV* framework may be overkill. There certainly are complex web applications where the partial rendering of views can be coupled with a single-page application effectively, but for everything else, you may be better off sticking to a simpler setup.

Maturity in software (framework) development isn't simply about how long a framework has been around; it's about how solid the framework is and, more importantly, how well it's evolved to fill its role. Has it become more effective at solving common problems? Does it continue to improve as developers build larger and more complex applications with it?

Why Consider Backbone.js?

Backbone provides a minimal set of data-structuring (models, collections) and user interface (views, URLs) primitives that are helpful when you're building dynamic applications using JavaScript. It's not opinionated, meaning you have the freedom and flexibility to build the best experience for your web application however you see fit. You can either use the prescribed architecture it offers out of the box or extend it to meet your requirements.

The library doesn't focus on widgets or replacing the way you structure objects—it just supplies you with utilities for manipulating and querying data in your application. It also doesn't prescribe a specific template engine; while you are free to use the micro-templating offered by Underscore.js (one of its dependencies), views can bind to HTML constructed via your templating solution of choice.

When we look at the large number of applications (*http://backbonejs.org/#examples*) built with Backbone, it's clear that it scales well. Backbone also works quite well with other libraries, meaning you can embed Backbone widgets in an application written with AngularJS, use it with TypeScript, or just use an individual class (like models) as a data backer for simpler apps.

There are no performance drawbacks to using Backbone to structure your application. It avoids run loops, two-way binding, and constant polling of your data structures for updates, and it tries to keep things simple where possible. That said, should you wish to go against the grain, you can, of course, implement such things on top of it. Backbone won't stop you.

With a vibrant community of plug-in and extension authors, it's likely that if you're looking to achieve some behavior Backbone is lacking, there's a complementary project that works well with it. In addition, Backbone offers literate documentation of its source code, allowing anyone an opportunity to easily understand what is going on behind the scenes.

Having been refined over two and a half years of development, Backbone is a mature library that will continue to offer a minimalist solution for building better web applications. I regularly use it and hope that you find it as useful an addition to your toolbelt as I have.

Setting Expectations

The goal of this book is to create an authoritative and centralized repository of information that can help those developing real-world apps with Backbone. If you come across a section or topic that you think could be improved or expanded, please feel free to submit an issue (or better yet, a pull-request) on the book's GitHub site (*https:// github.com/addyosmani/backbone-fundamentals*). It won't take long, and you'll be helping other developers avoid the problems you ran into.

Topics will include MVC theory and how to build applications using Backbone's models, views, collections, and routers. I'll also be taking you through advanced topics like modular development with Backbone.js and AMD (via RequireJS), solutions to common problems like nested views, how to solve routing problems with Backbone and jQuery Mobile, and much more.

Here is a peek at what you will be learning in each chapter:

Chapter 2, *Fundamentals*
> Traces the history of the MVC design pattern and introduces how it is implemented by Backbone.js and other JavaScript frameworks.

Chapter 3, *Backbone Basics*
> Covers the major features of Backbone.js and the technologies and techniques you will need to know in order to use it effectively.

Chapter 4, *Exercise 1: Todos—Your First Backbone.js App*
    Takes you step by step through development of a simple client-side todo list application.

Chapter 5, *Exercise 2: Book Library—Your First RESTful Backbone.js App*
    Walks you through development of a book library application that persists its model to a server using a REST API.

Chapter 6, *Backbone Extensions*
    Describes Backbone.Marionette and Thorax, two extension frameworks that add features to Backbone.js that are useful for developing large-scale applications.

Chapter 7, *Common Problems and Solutions*
    Reviews common issues you may encounter when using Backbone.js and ways to address them.

Chapter 8, *Modular Development*
    Looks at how AMD modules and RequireJS can be used to modularize your code.

Chapter 9, *Exercise 3: Your First Modular Backbone and RequireJS App*
    Takes you through rewriting the app created in Exercise 1 to be more modular, with the help of RequireJS.

Chapter 10, *Paginating Backbone.js Requests and Collections*
    Walks through how to use the Backbone.Paginator plug-in to paginate data for your collections.

Chapter 11, *Backbone Boilerplate and Grunt-BBB*
    Introduces powerful tools you can use to bootstrap a new Backbone.js application with boilerplate code.

Chapter 12, *Backbone and jQuery Mobile*
    Addresses the issues that arise when you are using Backbone with jQuery Mobile.

Chapter 13, *Jasmine*
    Covers how to unit-test Backbone code using the Jasmine test framework.

Chapter 14, *QUnit*
    Discusses how to use the QUnit for unit testing.

Chapter 15, *SinonJS*
    Discusses how to use SinonJS to unit-text your Backbone apps.

Appendix B
    Provides references to additional Backbone-related resources.

Chapter 16, *Conclusions*

Wraps up our tour through the world of Backbone.js development.

Appendix A

Returns to our design pattern discussion by contrasting MVC with the Model-View-Presenter (MVP) pattern and examines how Backbone.js relates to both. Also includes a walkthrough of writing a Backbone-like library from scratch and covers other topics.

CHAPTER 2

Fundamentals

Design patterns are proven solutions to common development problems that can help us improve the organization and structure of our applications. By using patterns, we benefit from the collective experience of skilled developers who have repeatedly solved similar problems.

Historically, developers creating desktop and server-class applications have had a wealth of design patterns available for them to lean on, but it's only been in the last few years that such patterns have been applied to client-side development.

In this chapter, we're going to explore the evolution of the Model-View-Controller (MVC) design pattern and get our first look at how Backbone.js allows us to apply this pattern to client-side development.

MVC

MVC is an architectural design pattern that encourages improved application organization through a separation of concerns. It enforces the isolation of business data (models) from user interfaces (views), with a third component (controllers) traditionally managing logic, user input, and coordination of models and views. The pattern was originally designed by Trygve Reenskaug (*http://en.wikipedia.org/wiki/Trygve_Reen skaug*) while he was working on Smalltalk-80 (1979), where it was initially called Model-View-Controller-Editor. MVC was described in depth in the Gang of Four's 1994 book *Design Patterns: Elements of Reusable Object-Oriented Software* (*http://amzn.com/ 0201633612*), which played a role in popularizing its use.

Smalltalk-80 MVC

It's important to understand the issues that the original MVC pattern was aiming to solve, as it has changed quite heavily since the days of its origin. Back in the 70s, graphical user interfaces were few and far between. An approach known as *separated presentation (http://martinfowler.com/eaaDev/SeparatedPresentation.html)* began to be used to make a clear division between domain objects, which modeled concepts in the real world (such as a photo, a person), and the presentation objects that were rendered to the user's screen.

The Smalltalk-80 implementation of MVC took this concept further and had the objective of separating out the application logic from the user interface. The idea was that decoupling these parts of the application would also allow the reuse of models for other interfaces in the application. There are some interesting points worth noting about Smalltalk-80's MVC architecture:

- A domain element was known as a model and was ignorant of the user interface (views and controllers).
- Presentation was taken care of by the view and the controller, but there wasn't just a single view and controller—a view-controller pair was required for each element being displayed on the screen, so there was no true separation between them.
- The controller's role in this pair was handling user input (such as keypresses and click events) and doing something sensible with them.
- The Observer pattern was used to update the view whenever the model changed.

Developers are sometimes surprised when they learn that the Observer pattern (nowadays commonly implemented as a publish/subscribe system) was included as a part of MVC's architecture decades ago. In Smalltalk-80's MVC, the view and controller both observe the model: anytime the model changes, the views react. A simple example of this is an application backed by stock market data: for the application to show real-time information, any change to the data in its model should result in the view being refreshed instantly.

Martin Fowler has done an excellent job of writing about MVC's origins (*http://martin fowler.com/eaaDev/uiArchs.html*), so if you are interested in further historical information about Smalltalk-80's MVC, I recommend reading his work.

MVC Applied to the Web

The Web relies heavily on the HTTP protocol, which is stateless. This means that there is not a constantly open connection between the browser and server; each request instantiates a new communication channel between the two. Once the request initiator (such as a browser) gets a response, the connection is closed. This fact creates a completely different context when compared to the one of the operating systems on which many of the original MVC ideas were developed. The MVC implementation has to conform to the web context.

An example of a server-side web application framework that tries to apply MVC to the web context is Ruby on Rails (*http://guides.rubyonrails.org/*), shown in Figure 2-1.

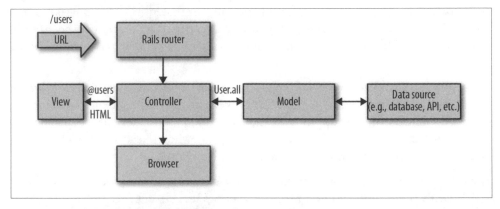

Figure 2-1. The Ruby on Rails framework

At its core are the three MVC components we would expect: the Model-View-Controller architecture. In Rails:

- Models represent the data in an application and are typically used to manage rules for interacting with a specific database table. You generally have one table corresponding to one model with much of your application's business logic living within these models.

- Views represent your user interface, often taking the form of HTML that will be sent down to the browser. They're used to present application data to anything making requests from your application.

- Controllers offer the glue between models and views. Their responsibility is to process requests from the browser, ask your models for data, and then supply this data to views so that they may be presented to the browser.

Although there's a clear separation of concerns that is MVC-like in Rails, it is actually using a different pattern called Model2 (*http://en.wikipedia.org/wiki/Model2*). Justifications for this include that Rails does not notify views from the model, and controllers just pass model data directly to the view.

That said, even for the server-side workflow of receiving a request from a URL, baking out an HTML page as a response and separating your business logic from your interface has many benefits. In the same way that keeping your UI cleanly separate from your database records is useful in server-side frameworks, it's equally useful to keep your UI cleanly separated from your data models in JavaScript (as we will read more about shortly).

Other server-side implementations of MVC, such as the PHP Zend (*http://zend.com*) framework, also implement the Front Controller (*http://en.wikipedia.org/wiki/Front_Controller_pattern*) design pattern. This pattern layers an MVC stack behind a single point of entry. This single point of entry means that all HTTP requests (for example, `http://www.example.com`, `http://www.example.com/whichever-page/`, and so on) are routed by the server's configuration to the same handler, independent of the URI.

When the Front Controller receives an HTTP request, it analyzes it and decides which class (controller) and method (action) to invoke. The selected controller action takes over and interacts with the appropriate model to fulfill the request. The controller receives data back from the model, loads an appropriate view, injects the model data into it, and returns the response to the browser.

For example, let's say we have our blog on `www.example.com` and we want to edit an article (with `id=43`) and request `http://www.example.com/article/edit/43`.

On the server side, the Front Controller would analyze the URL and invoke the article controller (corresponding to the */article/* part of the URI) and its edit action (corresponding to the */edit/* part of the URI). Within the action there would be a call to, let's say, the articles model and its `Articles::getEntry(43)` method (43 corresponding to the */43* at the end of the URI). This would return the blog article data from the database for edit. The article controller would then load the (*article/edit*) view, which would include logic for injecting the article's data into a form suitable for editing its content, title, and other (meta) data. Finally, the resulting HTML response would be returned to the browser.

As you can imagine, a similar flow is necessary with POST requests after we click a save button in a form. The POST action URI would look like */article/save/43*. The request would go through the same controller, but this time the save action would be invoked (due to the */save/* URI chunk), the articles model would save the edited article to the database with `Articles::saveEntry(43)`, and the browser would be redirected to the */article/edit/43* URI for further editing.

Finally, if the user requested `http://www.example.com/` the Front Controller would invoke the default controller and action (for example, the index controller and its index action). Within index action there would be a call to the articles model and its `Articles::getLastEntries(10)` method, which would return the last 10 blog posts. The controller would load the blog/index view, which would have basic logic for listing the blog posts.

Figure 2-2 shows this typical HTTP request/response lifecycle for server-side MVC.

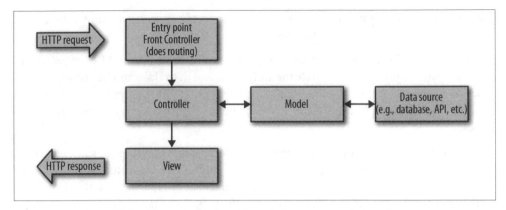

Figure 2-2. The HTTP request/response lifecycle for server-side MVC

The server receives an HTTP request and routes it through a single entry point. At that entry point, the Front Controller analyzes the request and invokes an action of the appropriate controller. This process is called *routing*. The action model is asked to return and/or save submitted data. The model communicates with the data source (for example, database or API). Once the model completes its work it returns data to the controller, which then loads the appropriate view. The view executes presentation logic (loops through articles and prints titles, content, etc.) using the supplied data. In the end, an HTTP response is returned to the browser.

Client-Side MVC and Single-Page Apps

Several studies (*http://radar.oreilly.com/2009/07/velocity-making-your-site-fast.html*) have confirmed that improvements to latency can have a positive impact on the usage and user engagement of sites and apps. This is at odds with the traditional approach to web app development, which is very server-centric, requiring a complete page reload to move from one page to the next. Even with heavy caching in place, the browser still has to parse the CSS, JavaScript, and HTML and render the interface to the screen.

In addition to resulting in a great deal of duplicated content being served back to the user, this approach affects both latency and the general responsiveness of the user experience. A trend to improve perceived latency in the past few years has been to move toward building single-page applications (SPAs)—apps that after an initial page load, are able to handle subsequent navigations and requests for data without the need for a complete reload.

When a user navigates to a new view, the application requests additional content required for the view using an XHR (XMLHttpRequest), typically communicating with a server-side REST API or endpoint. Ajax, short for Asynchronous JavaScript and XML) (*https://en.wikipedia.org/wiki/Ajax_(programming)*), makes communication with the server asynchronous so that data is transferred and processed in the background, allowing the user to work on other parts of a page without interaction. This improves usability and responsiveness.

SPAs can also take advantage of browser features like the History API (*http://divein tohtml5.info/history.html*) to update the address shown in the location bar when moving from one view to another. These URLs also make it possible for users to bookmark and share a particular application state, without the need to navigate to completely new pages.

The typical SPA consists of smaller pieces of interface representing logical entities, all of which have their own UI, business logic, and data. A good example is a basket in a shopping web application that can have items added to it. This basket might be presented to the user in a box in the top-right corner of the page (see Figure 2-3).

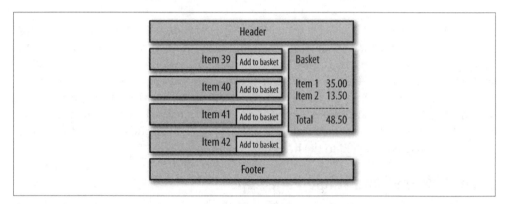

Figure 2-3. A shopping basket forming a region of a single-page application

The basket and its data are presented in HTML. The data and its associated View in HTML change over time. There was a time when we used jQuery (or a similar DOM manipulation library) and a bunch of Ajax calls and callbacks to keep the two in sync. That often produced code that was not well structured or easy to maintain. Bugs were frequent and perhaps even unavoidable.

The need for fast, complex, and responsive Ajax-powered web applications demands replication of a lot of this logic on the client side, dramatically increasing the size and complexity of the code residing there. Eventually this has brought us to the point where we need MVC (or a similar architecture) implemented on the client side to better structure the code and make it easier to maintain and further extend during the application lifecycle.

Through evolution and trial and error, JavaScript developers have harnessed the power of the traditional MVC pattern, leading to the development of several MVC-inspired JavaScript frameworks, such as Backbone.js.

Client-Side MVC: Backbone Style

Let's take our first look at how Backbone.js brings the benefits of MVC to client-side development using a todo application as our example. We will build on this example in the coming chapters when we explore Backbone's features, but for now we will just focus on the core components' relationships to MVC.

Our example will need a div element to which we can attach a list of todos. It will also need an HTML template containing a placeholder for a todo item title and a completion checkbox that can be instantiated for todo item instances. These are provided by the following HTML:

```html
<!doctype html>
<html lang="en">
<head>
  <meta charset="utf-8">
  <title></title>
  <meta name="description" content="">
</head>
<body>
  <div id="todo">
  </div>
  <script type="text/template" id="item-template">
    <div>
      <input id="todo_complete" type="checkbox" <%= completed ?
       'checked="checked"' : '' %>>
      <%- title %>
    </div>
  </script>
  <script src="jquery.js"></script>
  <script src="underscore.js"></script>
  <script src="backbone.js"></script>
  <script src="demo.js"></script>
</body>
</html>
```

In our Todo application (*demo.js*), Backbone model instances are used to hold the data for each todo item:

```javascript
// Define a Todo model
var Todo = Backbone.Model.extend({
  // Default todo attribute values
  defaults: {
    title: '',
    completed: false
  }
});

// Instantiate the Todo model with a title, allowing completed attribute
// to default to false
var myTodo = new Todo({
```

```
      title: 'Check attributes property of the logged models in the console.'
  });
```

Our Todo model extends Backbone.Model and simply defines default values for two data attributes. As you will discover in the upcoming chapters, Backbone models provide many more features, but this simple model illustrates that first and foremost a model is a data container.

Each todo instance will be rendered on the page by a TodoView:

```
  var TodoView = Backbone.View.extend({

    tagName:  'li',

    // Cache the template function for a single item.
    todoTpl: _.template( $('#item-template').html() ),

    events: {
      'dblclick label': 'edit',
      'keypress .edit': 'updateOnEnter',
      'blur .edit':    'close'
    },

    // Called when the view is first created
    initialize: function () {
      this.$el = $('#todo');
      // Later we'll look at:
      // this.listenTo(someCollection, 'all', this.render);
      // but you can actually run this example right now by
      // calling TodoView.render();
    },

    // Rerender the titles of the todo item.
    render: function() {
      this.$el.html( this.todoTpl( this.model.toJSON() ) );
      // $el here is a reference to the jQuery element
      // associated with the view, todoTpl is a reference
      // to an Underscore template and toJSON() returns an
      // object containing the model's attributes
      // Altogether, the statement is replacing the HTML of
      // a DOM element with the result of instantiating a
      // template with the model's attributes.
      this.input = this.$('.edit');
      return this;
    },

    edit: function() {
      // executed when todo label is double-clicked
    },

    close: function() {
      // executed when todo loses focus
```

```
  },

  updateOnEnter: function( e ) {
    // executed on each keypress when in todo edit mode,
    // but we'll wait for enter to get in action
  }
});

// create a view for a todo
var todoView = new TodoView({model: myTodo});
```

We define TodoView by extending Backbone.View and instantiate it with an associated model. In our example, the render() method uses a template to construct the HTML for the todo item, which is placed inside a li element. Each call to render() will replace the content of the li element using the current model data. Thus, a view instance renders the content of a DOM element using the attributes of an associated model. Later we will see how a view can bind its render() method to model change events, causing the view to rerender whenever the model changes.

So far, we have seen that Backbone.Model implements the model aspect of MVC and Backbone.View implements the view. However, as we noted earlier, Backbone departs from traditional MVC when it comes to controllers—there is no Backbone.Controller!

Instead, the controller responsibility is addressed within the view. Recall that controllers respond to requests and perform appropriate actions, which may result in changes to the model and updates to the view. In an SPA, rather than having requests in the traditional sense, we have events. Events can be traditional browser DOM events (such as clicks) or internal application events (such as model changes).

In our TodoView, the events attribute fulfills the role of the controller configuration, defining how events occurring within the view's DOM element are to be routed to event-handling methods defined in the View.

While in this instance events help us relate Backbone to the MVC pattern, we will see them playing a much larger role in our SPA applications. Backbone.Event is a fundamental Backbone component that is mixed into both Backbone.Model and Backbone.View, providing them with rich event management capabilities. Note that the traditional view role (Smalltalk-80-style) is performed by the template, not by the Backbone.View.

This completes our first encounter with Backbone.js. The remainder of this book will explore the many features of the framework that build on these simple constructs. Before moving on, let's take a look at common features of JavaScript MV* frameworks.

Implementation Specifics

An SPA is loaded into the browser through a normal HTTP request and response. The page may simply be an HTML file, as in the preceding example, or it could be a view constructed by a server-side MVC implementation.

Once the SPA is loaded, a client-side router intercepts URLs and invokes client-side logic in place of sending a new request to the server. Figure 2-4 shows typical request handling for client-side MVC as implemented by Backbone.

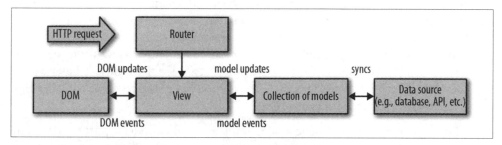

Figure 2-4. Backbone's approach to request handling

URL routing, DOM events (such as mouse clicks), and model events (such as attribute changes) all trigger handling logic in the view. The handlers update the DOM and models, which may trigger additional events. Models are synced with data sources, which may involve communicating with backend servers.

Models

- The built-in capabilities of models vary across frameworks; however, it's common for them to support validation of attributes, where attributes represent the properties of the model, such as a model identifier.

- When using models in real-world applications we generally also need a way of persisting models. Persistence allows us to edit and update models with the knowledge that their most recent states will be saved somewhere—for example, in a web browser's localStorage datastore or synchronized with a database.

- A model may have multiple views observing it for changes. By *observing*, I mean that a view has registered an interest in being informed whenever an update is made to the model. This allows the view to ensure that what is displayed on screen is kept in sync with the data contained in the model. Depending on your requirements, you might create a single view displaying all model attributes, or create separate views displaying different attributes. The important point is that the model doesn't care how these views are organized; it simply announces updates to its data as necessary through the framework's event system.

- It is not uncommon for modern MVC/MV* frameworks to provide a means of grouping models together. In Backbone, these groups are called collections. Managing models in groups allows us to write application logic based on notifications from the group when a model within the group changes. This avoids the need to manually observe individual model instances. We'll see this in action later in the book. Collections are also useful for performing any aggregate computations across more than one model.

Views

- Users interact with views, which usually means reading and editing model data. For example, in our Todo application, Todo model viewing happens in the user interface in the list of all todo items. Within it, each todo is rendered with its title and completed checkbox. Model editing is done through an edit view, where a user who has selected a specific todo edits its title in a form.

- We define within our view a render() utility, which is responsible for rendering the contents of the Model using a JavaScript templating engine (provided by Underscore.js) and updating the contents of our view, referenced by this.el.

- We then add our render() callback as a model subscriber, so the view can be triggered to update when the model changes.

- You may wonder where user interaction comes into play here. When users click on a todo element within the view, it's not the view's responsibility to know what to do next. A controller makes this decision. In Backbone, we achieve this by adding an event listener to the todo's element, which delegates handling of the click to an event handler.

Templating

In the context of JavaScript frameworks that support MVC/MV*, it is worth looking more closely at JavaScript templating and its relationship to views.

It has long been considered bad practice (and computationally expensive) to manually create large blocks of HTML markup in-memory through string concatenation. Developers using this technique often find themselves iterating through their data, wrapping it in nested divs and using outdated techniques such as document.write to inject the template into the DOM. This approach often means keeping scripted markup inline with standard markup, which can quickly become difficult to read and maintain, especially when you're building large applications.

JavaScript templating libraries (such as Mustache or Handlebars.js) are often used to define templates for views as HTML markup containing template variables. These template blocks can be either stored externally or within <script> tags with a custom type (such as text/template). Variables are delimited through a variable syntax (for example, `<%= title %>` for Underscore and `{{title}}` for Handlebars).

JavaScript template libraries typically accept data in a number of formats, including JSON, a serialization format that is always a string. The grunt work of populating templates with data is generally taken care of by the framework itself. This has several benefits, particularly when you opt to store templates externally, which enables applications to load templates dynamically on an as-needed basis.

Let's compare two examples of HTML templates. One is implemented using the popular Handlebars.js library, and the other uses Underscore's microtemplates.

Handlebars.js

```
<div class="view">
  <input class="toggle" type="checkbox" {{#if completed}} "checked" {{/if}}>
  <label>{{title}}</label>
  <button class="destroy"></button>
</div>
<input class="edit" value="{{title}}">
```

Underscore.js microtemplates

```
<div class="view">
  <input class="toggle" type="checkbox" <%= completed ? 'checked' : '' %>>
  <label><%- title %></label>
  <button class="destroy"></button>
</div>
<input class="edit" value="<%= title %>">
```

 It is also worth noting that in classical web development, navigating between independent views required the use of a page refresh. In single-page JavaScript applications, however, once data is fetched from a server via Ajax, it can be dynamically rendered in a new view within the same page. Since this doesn't automatically update the URL, the role of navigation thus falls to a router, which assists in managing application state (e.g., allowing users to bookmark a particular view they have navigated to). As routers are neither a part of MVC nor present in every MVC-like framework, I will not be going into them in greater detail in this section.

Controllers

In our Todo application, a controller would be responsible for handling changes the user made in the edit view for a particular todo, updating a specific todo model when a user had finished editing.

It's with controllers that most JavaScript MVC frameworks depart from the traditional interpretation of the MVC pattern. The reasons for this vary, but in my opinion, JavaScript framework authors likely initially looked at server-side interpretations of MVC (such as Ruby on Rails), realized that the approach didn't translate 1:1 on the client side, and so reinterpreted the C in MVC to solve their state management problem. This was a clever approach, but it can make it hard for developers coming to MVC for the first time to understand both the classical MVC pattern and the proper role of controllers in other JavaScript frameworks.

So does Backbone.js have controllers? Not really. Backbone's views typically contain controller logic, and routers are used to help manage application state, but neither are true controllers according to classical MVC.

In this respect, contrary to what might be mentioned in the official documentation or in blog posts, Backbone isn't truly an MVC framework. It's in fact better to view it a member of the MV* family that approaches architecture in its own way. There is, of course, nothing wrong with this, but it is important to distinguish between classical MVC and MV* should you be relying on discussions of MVC to help with your Backbone projects.

What Does MVC Give Us?

To summarize, the MVC pattern helps you keep your application logic separate from your user interface, making it easier to change and maintain both. Thanks to this separation of logic, it is more clear where changes to your data, interface, or business logic need to be made and for what your unit tests should be written.

Delving Deeper into MVC

Right now, you likely have a basic understanding of what the MVC pattern provides, but for the curious, we'll explore it a little further.

The GoF (Gang of Four) do not refer to MVC as a design pattern, but rather consider it a set of classes to build a user interface. In their view, it's actually a variation of three other classical design patterns: the Observer (publish/subscribe), Strategy, and Composite patterns. Depending on how MVC has been implemented in a framework, it may also use the Factory and Decorator patterns. I've covered some of these patterns in my other book, *JavaScript Design Patterns for Beginners*, if you would like to read about them further.

As we've discussed, models represent application data, while views handle what the user is presented with on screen. As such, MVC relies on publish/subscribe for some of its core communication (something that surprisingly isn't covered in many articles about the MVC pattern). When a model is changed, it publishes to the rest of the application that it has been updated. The subscriber, generally a controller, then updates the view accordingly. The observer-viewer nature of this relationship is what facilitates multiple views being attached to the same model.

For developers interested in knowing more about the decoupled nature of MVC (once again, depending on the implementation), one of the goals of the pattern is to help define one-to-many relationships between a topic and its observers. When a topic changes, its observers are updated. Views and controllers have a slightly different relationship. Controllers facilitate views' responses to different user input and are an example of the Strategy pattern.

Summary

Having reviewed the classical MVC pattern, you should now understand how it allows developers to cleanly separate concerns in an application. You should also now appreciate how JavaScript MVC frameworks may differ in their interpretation of MVC, and how they share some of the fundamental concepts of the original pattern.

When reviewing a new JavaScript MVC/MV* framework, remember that it can be useful to step back and consider how it's opted to approach models, views, controllers, or other alternatives, as this can better help you understand how the framework is intended to be used.

Further Reading

If you are interested in learning more about the variation of MVC that Backbone.js uses, please see "MVP" on page 324.

Fast Facts

Backbone.js

- Contains these core components: model, view, collection, router. Enforces its own flavor of MV*.

- Supports event-driven communication between views and models. As we'll see, it's relatively straightforward to add event listeners to any attribute in a model, giving developers fine-grained control over what changes in the view.

- Supports data bindings through manual events or a separate Key-value observing (KVO) library.

- Offers support for RESTful interfaces out of the box, so models can be easily tied to a backend.

- Possesses an extensive eventing system. It's trivial (*http://bit.ly/11eUlKq*) to add support for Publish/Subscribe in Backbone.

- Instantiates prototypes with the new keyword, which some developers prefer.
- Is agnostic about templating frameworks; however, Underscore's microtemplating is available by default.
- Provides clear and flexible conventions for structuring applications. Backbone doesn't force usage of all of its components and can work with only those needed.

Used by

Disqus

Disqus chose Backbone.js to power the latest version of its commenting widget (shown in Figure 2-5). It felt it was the right choice for its distributed web app, given Backbone's small footprint and ease of extensibility.

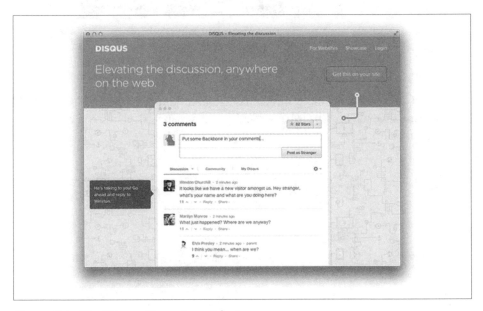

Figure 2-5. The Disqus discussion widget

Khan Academy

Offering a web app that aims to provide free world-class education to anyone anywhere, Khan uses Backbone to keep its frontend code both modular and organized (Figure 2-6).

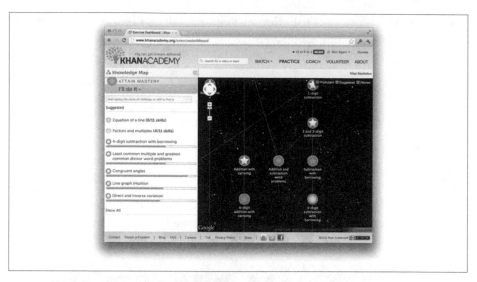

Figure 2-6. The Khan Academy Knowledge Map

MetaLab

MetaLab created Flow, a task management app for teams using Backbone (Figure 2-7). Its workspace uses Backbone to create task views, activities, accounts, tags, and more.

Figure 2-7. The Flow online task management application

Walmart Mobile

Walmart chose Backbone to power its mobile web applications (Figure 2-8), cre-ating two new extension frameworks in the process: Thorax and Lumbar. We'll be discussing both of these later in the book.

Figure 2-8. Walmart Mobile

Airbnb

Airbnb (Figure 2-9) developed its mobile web app using Backbone and now uses it across many of its products.

Figure 2-9. The Airbnb home page

Code School

Code School's course challenge app (Figure 2-10) was built from the ground up using Backbone, taking advantage of all the pieces it has to offer: routers, collections, models, and complex event handling.

Figure 2-10. The Code School learning environment

CHAPTER 3

Backbone Basics

In this section, you'll learn the essentials of Backbone's models, views, collections, events, and routers. This isn't by any means a replacement for the official documentation, but it will help you understand many of the core concepts behind Backbone before you start building applications using it.

Getting Set Up

Before we dive into more code examples, let's define some boilerplate markup you can use to specify the dependencies Backbone requires. This boilerplate can be reused in many ways with little to no alteration and will allow you to run code from examples with ease.

You can paste the following into your text editor of choice, replacing the commented line between the <script> tags with the JavaScript from any given example:

```
<!DOCTYPE HTML>
<html>
<head>
    <meta charset="UTF-8">
    <title>Title</title>
</head>
<body>

<script src="https://ajax.googleapis.com/ajax/libs/jquery/1.9.1/jquery.min.js">
</script>
<script src="http://documentcloud.github.com/underscore/underscore-min.js">
</script>
<script src="http://documentcloud.github.com/backbone/backbone-min.js">
</script>
<script>
  // Your code goes here
</script>
```

```
</body>
</html>
```

You can then save and run the file in your browser of choice, such as Chrome or Firefox. Alternatively, if you prefer working with an online code editor, jsFiddle (*http://bit.ly/18ZzHvy*) and jsBin (*http://bit.ly/11TjCoC*) versions of this boilerplate are also available.

Most examples can also be run directly from within the console in your browser's developer tools, assuming you've loaded the boilerplate HTML page so that Backbone and its dependencies are available for use.

For Chrome, you can open up the DevTools via the Chrome menu in the top-right corner: select Tools→Developer Tools or alternatively use the Ctrl+Shift+I shortcut on Windows/Linux or ⌘-Alt-I on Mac. See Figure 3-1.

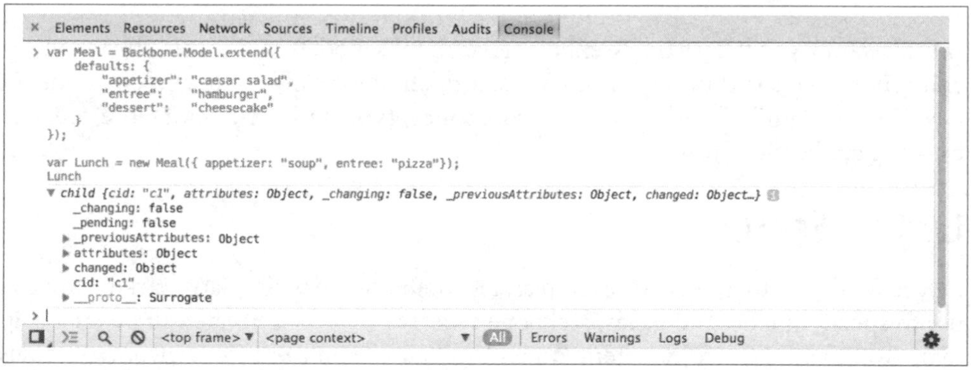

Figure 3-1. The Chrome DevTools console

Next, switch to the Console tab, from which you can enter and run any piece of JavaScript code by pressing the return key. You can also use the Console as a multiline editor using the Shift+Enter shortcut on Windows, or Ctrl-Enter shortcut on Mac, to move from the end of one line to the start of another.

Models

Backbone models contain data for an application as well as the logic around this data. For example, we can use a model to represent the concept of a todo item, including its attributes like `title` (todo content) and `completed` (current state of the todo).

We can create models by extending `Backbone.Model` as follows:

```
var Todo = Backbone.Model.extend({});

// We can then create our own concrete instance of a (Todo) model
// with no values at all:
var todo1 = new Todo();
```

```
// Following logs: {}
console.log(JSON.stringify(todo1));

// or with some arbitrary data:
var todo2 = new Todo({
  title: 'Check the attributes of both model instances in the console.',
  completed: true
});

// Following logs: {"title":"Check the attributes of both model
// instances in the console.","completed":true}
console.log(JSON.stringify(todo2));
```

Initialization

The `initialize()` method is called when a new instance of a model is created. Its use is optional; however, here you'll see why it's good practice to use it.

```
var Todo = Backbone.Model.extend({
  initialize: function(){
      console.log('This model has been initialized.');
  }
});

var myTodo = new Todo();
// Logs: This model has been initialized.
```

Default values

There are times when you want your model to have a set of default values (e.g., in a scenario where a complete set of data isn't provided by the user). You can set these using a property called `defaults` in your model.

```
var Todo = Backbone.Model.extend({
  // Default todo attribute values
  defaults: {
    title: '',
    completed: false
  }
});

// Now we can create our concrete instance of the model
// with default values as follows:
var todo1 = new Todo();

// Following logs: {"title":"","completed":false}
console.log(JSON.stringify(todo1));

// Or we could instantiate it with some of the attributes (e.g., with
// custom title):
var todo2 = new Todo({
  title: 'Check attributes of the logged models in the console.'
```

```
  });

  // Following logs: {"title":"Check attributes of the logged models
  // in the console.","completed":false}
  console.log(JSON.stringify(todo2));

  // Or override all of the default attributes:
  var todo3 = new Todo({
    title: 'This todo is done, so take no action on this one.',
    completed: true
  });

  // Following logs: {"title":"This todo is done, so take no action on
  // this one.","completed":true}
  console.log(JSON.stringify(todo3));
```

Getters and Setters

Model.get()

Model.get() provides easy access to a model's attributes.

```
  var Todo = Backbone.Model.extend({
    // Default todo attribute values
    defaults: {
      title: '',
      completed: false
    }
  });

  var todo1 = new Todo();
  console.log(todo1.get('title')); // empty string
  console.log(todo1.get('completed')); // false

  var todo2 = new Todo({
    title: "Retrieved with model's get() method.",
    completed: true
  });
  console.log(todo2.get('title')); // Retrieved with model's get() method.
  console.log(todo2.get('completed')); // true
```

If you need to read or clone all of a model's data attributes, use its toJSON() method.
This method returns a copy of the attributes as an object (not a JSON string, despite its
name). (When JSON.stringify() is passed an object with a toJSON() method, it
stringifies the return value of toJSON() instead of the original object. The examples in
the previous section took advantage of this feature when they called JSON.stringi
fy() to log model instances.)

```
  var Todo = Backbone.Model.extend({
    // Default todo attribute values
    defaults: {
```

```
      title: '',
      completed: false
  }
});

var todo1 = new Todo();
var todo1Attributes = todo1.toJSON();
// Following logs: {"title":"","completed":false}
console.log(todo1Attributes);

var todo2 = new Todo({
  title: "Try these examples and check results in console.",
  completed: true
});

// logs: {"title":"Try these examples and check results in console.",
// "completed":true}
console.log(todo2.toJSON());
```

Model.set()

Model.set() sets a hash containing one or more attributes on the model. When any of these attributes alter the state of the model, a change event is triggered on it. Change events for each attribute are also triggered and can be bound to the model (such as change:name, change:age).

```
var Todo = Backbone.Model.extend({
  // Default todo attribute values
  defaults: {
    title: '',
    completed: false
  }
});

// Setting the value of attributes via instantiation
var myTodo = new Todo({
  title: "Set through instantiation."
});
console.log('Todo title: ' + myTodo.get('title'));
// Todo title: Set through instantiation.
console.log('Completed: ' + myTodo.get('completed'));
// Completed: false

// Set single attribute value at a time through Model.set():
myTodo.set("title", "Title attribute set through Model.set().");
console.log('Todo title: ' + myTodo.get('title'));
// Todo title: Title attribute set through Model.set().
console.log('Completed: ' + myTodo.get('completed'));
// Completed: false

// Set map of attributes through Model.set():
myTodo.set({
```

```
    title: "Both attributes set through Model.set().",
      completed: true
  });
  console.log('Todo title: ' + myTodo.get('title'));
  // Todo title: Both attributes set through Model.set().
  console.log('Completed: ' + myTodo.get('completed'));
  // Completed: true
```

Direct access

Models expose an `.attributes` attribute, which represents an internal hash containing the state of that model. This is generally in the form of a JSON object similar to the model data you might find on the server, but it can take other forms.

Setting values through the `.attributes` attribute on a model bypasses triggers bound to the model.

Passing `{silent:true}` on change doesn't delay individual `"change:attr"` events; instead, they are silenced entirely:

```
  var Person = new Backbone.Model();
  Person.set({name: 'Jeremy'}, {silent: true});

  console.log(!Person.hasChanged(0));
  // true
  console.log(!Person.hasChanged(''));
  // true
```

Remember, where possible it is best practice to use `Model.set()`, or direct instantiation as explained earlier.

Listening for Changes to Your Model

If you want to receive a notification when a Backbone model changes, you can bind a listener to the model for its change event. A convenient place to add listeners is in the `initialize()` function, as shown here:

```
  var Todo = Backbone.Model.extend({
    // Default todo attribute values
    defaults: {
      title: '',
      completed: false
    },
    initialize: function(){
      console.log('This model has been initialized.');
      this.on('change', function(){
          console.log('- Values for this model have changed.');
      });
    }
  });
```

```
var myTodo = new Todo();

myTodo.set('title', 'The listener is triggered whenever an attribute
// value changes.');
console.log('Title has changed: ' + myTodo.get('title'));


myTodo.set('completed', true);
console.log('Completed has changed: ' + myTodo.get('completed'));

myTodo.set({
  title: 'Changing more than one attribute at the same time only triggers
// the listener once.',
  completed: true
});

// Above logs:
// This model has been initialized.
// - Values for this model have changed.
// Title has changed: The listener is triggered when an attribute value changes.
// - Values for this model have changed.
// Completed has changed: true
// - Values for this model have changed.
```

You can also listen for changes to individual attributes in a Backbone model. In the following example, we log a message whenever a specific attribute (the title of our Todo model) is altered.

```
var Todo = Backbone.Model.extend({
  // Default todo attribute values
  defaults: {
    title: '',
    completed: false
  },

  initialize: function(){
    console.log('This model has been initialized.');
    this.on('change:title', function(){
        console.log('Title value for this model has changed.');
    });
  },

  setTitle: function(newTitle){
    this.set({ title: newTitle });
  }
});

var myTodo = new Todo();

// Both of the following changes trigger the listener:
myTodo.set('title', 'Check what\'s logged.');
myTodo.setTitle('Go fishing on Sunday.');
```

```
// But this change type is not observed, so no listener is triggered:
myTodo.set('completed', true);
console.log('Todo set as completed: ' + myTodo.get('completed'));

// Above logs:
// This model has been initialized.
// Title value for this model has changed.
// Title value for this model has changed.
// Todo set as completed: true
```

Validation

Backbone supports model validation through model.validate(), which allows checking the attribute values for a model prior to setting them. By default, validation occurs
when the model is persisted via the save() method or when set() is called if {vali
date:true} is passed as an argument.

```
var Person = new Backbone.Model({name: 'Jeremy'});

// Validate the model name
Person.validate = function(attrs) {
  if (!attrs.name) {
    return 'I need your name';
  }
};

// Change the name
Person.set({name: 'Samuel'});
console.log(Person.get('name'));
// 'Samuel'

// Remove the name attribute, force validation
Person.unset('name', {validate: true});
// false
```

We also make use of the unset() method, which removes an attribute by deleting it
from the internal model attribute's hash.

Validation functions can be as simple or complex as necessary. If the attributes provided
are valid, nothing should be returned from .validate(). If they are invalid, an error
value should be returned instead.

Should an error be returned:

- An invalid event will be triggered, setting the validationError property on the
  model with the value that is returned by this method.
- .save() will not continue and the attributes of the model will not be modified on
  the server.

Here is a more complete validation example:

```
var Todo = Backbone.Model.extend({
  defaults: {
    completed: false
  },

  validate: function(attribs){
    if(attribs.title === undefined){
        return "Remember to set a title for your todo.";
    }
  },

  initialize: function(){
    console.log('This model has been initialized.');
    this.on("invalid", function(model, error){
        console.log(error);
    });
  }
});

var myTodo = new Todo();
myTodo.set('completed', true, {validate: true});
// logs: Remember to set a title for your todo.
console.log('completed: ' + myTodo.get('completed')); // completed: false
```

 The attributes object passed to the validate function represents what the attributes would be after the current set() or save() completes. This object is distinct from the current attributes of the model and from the parameters passed to the operation. Since it is created by shallow copy, it is not possible to change any Number, String, or Boolean attribute of the input within the function, but it *is* possible to change attributes in nested objects.

An example of this (by @fivetanley) is available at *http://jsfiddle.net/2NdDY/7/*.

Views

Views in Backbone don't contain the HTML markup for your application; they contain the logic behind the presentation of the model's data to the user. They achieve this using JavaScript templating (for example, Underscore microtemplates, Mustache, jQuery-tmpl, and so on). A view's render() method can be bound to a model's change() event, enabling the view to instantly reflect model changes without requiring a full page refresh.

Creating New Views

Creating a new view is relatively straightforward and similar to creating new models. To create a new view, simply extend Backbone.View. We introduced the following sample TodoView in the previous chapter; now let's take a closer look at how it works.

```
var TodoView = Backbone.View.extend({

  tagName:  'li',

  // Cache the template function for a single item.
  todoTpl: _.template( "An example template" ),

  events: {
    'dblclick label': 'edit',
    'keypress .edit': 'updateOnEnter',
    'blur .edit':    'close'
  },

  // Rerender the titles of the todo item.
  render: function() {
    this.$el.html( this.todoTpl( this.model.toJSON() ) );
    this.input = this.$('.edit');
    return this;
  },

  edit: function() {
    // executed when todo label is double-clicked
  },

  close: function() {
    // executed when todo loses focus
  },

  updateOnEnter: function( e ) {
    // executed on each keypress when in todo edit mode,
    // but we'll wait for enter to get in action
  }
});

var todoView = new TodoView();

// log reference to a DOM element that corresponds to the view instance
console.log(todoView.el); // logs <li></li>
```

What Is el?

The central property of a view is el (the value logged in the last statement of the example). What is el and how is it defined?

el is basically a reference to a DOM element, and all views must have one. Views can use el to compose their element's content and then insert it into the DOM all at once, which makes for faster rendering because the browser performs the minimum required number of reflows and repaints.

There are two ways to associate a DOM element with a view: a new element can be created for the view and subsequently added to the DOM, or a reference can be made to an element that already exists in the page.

If you want to create a new element for your view, set any combination of the following properties on the view: tagName, id, and className. The framework will create a new element for you, and a reference to it will be available at the el property. If nothing is specified, tagName defaults to div.

In the preceding example, tagName is set to li, resulting in the creation of a li element. The following example creates a ul element with id and class attributes:

```
var TodosView = Backbone.View.extend({
  tagName: 'ul', // required, but defaults to 'div' if not set
  className: 'container', // optional, you can assign multiple classes to
// this property like so: 'container homepage'
  id: 'todos', // optional
});
```

```
var todosView = new TodosView();
console.log(todosView.el); // logs <ul id="todos" class="container"></ul>
```

The preceding code creates the following DOM element but doesn't append it to the DOM.

```
<ul id="todos" class="container"></ul>
```

If the element already exists in the page, you can set el as a CSS selector that matches the element.

```
el: '#footer'
```

Alternatively, you can set el to an existing element when creating the view:

```
var todosView = new TodosView({el: $('#footer')});
```

 When declaring a view, you can define options, el, tagName, id, and className as functions, if you want their values to be determined at runtime.

$el and $()

View logic often needs to invoke jQuery or Zepto functions on the el element and elements nested within it. Backbone makes it easy to do so by defining the $el property and $() function. The view.$el property is equivalent to $(view.el), and view.$ (selector) is equivalent to $(view.el).find(selector). In our TodosView example's render method, we see this.$el used to set the HTML of the element and this.$() used to find subelements of class edit.

setElement

If you need to apply an existing Backbone view to a different DOM element, you can use setElement. Overriding this.el needs to both change the DOM reference and rebind events to the new element (and unbind from the old).

setElement will create a cached $el reference for you, moving the delegated events for a view from the old element to the new one.

```
// We create two DOM elements representing buttons
// which could easily be containers or something else
var button1 = $('<button></button>');
var button2 = $('<button></button>');

// Define a new view
var View = Backbone.View.extend({
    events: {
      click: function(e) {
        console.log(view.el === e.target);
      }
    }
});

// Create a new instance of the view, applying it
// to button1
var view = new View({el: button1});

// Apply the view to button2 using setElement
view.setElement(button2);

button1.trigger('click');
button2.trigger('click'); // returns true
```

The el property represents the markup portion of the view that will be rendered; to get the view to actually render to the page, you need to add it as a new element or append it to an existing element.

```
// We can also provide raw markup to setElement
// as follows (just to demonstrate it can be done):
var view = new Backbone.View;
view.setElement('<p><a><b>test</b></a></p>');
view.$('a b').html(); // outputs "test"
```

Understanding render()

render() is an optional function that defines the logic for rendering a template. We'll use Underscore's microtemplating in these examples, but remember you can use other templating frameworks if you prefer. Our example will reference the following HTML markup:

```
<!doctype html>
<html lang="en">
<head>
  <meta charset="utf-8">
  <title></title>
  <meta name="description" content="">
</head>
<body>
  <div id="todo">
  </div>
  <script type="text/template" id="item-template">
    <div>
      <input id="todo_complete" type="checkbox" <%= completed ?
       'checked="checked"' : '' %>>
      <%= title %>
    </div>
  </script>
  <script src="underscore-min.js"></script>
  <script src="backbone-min.js"></script>
  <script src="jquery-min.js"></script>
  <script src="example.js"></script>
</body>
</html>
```

The _.template method in Underscore compiles JavaScript templates into functions that can be evaluated for rendering. In the TodoView, I'm passing the markup from the template with an id of item-template to _.template() to be compiled and stored in the todoTpl property when the view is created.

The render() method uses this template by passing it the toJSON() encoding of the attributes of the model associated with the view. The template returns its markup after using the model's title and completed flag to evaluate the expressions containing them. I then set this markup as the HTML content of the el DOM element using the $el property.

Presto! This populates the template, giving you a data-complete set of markup in just a few short lines of code.

A common Backbone convention is to return this at the end of render(). This is useful for a number of reasons, including:

- Making views easily reusable in other parent views
- Creating a list of elements without rendering and painting each of them individually, only to be drawn once the entire list is populated

Let's try to implement the latter of these. The render method of a simple ListView that doesn't use an ItemView for each item could be written as follows:

```
var ListView = Backbone.View.extend({
  render: function(){
    this.$el.html(this.model.toJSON());
  }
});
```

Simple enough. Let's now assume we've decided to construct the items using an Item View to provide enhanced behavior to our list. The ItemView could be written like so:

```
var ItemView = Backbone.View.extend({
  events: {},
  render: function(){
    this.$el.html(this.model.toJSON());
    return this;
  }
});
```

Note the usage of return this; at the end of render. This common pattern enables us to reuse the view as a subview. We can also use it to prerender the view prior to rendering. Doing so requires that we make a change to our ListView's render method as follows:

```
var ListView = Backbone.View.extend({
  render: function(){

    // Assume our model exposes the items we will
    // display in our list
    var items = this.model.get('items');

    // Loop through each of our items using the Underscore
    // _.each iterator
    _.each(items, function(item){

      // Create a new instance of the ItemView, passing
      // it a specific model item
      var itemView = new ItemView({ model: item });
      // The itemView's DOM element is appended after it
      // has been rendered. Here, the 'return this' is helpful
      // as the itemView renders its model. Later, we ask for
      // its output ("el")
      this.$el.append( itemView.render().el );
    }, this);
```

```
  }
});
```

The events hash

The Backbone events hash allows us to attach event listeners to either el-relative custom selectors, or directly to el if no selector is provided. An event takes the form of a key-value pair 'eventName selector': 'callbackFunction', and a number of DOM event types are supported, including click, submit, mouseover, dblclick, and more.

```
// A sample view
var TodoView = Backbone.View.extend({
  tagName: 'li',

  // with an events hash containing DOM events
  // specific to an item:
  events: {
    'click .toggle': 'toggleCompleted',
    'dblclick label': 'edit',
    'click .destroy': 'clear',
    'blur .edit': 'close'
  },
```

What isn't instantly obvious is that while Backbone uses jQuery's .delegate() underneath, it goes further by extending it so that this always refers to the current view object within callback functions. The only thing to really keep in mind is that any string callback supplied to the events attribute must have a corresponding function with the same name within the scope of your view.

The declarative, delegated jQuery events means that you don't have to worry about whether a particular element has been rendered to the DOM yet or not. Usually with jQuery you have to worry about presence or absence in the DOM all the time when binding events.

In our TodoView example, the edit callback is invoked when the user double-clicks a label element within the el element, updateOnEnter is called for each keypress in an element with class edit, and close executes when an element with class edit loses focus. Each of these callback functions can use this to refer to the TodoView object.

Note that you can also bind methods yourself using _.bind(this.viewEvent, this), which is effectively what the value in each event's key-value pair is doing. Here we use _.bind to rerender our view when a model changes:

```
var TodoView = Backbone.View.extend({
  initialize: function() {
    this.model.bind('change', _.bind(this.render, this));
  }
});
```

_.bind works on only one method at a time, but it supports currying; because it returns the bound function, you can use _.bind on an anonymous function.

Collections

Collections are sets of models, and you create them by extending Backbone.Collection.

Normally, when creating a collection you'll also want to define a property specifying the type of model that your collection will contain, along with any instance properties required.

In the following example, we create a TodoCollection that will contain our Todo models:

```
var Todo = Backbone.Model.extend({
  defaults: {
    title: '',
    completed: false
  }
});

var TodosCollection = Backbone.Collection.extend({
  model: Todo
});

var myTodo = new Todo({title:'Read the whole book', id: 2});

// pass array of models on collection instantiation
var todos = new TodosCollection([myTodo]);
console.log("Collection size: " + todos.length); // Collection size: 1
```

Adding and Removing Models

The preceding example populated the collection using an array of models when it was instantiated. After a collection has been created, you can add and remove models using the add() and remove() methods:

```
var Todo = Backbone.Model.extend({
  defaults: {
    title: '',
    completed: false
  }
});

var TodosCollection = Backbone.Collection.extend({
  model: Todo,
});

var a = new Todo({ title: 'Go to Jamaica.'}),
    b = new Todo({ title: 'Go to China.'}),
```

```
        c = new Todo({ title: 'Go to Disneyland.'});

    var todos = new TodosCollection([a,b]);
    console.log("Collection size: " + todos.length);
    // Logs: Collection size: 2

    todos.add(c);
    console.log("Collection size: " + todos.length);
    // Logs: Collection size: 3

    todos.remove([a,b]);
    console.log("Collection size: " + todos.length);
    // Logs: Collection size: 1

    todos.remove(c);
    console.log("Collection size: " + todos.length);
    // Logs: Collection size: 0
```

Note that add() and remove() accept both individual models and lists of models.

Also note that when you are using add() on a collection, passing {merge: true} causes duplicate models to have their attributes merged into the existing models, instead of being ignored.

```
    var items = new Backbone.Collection;
    items.add([{ id : 1, name: "Dog" , age: 3}, { id : 2, name: "cat" , age: 2}]);
    items.add([{ id : 1, name: "Bear" }], {merge: true });
    items.add([{ id : 2, name: "lion" }]); // merge: false

    console.log(JSON.stringify(items.toJSON()));
    // [{"id":1,"name":"Bear","age":3},{"id":2,"name":"cat","age":2}]
```

Retrieving Models

There are a few different ways to retrieve a model from a collection. The most straight-forward is to use Collection.get(), which accepts a single id as follows:

```
    var myTodo = new Todo({title:'Read the whole book', id: 2});

    // pass array of models on collection instantiation
    var todos = new TodosCollection([myTodo]);

    var todo2 = todos.get(2);

    // Models, as objects, are passed by reference
    console.log(todo2 === myTodo); // true
```

In client-server applications, collections contain models obtained from the server. Any-time you're exchanging data between the client and a server, you will need a way to uniquely identify models. In Backbone, you do so using the id, cid, and idAttribute properties.

Each model in Backbone has an id, which is a unique identifier that is either an integer or string (for example, a UUID). Models also have a cid (client ID) which is automatically generated by Backbone when the model is created. Either identifier can be used to retrieve a model from a collection.

The main difference between them is that the cid is generated by Backbone, which is helpful when you don't have a true id; this may be the case if your model has yet to be saved to the server or you aren't saving it to a database.

The idAttribute is the identifying attribute of the model returned from the server (i.e., the id in your database). This tells Backbone which data field from the server should be used to populate the id property (think of it as a mapper). By default, it assumes id, but this can be customized as needed. For instance, if your server sets a unique attribute on your model named userId, then you would set idAttribute to userId in your model definition.

The value of a model's idAttribute should be set by the server when the model is saved. After this point, you shouldn't need to set it manually, unless further control is required.

Internally, Backbone.Collection contains an array of models enumerated by their id property, if the model instances happen to have one. When collection.get(id) is called, this array is checked for the existence of the model instance with the corresponding id.

```
// extends the previous example

var todoCid = todos.get(todo2.cid);

// As mentioned in previous example,
// models are passed by reference
console.log(todoCid === myTodo); // true
```

Listening for Events

Because collections represent a group of items, we can listen for add and remove events, which occur when models are added to or removed from a collection. Here's an example:

```
var TodosCollection = new Backbone.Collection();

TodosCollection.on("add", function(todo) {
  console.log("I should " + todo.get("title") + ". Have I done it before? "
  + (todo.get("completed") ? 'Yeah!': 'No.' ));
});

TodosCollection.add([
  { title: 'go to Jamaica', completed: false },
  { title: 'go to China', completed: false },
  { title: 'go to Disneyland', completed: true }
]);
```

```
// The above logs:
// I should go to Jamaica. Have I done it before? No.
// I should go to China. Have I done it before? No.
// I should go to Disneyland. Have I done it before? Yeah!
```

In addition, we're also able to bind to a change event to listen for changes to any of the models in the collection.

```
var TodosCollection = new Backbone.Collection();

// log a message if a model in the collection changes
TodosCollection.on("change:title", function(model) {
    console.log("Changed my mind! I should " + model.get('title'));
});

TodosCollection.add([
  { title: 'go to Jamaica.', completed: false, id: 3 },
]);

var myTodo = TodosCollection.get(3);

myTodo.set('title', 'go fishing');
// Logs: Changed my mind! I should go fishing
```

jQuery-style event maps of the form obj.on({click: action}) can also be used. These can be clearer than using three separate calls to .on, and should align better with the events hash used in views:

```
var Todo = Backbone.Model.extend({
  defaults: {
    title: '',
    completed: false
  }
});

var myTodo = new Todo();
myTodo.set({title: 'Buy some cookies', completed: true});

myTodo.on({
    'change:title' : titleChanged,
    'change:completed' : stateChanged
});

function titleChanged(){
  console.log('The title was changed!');
}

function stateChanged(){
  console.log('The state was changed!');
}
```

```
myTodo.set({title: 'Get the groceries'});
// The title was changed!
```

Backbone events also support a once() method (*http://backbonejs.org/#Events-once*), which ensures that a callback fires only one time when a notification arrives. It is similar to Node's once (*http://nodejs.org/api/events.html#events_emitter_once_event_listener*), or jQuery's one (*http://api.jquery.com/one/*). This is particularly useful for when you want to say, "The next time something happens, do this."

```
// Define an object with two counters
var TodoCounter = { counterA: 0, counterB: 0 };
// Mix in Backbone Events
_.extend(TodoCounter, Backbone.Events);

// Increment counterA, triggering an event
var incrA = function(){
  TodoCounter.counterA += 1;
  TodoCounter.trigger('event');
};

// Increment counterB
var incrB = function(){
  TodoCounter.counterB += 1;
};

// Use once rather than having to explicitly unbind
// our event listener
TodoCounter.once('event', incrA);
TodoCounter.once('event', incrB);

// Trigger the event once again
TodoCounter.trigger('event');

// Check our output
console.log(TodoCounter.counterA === 1); // true
console.log(TodoCounter.counterB === 1); // true
```

counterA and counterB should have been incremented only once.

Resetting/Refreshing Collections

Rather than adding or removing models individually, you might want to update an entire collection at once. Collection.set() takes an array of models and performs the necessary add, remove, and change operations required to update the collection.

```
var TodosCollection = new Backbone.Collection();

TodosCollection.add([
    { id: 1, title: 'go to Jamaica.', completed: false },
    { id: 2, title: 'go to China.', completed: false },
    { id: 3, title: 'go to Disneyland.', completed: true }
]);
```

```
// we can listen for add/change/remove events
TodosCollection.on("add", function(model) {
  console.log("Added " + model.get('title'));
});

TodosCollection.on("remove", function(model) {
  console.log("Removed " + model.get('title'));
});

TodosCollection.on("change:completed", function(model) {
  console.log("Completed " + model.get('title'));
});

TodosCollection.set([
    { id: 1, title: 'go to Jamaica.', completed: true },
    { id: 2, title: 'go to China.', completed: false },
    { id: 4, title: 'go to Disney World.', completed: false }
]);

// Above logs:
// Removed go to Disneyland.
// Completed go to Jamaica.
// Added go to Disney World.
```

If you need to simply replace the entire content of the collection, then you can use
Collection.reset() as follows:

```
var TodosCollection = new Backbone.Collection();

// we can listen for reset events
TodosCollection.on("reset", function() {
  console.log("Collection reset.");
});

TodosCollection.add([
  { title: 'go to Jamaica.', completed: false },
  { title: 'go to China.', completed: false },
  { title: 'go to Disneyland.', completed: true }
]);

console.log('Collection size: ' + TodosCollection.length); // Collection size: 3

TodosCollection.reset([
  { title: 'go to Cuba.', completed: false }
]);
// Above logs 'Collection reset.'

console.log('Collection size: ' + TodosCollection.length); // Collection size: 1
```

Another useful tip is to use `reset` with no arguments to clear out a collection completely. This is handy when you're dynamically loading a new page of results where you want to blank out the current page of results.

```
myCollection.reset();
```

Note that using `Collection.reset()` doesn't fire any `add` or `remove` events. A `reset` event is fired instead, as shown in the previous example. The reason you might want to use this is to perform super-optimized rendering in extreme cases where individual events are too expensive.

Also note that when you're listening to a reset event (*http://backbonejs.org/#Collection-reset*), the list of previous models is available in `options.previousModels`, for convenience.

```
var Todo = new Backbone.Model();
var Todos = new Backbone.Collection([Todo])
.on('reset', function(Todos, options) {
  console.log(options.previousModels);
  console.log([Todo]);
  console.log(options.previousModels[0] === Todo); // true
});
Todos.reset([]);
```

An `update()` method is available for collections (and is also available as an option to fetch) for smart updating of sets of models. This method attempts to perform smart updating of a collection using a specified list of models. When a model in this list isn't present in the collection, it is added. If it is present, its attributes will be merged. Models that are present in the collection but not in the list are removed.

```
var theBeatles = new Collection(['john', 'paul', 'george', 'ringo']);

theBeatles.update(['john', 'paul', 'george', 'pete']);

// Fires a `remove` event for 'ringo', and an `add` event for 'pete'.
// Updates any of john, paul, and george's attributes that may have
// changed over the years.
```

Underscore Utility Functions

Backbone takes full advantage of its hard dependency on Underscore by making many of its utilities directly available on collections.

forEach: Iterate over collections

```
var Todos = new Backbone.Collection();

Todos.add([
  { title: 'go to Belgium.', completed: false },
  { title: 'go to China.', completed: false },
  { title: 'go to Austria.', completed: true }
```

```
]);

// iterate over models in the collection
Todos.forEach(function(model){
  console.log(model.get('title'));
});
// Above logs:
// go to Belgium.
// go to China.
// go to Austria.
```

sortBy(): Sort a collection on a specific attribute

```
// sort collection
var sortedByAlphabet = Todos.sortBy(function (todo) {
    return todo.get("title").toLowerCase();
});

console.log("- Now sorted: ");

sortedByAlphabet.forEach(function(model){
  console.log(model.get('title'));
});
// Above logs:
// go to Austria.
// go to Belgium.
// go to China.
```

map(): Create a new collection by mapping each value in a list through a transformation function

```
var count = 1;
console.log(Todos.map(function(model){
  return count++ + ". " + model.get('title');
}));
// Above logs:
//1. go to Belgium.
//2. go to China.
//3. go to Austria.
```

min()/max(): Retrieve item with the min or max value of an attribute

```
Todos.max(function(model){
  return model.id;
}).id;

Todos.min(function(model){
  return model.id;
}).id;
```

pluck(): Extract a specific attribute

```
var captions = Todos.pluck('caption');
// returns list of captions
```

filter(): Filter a collection

Filter by an array of model IDs.

```
var Todos = Backbone.Collection.extend({
  model: Todo,
  filterById: function(ids){
    return this.models.filter(
      function(c) {
        return _.contains(ids, c.id);
      })
  }
});
```

indexOf(): Return the item at a particular index within a collection

```
var People = new Backbone.Collection;

People.comparator = function(a, b) {
  return a.get('name') < b.get('name') ? -1 : 1;
};

var tom = new Backbone.Model({name: 'Tom'});
var rob = new Backbone.Model({name: 'Rob'});
var tim = new Backbone.Model({name: 'Tim'});

People.add(tom);
People.add(rob);
People.add(tim);

console.log(People.indexOf(rob) === 0); // true
console.log(People.indexOf(tim) === 1); // true
console.log(People.indexOf(tom) === 2); // true
```

any() : Confirm if any of the values in a collection pass an iterator truth test

```
Todos.any(function(model){
  return model.id === 100;
});

// or
Todos.some(function(model){
  return model.id === 100;
});
```

size(): Return the size of a collection

```
Todos.size();

// equivalent to
Todos.length;
```

isEmpty(): Determine whether a collection is empty

```
var isEmpty = Todos.isEmpty();
```

groupBy(): Group a collection into groups like items

```
var Todos = new Backbone.Collection();

Todos.add([
  { title: 'go to Belgium.', completed: false },
  { title: 'go to China.', completed: false },
  { title: 'go to Austria.', completed: true }
]);

// create groups of completed and incomplete models
var byCompleted = Todos.groupBy('completed');
var completed = new Backbone.Collection(byCompleted[true]);
console.log(completed.pluck('title'));
// logs: ["go to Austria."]
```

In addition, several of the Underscore operations on objects are available as methods on models.

pick(): Extract a set of attributes from a model

```
var Todo = Backbone.Model.extend({
  defaults: {
    title: '',
    completed: false
  }
});

var todo = new Todo({title: 'go to Austria.'});
console.log(todo.pick('title'));
// logs {title: "go to Austria"}
```

omit(): Extract all attributes from a model except those listed

```
var todo = new Todo({title: 'go to Austria.'});
console.log(todo.omit('title'));
// logs {completed: false}
```

keys() and values(): Get lists of attribute names and values

```
var todo = new Todo({title: 'go to Austria.'});
console.log(todo.keys());
```

```
// logs: ["title", "completed"]

console.log(todo.values());
//logs: ["go to Austria.", false]
```

pairs(): Get list of attributes as [key, value] pairs

```
var todo = new Todo({title: 'go to Austria.'});
var pairs = todo.pairs();

console.log(pairs[0]);
// logs: ["title", "go to Austria."]
console.log(pairs[1]);
// logs: ["completed", false]
```

invert(): Create object in which the values are keys and the attributes are values

```
var todo = new Todo({title: 'go to Austria.'});
console.log(todo.invert());

// logs: {go to Austria.: "title", false: "completed"}
```

You can find the complete list of what Underscore can do in its official docs (*http://documentcloud.github.com/underscore/*).

Chainable API

Speaking of utility methods, another bit of sugar in Backbone is its support for Underscore's chain() method. Chaining is a common idiom in object-oriented languages; a *chain* is a sequence of method calls on the same object that are performed in a single statement. While Backbone makes Underscore's array manipulation operations available as methods of collection objects, they cannot be directly chained since they return arrays rather than the original collection.

Fortunately, the inclusion of Underscore's chain() method enables you to chain calls to these methods on collections.

The chain() method returns an object that has all of the Underscore array operations attached as methods that return that object. The chain ends with a call to the value() method, which simply returns the resulting array value. In case you haven't seen it before, the chainable API looks like this:

```
var collection = new Backbone.Collection([
  { name: 'Tim', age: 5 },
  { name: 'Ida', age: 26 },
  { name: 'Rob', age: 55 }
]);

var filteredNames = collection.chain()
// start chain, returns wrapper around collection's models
  .filter(function(item) { return item.get('age') > 10; })
```

```
   // returns wrapped array excluding Tim
   .map(function(item) { return item.get('name'); })
   // returns wrapped array containing remaining names
   .value(); // terminates the chain and returns the resulting array

console.log(filteredNames); // logs: ['Ida', 'Rob']
```

Some of the Backbone-specific methods do return this, which means they can be chained as well:

```
var collection = new Backbone.Collection();

collection
    .add({ name: 'John', age: 23 })
    .add({ name: 'Harry', age: 33 })
    .add({ name: 'Steve', age: 41 });

var names = collection.pluck('name');

console.log(names); // logs: ['John', 'Harry', 'Steve']
```

RESTful Persistence

Thus far, all of our example data has been created in the browser. For most single-page applications, the models are derived from a data set residing on a server. This is an area in which Backbone dramatically simplifies the code you need to write to perform RESTful synchronization with a server through a simple API on its models and collections.

Fetching Models from the Server

Collections.fetch() retrieves a set of models from the server in the form of a JSON array by sending an HTTP GET request to the URL specified by the collection's url property (which may be a function). When this data is received, a set() will be executed to update the collection.

```
var Todo = Backbone.Model.extend({
  defaults: {
    title: '',
    completed: false
  }
});

var TodosCollection = Backbone.Collection.extend({
  model: Todo,
  url: '/todos'
});

var todos = new TodosCollection();
todos.fetch(); // sends HTTP GET to /todos
```

Saving Models to the Server

While Backbone can retrieve an entire collection of models from the server at once, updates to models are performed individually via the model's save() method. When save() is called on a model that was fetched from the server, it constructs a URL by appending the model's id to the collection's URL and sends an HTTP PUT to the server. If the model is a new instance that was created in the browser (it doesn't have an id), then an HTTP POST is sent to the collection's URL. Collections.create() can be used to create a new model, add it to the collection, and send it to the server in a single method call.

```
var Todo = Backbone.Model.extend({
  defaults: {
    title: '',
    completed: false
  }
});

var TodosCollection = Backbone.Collection.extend({
  model: Todo,
  url: '/todos'
});

var todos = new TodosCollection();
todos.fetch();

var todo2 = todos.get(2);
todo2.set('title', 'go fishing');
todo2.save(); // sends HTTP PUT to /todos/2

todos.create({title: 'Try out code samples'});
// sends HTTP POST to /todos and adds to collection
```

As mentioned earlier, a model's validate() method is called automatically by save() and will trigger an invalid event on the model if validation fails.

Deleting Models from the Server

You can remove a model from the containing collection and the server by calling its destroy() method. Unlike Collection.remove(), which only removes a model from a collection, Model.destroy() will also send an HTTP DELETE to the collection's URL.

```
var Todo = Backbone.Model.extend({
  defaults: {
    title: '',
    completed: false
  }
});

var TodosCollection = Backbone.Collection.extend({
```

```
  model: Todo,
  url: '/todos'
});

var todos = new TodosCollection();
todos.fetch();

var todo2 = todos.get(2);
todo2.destroy(); // sends HTTP DELETE to /todos/2 and removes from collection
```

Calling destroy on a model will return false if the model isNew:

```
var Todo = new Backbone.Model();
console.log(Todo.destroy());
// false
```

Options

Each RESTful API method accepts a variety of options. Most importantly, all methods accept success and error callbacks that can be used to customize the handling of server responses.

Specifying the {patch: true} option to Model.save() will cause it to use HTTP PATCH to send only the changed attributes (such as partial updates) to the server instead of the entire model—that is model.save(attrs, {patch: true}):

```
// Save partial using PATCH
model.clear().set({id: 1, a: 1, b: 2, c: 3, d: 4});
model.save();
model.save({b: 2, d: 4}, {patch: true});
console.log(this.syncArgs.method);
// 'patch'
```

Similarly, passing the {reset: true} option to Collection.fetch() will result in the collection being updated using reset() rather than set().

See the Backbone.js documentation for full descriptions of the supported options.

Events

Events are a basic inversion of control. Instead of having one function call another by name, the second function is registered as a handler to be called when a specific event occurs.

The part of your application that has to know how to call the other part of your app has been inverted. This is the core component that makes it possible for your business logic to not have to know about how your user interface works, and the most powerful thing about the Backbone events system.

Mastering events is one of the quickest ways to become more productive with Backbone, so let's take a closer look at Backbone's event model.

Backbone.Events is mixed into the other Backbone classes, including:

- Backbone
- Backbone.Model
- Backbone.Collection
- Backbone.Router
- Backbone.History
- Backbone.View

Note that Backbone.Events is mixed into the Backbone object. Since Backbone is globally visible, it can be used as a simple event bus:

```
Backbone.on('event', function() {
    console.log('Handled Backbone event');
});
```

on(), off(), and trigger()

Backbone.Events can give any object the ability to bind and trigger custom events. We can mix this module into any object easily, and there isn't a requirement for events to be declared before being bound to a callback handler. For example:

```
var ourObject = {};

// Mixin
_.extend(ourObject, Backbone.Events);

// Add a custom event
ourObject.on('dance', function(msg){
  console.log('We triggered ' + msg);
});

// Trigger the custom event
ourObject.trigger('dance', 'our event');
```

If you're familiar with jQuery custom events or the concept of publish/subscribe, Backbone.Events provides a very similar system, with on being analogous to subscribe and trigger being similar to publish.

on binds a callback function to an object, as we've done with dance in the preceding example. The callback is invoked whenever the event is triggered.

The official Backbone.js documentation recommends namespacing event names using colons if you end up having quite a few of these on your page. For example:

```
var ourObject = {};

// Mixin
_.extend(ourObject, Backbone.Events);

function dancing (msg) { console.log("We started " + msg); }

// Add namespaced custom events
ourObject.on("dance:tap", dancing);
ourObject.on("dance:break", dancing);

// Trigger the custom events
ourObject.trigger("dance:tap", "tap dancing. Yeah!");
ourObject.trigger("dance:break", "break dancing. Yeah!");

// This one triggers nothing as no listener listens for it
ourObject.trigger("dance", "break dancing. Yeah!");
```

A special all event is made available in case you would like notifications for every event that occurs on the object (for example, if you would like to screen events in a single location). The all event can be used as follows:

```
var ourObject = {};

// Mixin
_.extend(ourObject, Backbone.Events);

function dancing (msg) { console.log("We started " + msg); }

ourObject.on("all", function(eventName){
  console.log("The name of the event passed was " + eventName);
});

// This time each event will be caught with a catch 'all' event listener
ourObject.trigger("dance:tap", "tap dancing. Yeah!");
ourObject.trigger("dance:break", "break dancing. Yeah!");
ourObject.trigger("dance", "break dancing. Yeah!");
```

off removes callback functions that were previously bound to an object. Going back to our publish/subscribe comparison, think of it as an unsubscribe for custom events.

To remove the dance event we previously bound to ourObject, we would simply do:

```
var ourObject = {};

// Mixin
_.extend(ourObject, Backbone.Events);

function dancing (msg) { console.log("We " + msg); }

// Add namespaced custom events
ourObject.on("dance:tap", dancing);
ourObject.on("dance:break", dancing);
```

```
// Trigger the custom events. Each will be caught and acted upon.
ourObject.trigger("dance:tap", "started tap dancing. Yeah!");
ourObject.trigger("dance:break", "started break dancing. Yeah!");

// Removes event bound to the object
ourObject.off("dance:tap");

// Trigger the custom events again, but one is logged.
ourObject.trigger("dance:tap", "stopped tap dancing.");
// won't be logged as it's not listened for
ourObject.trigger("dance:break", "break dancing. Yeah!");
```

To remove all callbacks for the event, we pass an event name (such as move) to the off() method on the object the event is bound to. If we wish to remove a specific callback, we can pass that callback as the second parameter:

```
var ourObject = {};

// Mixin
_.extend(ourObject, Backbone.Events);

function dancing (msg) { console.log("We are dancing. " + msg); }
function jumping (msg) { console.log("We are jumping. " + msg); }

// Add two listeners to the same event
ourObject.on("move", dancing);
ourObject.on("move", jumping);

// Trigger the events. Both listeners are called.
ourObject.trigger("move", "Yeah!");

// Removes specified listener
ourObject.off("move", dancing);

// Trigger the events again. One listener left.
ourObject.trigger("move", "Yeah, jump, jump!");
```

Finally, as we have seen in our previous examples, trigger triggers a callback for a specified event (or a space-separated list of events). For example:

```
var ourObject = {};

// Mixin
_.extend(ourObject, Backbone.Events);

function doAction (msg) { console.log("We are " + msg); }

// Add event listeners
ourObject.on("dance", doAction);
ourObject.on("jump", doAction);
ourObject.on("skip", doAction);
```

```
// Single event
ourObject.trigger("dance", 'just dancing.');

// Multiple events
ourObject.trigger("dance jump skip", 'very tired from so much action.');
```

trigger can pass multiple arguments to the callback function:

```
var ourObject = {};

// Mixin
_.extend(ourObject, Backbone.Events);

function doAction (action, duration) {
  console.log("We are " + action + ' for ' + duration );
}

// Add event listeners
ourObject.on("dance", doAction);
ourObject.on("jump", doAction);
ourObject.on("skip", doAction);

// Passing multiple arguments to single event
ourObject.trigger("dance", 'dancing', "5 minutes");

// Passing multiple arguments to multiple events
ourObject.trigger("dance jump skip", 'on fire', "15 minutes");
```

listenTo() and stopListening()

While on() and off() add callbacks directly to an observed object, listenTo() tells an object to listen for events on another object, allowing the listener to keep track of the events for which it is listening. stopListening() can subsequently be called on the listener to tell it to stop listening for events:

```
var a = _.extend({}, Backbone.Events);
var b = _.extend({}, Backbone.Events);
var c = _.extend({}, Backbone.Events);

// add listeners to A for events on B and C
a.listenTo(b, 'anything', function(event){
    console.log("anything happened"); });
a.listenTo(c, 'everything', function(event){
    console.log("everything happened"); });

// trigger an event
b.trigger('anything'); // logs: anything happened

// stop listening
a.stopListening();

// A does not receive these events
```

```
b.trigger('anything');
c.trigger('everything');
```

`stopListening()` can also be used to selectively stop listening based on the event, model, or callback handler.

If you use on and `off` and remove views and their corresponding models at the same time, there are generally no problems. But a problem arises when you remove a view that had registered to be notified about events on a model, but you don't remove the model or call `off` to remove the view's event handler. Since the model has a reference to the view's callback function, the JavaScript garbage collector cannot remove the view from memory. This is called a *ghost view* and is a common form of memory leak since the models generally tend to outlive the corresponding views during an application's lifecycle. For details on the topic and a solution, check out this excellent article by Derick Bailey (*http://bit.ly/ZN0Sci*).

Practically, every on called on an object also requires an `off` to be called in order for the garbage collector to do its job. `listenTo()` changes that, allowing views to bind to model notifications and unbind from all of them with just one call: `stopListening()`.

The default implementation of `View.remove()` makes a call to `stopListening()`, ensuring that any listeners bound via `listenTo()` are unbound before the view is destroyed.

```
var view = new Backbone.View();
var b = _.extend({}, Backbone.Events);

view.listenTo(b, 'all', function(){ console.log(true); });
b.trigger ('anything'); // logs: true

view.listenTo(b, 'all', function(){ console.log(false); });
view.remove(); // stopListening() implicitly called
b.trigger('anything');
// does not log anything
```

Events and Views

Within a view, there are two types of events you can listen for: DOM events and events triggered using the Event API. It is important to understand the differences in how views bind to these events and the context in which their callbacks are invoked.

You can bind DOM events using the view's events property or using jQuery.on(). Within callbacks bound using the events property, this refers to the view object; any callbacks bound directly using jQuery, however, will have this set to the handling DOM element by jQuery. All DOM event callbacks are passed an event object by jQuery. See `delegateEvents()` in the Backbone documentation for additional details.

Event API events are bound as described in this section. If you bind the event using on() on the observed object, you can pass a context parameter as the third argument. If you bind the event using listenTo(), then within the callback this refers to the listener. The arguments passed to Event API callbacks depend on the type of event. See the Catalog of Events in the Backbone documentation for details.

The following example illustrates these differences:

```
<div id="todo">
    <input type='checkbox' />
</div>

var View = Backbone.View.extend({

    el: '#todo',

    // bind to DOM event using events property
    events: {
        'click [type="checkbox"]': 'clicked',
    },

    initialize: function () {
        // bind to DOM event using jQuery
        this.$el.click(this.jqueryClicked);

        // bind to API event
        this.on('apiEvent', this.callback);
    },

    // 'this' is view
    clicked: function(event) {
        console.log("events handler for " + this.el.outerHTML);
        this.trigger('apiEvent', event.type);
    },

    // 'this' is handling DOM element
    jqueryClicked: function(event) {
        console.log("jQuery handler for " + this.outerHTML);
    },

    callback: function(eventType) {
        console.log("event type was " + eventType);
    }

});

var view = new View();
```

Routers

In Backbone, routers provide a way for you to connect URLs (either hash fragments, or real) to parts of your application. Any piece of your application that you want to be bookmarkable, shareable, and back-button-able needs a URL.

Here are some examples of routes using the hash mark:

```
http://example.com/#about
http://example.com/#search/seasonal-horns/page2
```

An application will usually have at least one route mapping a URL route to a function that determines what happens when a user reaches that route. This relationship is defined as follows:

```
'route' : 'mappedFunction'
```

Let's define our first router by extending Backbone.Router. For the purposes of this guide, we're going to continue pretending we're creating a complex todo application (something like a personal organizer/planner) that requires a complex TodoRouter.

Note the inline comments in the following code example, as they continue our lesson on routers.

```
var TodoRouter = Backbone.Router.extend({
    /* define the route and function maps for this router */
    routes: {
        "about" : "showAbout",
        /* Sample usage: http://example.com/#about */

        "todo/:id" : "getTodo",
        /* This is an example of using a ":param" variable, which allows us to
        match any of the components between two URL slashes */
        /* Sample usage: http://example.com/#todo/5 */

        "search/:query" : "searchTodos",
        /* We can also define multiple routes that are bound to the same map
        function, in this case searchTodos(). Note below how we're optionally
        passing in a reference to a page number if one is supplied */
        /* Sample usage: http://example.com/#search/job */

        "search/:query/p:page" : "searchTodos",
        /* As we can see, URLs may contain as many ":param"s as we wish */
        /* Sample usage: http://example.com/#search/job/p1 */

        "todos/:id/download/*documentPath" : "downloadDocument",
        /* This is an example of using a *splat. Splats are able to match
        any number of URL components and can be combined with ":param"s*/
        /* Sample usage: http://example.com/#todos/5/download/todos.doc */

        /* If you wish to use splats for anything beyond default routing,
        it's probably a good idea to leave them at the end of a URL;
```

```
    otherwise, you may need to apply regular expression parsing
    on your fragment */

    "*other"     : "defaultRoute"
    /* This is a default route that also uses a *splat. Consider the
    default route a wildcard for URLs that are either not matched or where
    the user has incorrectly typed in a route path manually */
    /* Sample usage: http://example.com/# <anything> */,

    "optional(/:item)": "optionalItem",
    "named/optional/(y:z)": "namedOptionalItem"
    /* Router URLs also support optional parts via parentheses, without
        having to use a regex.  */
},

showAbout: function(){
},

getTodo: function(id){
    /*
    Note that the id matched in the above route will be passed to this
    function */
    console.log("You are trying to reach todo " + id);
},

searchTodos: function(query, page){
    var page_number = page || 1;
    console.log("Page number: " + page_number + " of the results for todos
    containing the word: " + query);
},

downloadDocument: function(id, path){
},

defaultRoute: function(other){
    console.log('Invalid. You attempted to reach:' + other);
}
});

/* Now that we have a router setup, we need to instantiate it */

var myTodoRouter = new TodoRouter();
```

Backbone offers an opt-in for HTML5 pushState support via window.history.push
State. This permits you to define routes such as *http://backbonejs.org/just/an/example*. This will be supported with automatic degradation when a user's browser doesn't
support pushState. Note that it is vastly preferred if you're capable of also supporting
pushState on the server side, although it is a little more difficult to implement.

You might be wondering if there's a limit to the number of routers you should be using. Andrew de Andrade has pointed out that Document-Cloud, the creator of Backbone, usually only uses a single router in most of its applications. You're very likely to not require more than one or two routers in your own projects; the majority of your application routing can be kept organized in a single router without it getting unwieldy.

Backbone.history

Next, we need to initialize `Backbone.history`, as it handles `hashchange` events in our application. This will automatically handle routes that have been defined and trigger callbacks when they've been accessed.

The `Backbone.history.start()` method will simply tell Backbone that it's OK to begin monitoring all `hashchange` events as follows:

```
var TodoRouter = Backbone.Router.extend({
  /* define the route and function maps for this router */
  routes: {
    "about" : "showAbout",
    "search/:query" : "searchTodos",
    "search/:query/p:page" : "searchTodos"
  },

  showAbout: function(){},

  searchTodos: function(query, page){
    var page_number = page || 1;
    console.log("Page number: " + page_number + " of the results for todos
    containing the word: " + query);
  }
});

var myTodoRouter = new TodoRouter();

Backbone.history.start();

// Go to and check console:
// http://localhost/#search/job/p3    logs: Page number: 3 of the results for
// todos containing the word: job
// http://localhost/#search/job       logs: Page number: 1 of the results for
// todos containing the word: job
// etc.
```

 To run the preceding example, you'll need to create a local development environment and test project, which we will cover in Chapter 4.

If you would like to update the URL to reflect the application state at a particular point, you can use the router's .navigate() method. By default, it simply updates your URL fragment without triggering the hashchange event:

```
// Let's imagine we would like a specific fragment
// (edit) once a user opens a single todo
var TodoRouter = Backbone.Router.extend({
  routes: {
    "todo/:id": "viewTodo",
    "todo/:id/edit": "editTodo"
    // ... other routes
  },

  viewTodo: function(id){
    console.log("View todo requested.");
    this.navigate("todo/" + id + '/edit');
    // updates the fragment for us, but doesn't trigger the route
  },

  editTodo: function(id) {
    console.log("Edit todo opened.");
  }
});

var myTodoRouter = new TodoRouter();

Backbone.history.start();

// Go to: http://localhost/#todo/4
//
// URL is updated to: http://localhost/#todo/4/edit
// but editTodo() function is not invoked even though location we end up
// is mapped to it.
//
// logs: View todo requested.
```

It is also possible for Router.navigate() to trigger the route along with updating the URL fragment by passing the trigger:true option.

 This usage is discouraged. The recommended usage is the one previously described that creates a bookmarkable URL when your application transitions to a specific state.

```
var TodoRouter = Backbone.Router.extend({
  routes: {
    "todo/:id": "viewTodo",
    "todo/:id/edit": "editTodo"
    // ... other routes
  },
```

```
  viewTodo: function(id){
    console.log("View todo requested.");
    this.navigate("todo/" + id + '/edit', {trigger: true});
// updates the fragment and triggers the route as well
  },

  editTodo: function(id) {
    console.log("Edit todo opened.");
  }
});

var myTodoRouter = new TodoRouter();

Backbone.history.start();

// Go to: http://localhost/#todo/4
//
// URL is updated to: http://localhost/#todo/4/edit
// and this time editTodo() function is invoked.
//
// logs:
// View todo requested.
// Edit todo opened.
```

A route event is also triggered on the router in addition to being fired on Back
bone.history.

```
Backbone.history.on('route', onRoute);

// Trigger 'route' event on router instance."
router.on('route', function(name, args) {
  console.log(name === 'routeEvent');
});

location.replace('http://example.com#route-event/x');
Backbone.history.checkUrl();
```

Backbone's Sync API

We previously discussed how Backbone supports RESTful persistence via the fetch(),
save(), and destroy() methods on models, and the fetch() and create() methods
on collections. Now we are going to take a closer look at Backbone's sync method, which
underlies these operations.

The Backbone.sync method is an integral part of Backbone.js. It assumes a jQuery-like
$.ajax() method, so HTTP parameters are organized based on jQuery's API. Since
some legacy servers may not support JSON-formatted requests and HTTP PUT and
DELETE operations, we can configure Backbone to emulate these capabilities using the
two configuration variables shown here with their default values:

```
Backbone.emulateHTTP = false;
// set to true if server cannot handle HTTP PUT or HTTP DELETE
Backbone.emulateJSON = false;
// set to true if server cannot handle application/json requests
```

The inline `Backbone.emulateHTTP` option should be set to `true` if extended HTTP methods are not supported by the server. The `Backbone.emulateJSON` option should be set to `true` if the server does not understand the MIME type for JSON.

```
// Create a new library collection
var Library = Backbone.Collection.extend({
    url : function() { return '/library'; }
});

// Define attributes for our model
var attrs = {
    title  : "The Tempest",
    author : "Bill Shakespeare",
    length : 123
};

// Create a new library instance
var library = new Library;

// Create a new instance of a model within our collection
library.create(attrs, {wait: false});

// Update with just emulateHTTP
library.first().save({id: '2-the-tempest', author: 'Tim Shakespeare'}, {
  emulateHTTP: true
});

// Check the ajaxSettings being used for our request
console.log(this.ajaxSettings.url === '/library/2-the-tempest');
// true
console.log(this.ajaxSettings.type === 'POST'); // true
console.log(this.ajaxSettings.contentType === 'application/json');
// true

// Parse the data for the request to confirm it is as expected
var data = JSON.parse(this.ajaxSettings.data);
console.log(data.id === '2-the-tempest');  // true
console.log(data.author === 'Tim Shakespeare'); // true
console.log(data.length === 123); // true
```

Similarly, we could just update using `emulateJSON`:

```
library.first().save({id: '2-the-tempest', author: 'Tim Shakespeare'}, {
  emulateJSON: true
});

console.log(this.ajaxSettings.url === '/library/2-the-tempest'); // true
console.log(this.ajaxSettings.type === 'PUT'); // true
```

```
console.log(this.ajaxSettings.contentType ===
'application/x-www-form-urlencoded'); // true

var data = JSON.parse(this.ajaxSettings.data.model);
console.log(data.id === '2-the-tempest');
console.log(data.author ==='Tim Shakespeare');
console.log(data.length === 123);
```

Backbone.sync is called every time Backbone tries to read, save, or delete models. It uses jQuery or Zepto's $.ajax() implementations to make these RESTful requests, but you can override this as per your needs.

Overriding Backbone.sync

You can override the sync method globally as Backbone.sync, or at a finer-grained level, by adding a sync function to a Backbone collection or to an individual model.

Since all persistence is handled by the Backbone.sync function, we can use an alternative persistence layer by simply overriding Backbone.sync with a function that has the same signature:

```
Backbone.sync = function(method, model, options) {
};
```

The following methodMap is used by the standard sync implementation to map the method parameter to an HTTP operation and illustrates the type of action required by each method argument:

```
var methodMap = {
  'create': 'POST',
  'update': 'PUT',
  'patch':  'PATCH',
  'delete': 'DELETE',
  'read':   'GET'
};
```

If we wanted to replace the standard sync implementation with one that simply logged the calls to sync, we could do this:

```
var id_counter = 1;
Backbone.sync = function(method, model) {
  console.log("I've been passed " + method + " with " + JSON.stringify(model));
  if(method === 'create'){ model.set('id', id_counter++); }
};
```

Note that we assign a unique id to any created models.

The Backbone.sync method is intended to be overridden to support other persistence backends. The built-in method is tailored to a certain breed of RESTful JSON APIs—Backbone was originally extracted from a Ruby on Rails application, which uses HTTP methods like PUT in the same way.

The sync method is called with three parameters:

method
> One of create, update, patch, delete, or read

model
> The Backbone model object

options
> May include success and error methods

We can implement a new sync method using the following pattern:

```
Backbone.sync = function(method, model, options) {

  function success(result) {
    // Handle successful results from MyAPI
    if (options.success) {
      options.success(result);
    }
  }

  function error(result) {
    // Handle error results from MyAPI
    if (options.error) {
      options.error(result);
    }
  }

  options || (options = {});

  switch (method) {
    case 'create':
      return MyAPI.create(model, success, error);

    case 'update':
      return MyAPI.update(model, success, error);

    case 'patch':
      return MyAPI.patch(model, success, error);

    case 'delete':
      return MyAPI.destroy(model, success, error);

    case 'read':
      if (model.attributes[model.idAttribute]) {
        return MyAPI.find(model, success, error);
      } else {
        return MyAPI.findAll(model, success, error);
      }
  }
};
```

This pattern delegates API calls to a new object (`MyAPI`), which could be a Backbone-style class that supports events. This can be safely tested separately, and potentially used with libraries other than Backbone.

There are quite a few `sync` implementations out there. The following examples are all available on GitHub:

Backbone `localStorage`
> Persists to the browser's `localStorage`

Backbone offline
> Supports working offline

Backbone Redis
> Uses Redis key-value store

backbone-parse
> Integrates Backbone with Parse.com

backbone-websql
> Stores data to WebSQL

Backbone Caching Sync
> Uses `localStorage` as cache for other sync implementations

Dependencies

The official Backbone.js documentation (*http://backbonejs.org/*) states:

> Backbone's only hard dependency is either Underscore.js (>= 1.4.3) or Lo-Dash. For RESTful persistence, history support via Backbone.Router and DOM manipulation with Backbone.View, include json2.js, and either jQuery (>= 1.7.0) or Zepto.

What this translates to is that if you require working with anything beyond models, you will need to include a DOM manipulation library such as jQuery or Zepto. Underscore is primarily used for its utility methods (which Backbone relies upon heavily) and json2.js for legacy browser JSON support if `Backbone.sync` is used.

Summary

In this chapter I have introduced you to the components you will be using to build applications with Backbone: models, views, collections, and routers. We've explored the Events mixin that Backbone uses to enhance all components with publish-subscribe capabilities and seen how it can be used with arbitrary objects. Finally, we saw how Backbone leverages the Underscore.js and jQuery/Zepto APIs to add rich manipulation and persistence features to Backbone collections and models.

Backbone has many operations and options beyond those we have covered here and is always evolving, so be sure to visit the official documentation (*http://backbonejs.org/*) for more details and the latest features. In the next chapter, you will start to get your hands dirty as we walk through the implementation of your first Backbone application.

CHAPTER 4

Exercise 1: Todos—Your First Backbone.js App

Now that we've covered fundamentals, let's write our first Backbone.js application. We'll build the Backbone Todo List application exhibited on TodoMVC.com (*http://todomvc.com*). Building a todo list is a great way to learn Backbone's conventions (see Figure 4-1). It's a relatively simple application, yet technical challenges surrounding binding, persisting model data, routing, and template rendering provide opportunities to illustrate some core Backbone features.

Let's consider the application's architecture at a high level. We'll need:

- A Todo model to describe individual todo items
- A TodoList collection to store and persist todos
- A way of creating todos
- A way to display a listing of todos
- A way to edit existing todos
- A way to mark a todo as completed
- A way to delete todos
- A way to filter the items that have been completed or are remaining

Figure 4-1. A todo list—the first Backbone.js application we will be writing

Essentially, these features are classic CRUD (create, read, update, delete) (*http://bit.ly/YrWE99*) methods. Let's get started!

Static HTML

We'll place all of our HTML in a single file named *index.html*.

Header and Scripts

First, we'll set up the header and the basic application dependencies: jQuery (*http://jquery.com*), Underscore (*http://underscorejs.org*), Backbone.js, and the Backbone localStorage adapter (*http://bit.ly/16dX4op*).

```
<!doctype html>
<html lang="en">
<head>
  <meta charset="utf-8">
  <meta http-equiv="X-UA-Compatible" content="IE=edge,chrome=1">
  <title>Backbone.js • TodoMVC</title>
  <link rel="stylesheet" href="assets/base.css">
</head>
<body>
  <script type="text/template" id="item-template"></script>
  <script type="text/template" id="stats-template"></script>
  <script src="js/lib/jquery.min.js"></script>
```

```
<script src="js/lib/underscore-min.js"></script>
<script src="js/lib/backbone-min.js"></script>
<script src="js/lib/backbone.localStorage.js"></script>
<script src="js/models/todo.js"></script>
<script src="js/collections/todos.js"></script>
<script src="js/views/todos.js"></script>
<script src="js/views/app.js"></script>
<script src="js/routers/router.js"></script>
<script src="js/app.js"></script>
</body>
</html>
```

In addition to the aforementioned dependencies, note that a few other application-specific files are also loaded. These are organized into folders representing their application responsibilities: models, views, collections, and routers. An *app.js* file houses central initialization code.

If you want to follow along, create a directory structure as demonstrated in *index.html*:

1. Place the *index.html* in a top-level directory.

2. Download jQuery, Underscore, Backbone, and Backbone localStorage from their respective websites and place them under *js/lib*.

3. Create the directories *js/models*, *js/collections*, *js/views*, and *js/routers*.

You will also need *base.css (http://bit.ly/YePkgQ)* and *bg.png (http://bit.ly/11YarU3)*, which should live in an assets directory. And remember that you can see a demo of the final application at TodoMVC.com (*http://todomvc.com*).

We will be creating the application JavaScript files during the tutorial. Don't worry about the two text/template script elements—we will replace those soon!

Application HTML

Now let's populate the body of *index.html*. We'll need an <input> for creating new todos, a <ul id="todo-list" /> for listing the actual todos, and a footer where we can later insert statistics and links for performing operations such as clearing completed todos. We'll add the following markup immediately inside our <body> tag before the script elements:

```
<section id="todoapp">
  <header id="header">
    <h1>todos</h1>
    <input id="new-todo" placeholder="What needs to be done?" autofocus>
  </header>
  <section id="main">
    <input id="toggle-all" type="checkbox">
    <label for="toggle-all">Mark all as complete</label>
    <ul id="todo-list"></ul>
```

```
    </section>
    <footer id="footer"></footer>
  </section>
  <div id="info">
    <p>Double-click to edit a todo</p>
    <p>Written by <a href="https://github.com/addyosmani">Addy Osmani</a></p>
    <p>Part of <a href="http://todomvc.com">TodoMVC</a></p>
  </div>
```

Templates

To complete *index.html*, we need to add the templates, which we will use to dynamically create HTML by injecting model data into their placeholders. One way of including templates in the page is by using custom `<script>` tags. These don't get evaluated by the browser, which just interprets them as plain text. Underscore microtemplating can then access the templates, rendering fragments of HTML.

We'll start by filling in the `#item-template`, which will be used to display individual todo items.

```
<!-- index.html -->

<script type="text/template" id="item-template">
  <div class="view">
    <input class="toggle" type="checkbox" <%= completed ? 'checked' : '' %>>
    <label><%- title %></label>
    <button class="destroy"></button>
  </div>
  <input class="edit" value="<%- title %>">
</script>
```

The template tags in the preceding markup, such as `<%=` and `<%-`, are specific to Underscore.js and are documented on the Underscore site. In your own applications, you have a choice of template libraries, such as Mustache or Handlebars. Use whichever you prefer; Backbone doesn't mind.

We also need to define the `#stats-template`, which we will use to populate the footer.

```
<!-- index.html -->

<script type="text/template" id="stats-template">
  <span id="todo-count"><strong><%= remaining %></strong>
  <%= remaining === 1 ? 'item' : 'items' %> left</span>
  <ul id="filters">
    <li>
      <a class="selected" href="#/">All</a>
    </li>
    <li>
      <a href="#/active">Active</a>
    </li>
    <li>
```

```
        <a href="#/completed">Completed</a>
      </li>
    </ul>
    <% if (completed) { %>
    <button id="clear-completed">Clear completed (<%= completed %>)</button>
    <% } %>
</script>
```

The `#stats-template` displays the number of remaining incomplete items and contains a list of hyperlinks that will be used to perform actions when we implement our router. It also contains a button that can be used to clear all of the completed items.

Now that we have all the HTML that we will need, we'll start implementing our application by returning to the fundamentals: a Todo model.

Todo Model

The Todo model is remarkably straightforward. First, a todo has two attributes: a `title` stores a todo item's title, and a `completed` status indicates whether it's complete. These attributes are passed as defaults, as shown here:

```
// js/models/todo.js

var app = app || {};

// Todo Model
// ----------
// Our basic **Todo** model has 'title', 'order', and 'completed' attributes.

app.Todo = Backbone.Model.extend({

  // Default attributes ensure that each todo created has `title` and
  // `completed` keys.
  defaults: {
    title: '',
    completed: false
  },

  // Toggle the `completed` state of this todo item.
  toggle: function() {
    this.save({
      completed: !this.get('completed')
    });
  }

});
```

Second, the Todo model has a `toggle()` method through which a todo item's completion status can be set and simultaneously persisted.

Todo Collection

Next, a `TodoList` collection is used to group our models. The collection uses the localStorage adapter to override Backbone's default `sync()` operation with one that will persist our todo records to HTML5 localStorage. Through localStorage, they're saved between page requests.

```
// js/collections/todos.js

var app = app || {};

// Todo Collection
// ---------------

// The collection of todos is backed by *localStorage* instead of a remote
// server.
var TodoList = Backbone.Collection.extend({

  // Reference to this collection's model.
  model: app.Todo,

  // Save all of the todo items under the `"todos-backbone"` namespace.
  // Note that you will need to have the Backbone localStorage plug-in
  // loaded inside your page in order for this to work. If testing
  // in the console without this present, comment out the next line
  // to avoid running into an exception.
  localStorage: new Backbone.LocalStorage('todos-backbone'),

  // Filter down the list of all todo items that are finished.
  completed: function() {
    return this.filter(function( todo ) {
      return todo.get('completed');
    });
  },

  // Filter down the list to only todo items that are still not finished.
  remaining: function() {
  // apply allowsus to define the context of this within our function scope
    return this.without.apply( this, this.completed() );
  },

  // We keep the Todos in sequential order, despite being saved by unordered
  // GUID in the database. This generates the next order number for new items.
  nextOrder: function() {
    if ( !this.length ) {
      return 1;
    }
    return this.last().get('order') + 1;
  },

  // Todos are sorted by their original insertion order.
```

```
    comparator: function( todo ) {
      return todo.get('order');
    }
});

// Create our global collection of **Todos**.
app.Todos = new TodoList();
```

The collection's `completed()` and `remaining()` methods return an array of finished and unfinished todos, respectively.

A `nextOrder()` method implements a sequence generator while a `comparator()` sorts items by their insertion order.

 `this.filter`, `this.without`, and `this.last` are Underscore methods that are mixed in to `Backbone.Collection` so that the reader knows how to find out more about them.

Application View

Let's examine the core application logic that resides in the views. Each view supports functionality such as edit-in-place, and therefore contains a fair amount of logic. To help organize this logic, we'll use the element controller pattern. The element controller pattern consists of two views: one controls a collection of items, while the other deals with each individual item.

In our case, an `AppView` will handle the creation of new todos and rendering of the initial todo list. Instances of `TodoView` will be associated with each individual todo record. Todo instances can handle editing, updating, and destroying their associated todo.

To keep things short and simple, we won't be implementing all of the application's features in this tutorial; we'll just cover enough to get you started. Even so, there is a lot for us to cover in `AppView`, so we'll split our discussion into two sections.

```
// js/views/app.js

var app = app || {};

// The Application
// ---------------

// Our overall **AppView** is the top-level piece of UI.
app.AppView = Backbone.View.extend({

  // Instead of generating a new element, bind to the existing skeleton of
  // the app already present in the HTML.
  el: '#todoapp',
```

```
// Our template for the line of statistics at the bottom of the app.
statsTemplate: _.template( $('#stats-template').html() ),

// At initialization we bind to the relevant events on the `Todos`
// collection, when items are added or changed.
initialize: function() {
  this.allCheckbox = this.$('#toggle-all')[0];
  this.$input = this.$('#new-todo');
  this.$footer = this.$('#footer');
  this.$main = this.$('#main');

  this.listenTo(app.Todos, 'add', this.addOne);
  this.listenTo(app.Todos, 'reset', this.addAll);
},

// Add a single todo item to the list by creating a view for it, and
// appending its element to the `<ul>`.
addOne: function( todo ) {
  var view = new app.TodoView({ model: todo });
  $('#todo-list').append( view.render().el );
},

// Add all items in the **Todos** collection at once.
addAll: function() {
  this.$('#todo-list').html('');
  app.Todos.each(this.addOne, this);
}

});
```

There are a few notable features in our initial version of AppView, including a statsTem plate, an initialize method that's implicitly called on instantiation, and several view-specific methods.

An el (element) property stores a selector targeting the DOM element with an id of todoapp. In the case of our application, el refers to the matching <section id="to doapp" /> element in *index.html*.

The call to _.template uses Underscore's microtemplating to construct a statsTem plate object from our #stats-template. We will use this template later when we render our view.

Now let's take a look at the initialize function. First, it's using jQuery to cache the elements it will be using into local properties (recall that this.$() finds elements relative to this.$el). Then it's binding to two events on the Todos collection: add and reset. Since we're delegating handling of updates and deletes to the TodoView view, we don't need to worry about those here. The two pieces of logic are:

- When an `add` event is fired, the `addOne()` method is called and passed the new model. `addOne()` creates an instance of the `TodoView` view, renders it, and appends the resulting element to our todo list.

- When a `reset` event occurs (we update the collection in bulk as happens when the todos are loaded from localStorage), `addAll()` is called and iterates over all of the todos currently in our collection, firing `addOne()` for each item.

Note that we were able to use `this` within `addAll()` to refer to the view because `listenTo()` implicitly set the callback's context to the view when it created the binding.

Now, let's add some more logic to complete our `AppView`:

```
// js/views/app.js

var app = app || {};

// The Application
// ---------------

// Our overall **AppView** is the top-level piece of UI.
app.AppView = Backbone.View.extend({

  // Instead of generating a new element, bind to the existing skeleton of
  // the app already present in the HTML.
  el: '#todoapp',

  // Our template for the line of statistics at the bottom of the app.
  statsTemplate: _.template( $('#stats-template').html() ),

  // New
  // Delegated events for creating new items, and clearing completed ones.
  events: {
    'keypress #new-todo': 'createOnEnter',
    'click #clear-completed': 'clearCompleted',
    'click #toggle-all': 'toggleAllComplete'
  },

  // At initialization we bind to the relevant events on the `Todos`
  // collection, when items are added or changed. Kick things off by
  // loading any preexisting todos that might be saved in *localStorage*.
  initialize: function() {
    this.allCheckbox = this.$('#toggle-all')[0];
    this.$input = this.$('#new-todo');
    this.$footer = this.$('#footer');
    this.$main = this.$('#main');

    this.listenTo(app.Todos, 'add', this.addOne);
    this.listenTo(app.Todos, 'reset', this.addAll);

    // New
```

```javascript
    this.listenTo(app.Todos, 'change:completed', this.filterOne);
    this.listenTo(app.Todos,'filter', this.filterAll);
    this.listenTo(app.Todos, 'all', this.render);

    app.Todos.fetch();
  },

  // New
  // Rerendering the app just means refreshing the statistics -- the rest
  // of the app doesn't change.
  render: function() {
    var completed = app.Todos.completed().length;
    var remaining = app.Todos.remaining().length;

    if ( app.Todos.length ) {
      this.$main.show();
      this.$footer.show();

      this.$footer.html(this.statsTemplate({
        completed: completed,
        remaining: remaining
      }));

      this.$('#filters li a')
        .removeClass('selected')
        .filter('[href="#/' + ( app.TodoFilter || '' ) + '"]')
        .addClass('selected');
    } else {
      this.$main.hide();
      this.$footer.hide();
    }

    this.allCheckbox.checked = !remaining;
  },

  // Add a single todo item to the list by creating a view for it, and
  // appending its element to the `<ul>`.
  addOne: function( todo ) {
    var view = new app.TodoView({ model: todo });
    $('#todo-list').append( view.render().el );
  },

  // Add all items in the **Todos** collection at once.
  addAll: function() {
    this.$('#todo-list').html('');
    app.Todos.each(this.addOne, this);
  },

  // New
  filterOne : function (todo) {
    todo.trigger('visible');
  },
```

```
    // New
    filterAll : function () {
      app.Todos.each(this.filterOne, this);
    },


    // New
    // Generate the attributes for a new todo item.
    newAttributes: function() {
      return {
        title: this.$input.val().trim(),
        order: app.Todos.nextOrder(),
        completed: false
      };
    },

    // New
    // If you hit return in the main input field, create new Todo model,
    // persisting it to localStorage.
    createOnEnter: function( event ) {
      if ( event.which !== ENTER_KEY || !this.$input.val().trim() ) {
        return;
      }

      app.Todos.create( this.newAttributes() );
      this.$input.val('');
    },

    // New
    // Clear all completed todo items, destroying their models.
    clearCompleted: function() {
      _.invoke(app.Todos.completed(), 'destroy');
      return false;
    },

    // New
    toggleAllComplete: function() {
      var completed = this.allCheckbox.checked;

      app.Todos.each(function( todo ) {
        todo.save({
          'completed': completed
        });
      });
    }
});
```

We have added the logic for creating new todos, editing them, and filtering them based on their completed status.

We've defined an events hash containing declarative callbacks for our DOM events. It binds those events to the following methods:

createOnEnter()
> Creates a new Todo model and persists it in localStorage when a user presses Enter inside the <input/> field. Also resets the main <input/> field value to prepare it for the next entry. The model is populated by newAttributes(), which returns an object literal composed of the title, order, and completed state of the new item. Note that this is referring to the view and not the DOM element since the callback was bound using the events hash.

clearCompleted()
> Removes the items in the todo list that have been marked as completed when the user clicks the clear-completed checkbox (this checkbox will be in the footer populated by the #stats-template).

toggleAllComplete()
> Allows a user to mark all of the items in the todo list as completed by clicking the toggle-all checkbox.

initialize()
> We've bound callbacks to several additional events:
>
> - We've bound a filterOne() callback on the Todos collection for a change:com pleted event. This listens for changes to the completed flag for any model in the collection. The affected todo is passed to the callback, which triggers a custom visible event on the model.
>
> - We've bound a filterAll() callback for a filter event, which works a little like addOne() and addAll(). Its responsibility is to toggle which todo items are visible based on the filter currently selected in the UI (all, completed, or remaining) via calls to filterOne().
>
> - We've used the special all event to bind any event triggered on the Todos collection to the view's render method (discussed momentarily).

The initialize() method completes by fetching the previously saved todos from localStorage.

Several things are happening in our render() method:

1. The #main and #footer sections are displayed or hidden depending on whether there are any todos in the collection.

2. The footer is populated with the HTML produced by instantiating the statsTem plate with the number of completed and remaining todo items.

3. The HTML produced by the preceding step contains a list of filter links. The value of app.TodoFilter, which will be set by our router, is being used to apply the class selected to the link corresponding to the currently selected filter. This will result in conditional CSS styling being applied to that filter.

4. The allCheckbox is updated based on whether there are remaining todos.

Individual TodoView

Now let's look at the TodoView view. This will be in charge of individual todo records, making sure the view updates when the todo does. To enable this functionality, we will add event listeners to the view that listen for events on an individual todo's HTML representation.

```
// js/views/todos.js

var app = app || {};

// Todo Item View
// -------------

// The DOM element for a todo item...
app.TodoView = Backbone.View.extend({

  //... is a list tag.
  tagName: 'li',

  // Cache the template function for a single item.
  template: _.template( $('#item-template').html() ),

  // The DOM events specific to an item.
  events: {
    'dblclick label': 'edit',
    'keypress .edit': 'updateOnEnter',
    'blur .edit': 'close'
  },

  // The TodoView listens for changes to its model, rerendering. Since there's
  // a one-to-one correspondence between a **Todo** and a **TodoView** in this
  // app, we set a direct reference on the model for convenience.
  initialize: function() {
    this.listenTo(this.model, 'change', this.render);
  },

  // Rerenders the titles of the todo item.
  render: function() {
    this.$el.html( this.template( this.model.toJSON() ) );
    this.$input = this.$('.edit');
    return this;
```

```
      },

      // Switch this view into `"editing"` mode, displaying the input field.
      edit: function() {
        this.$el.addClass('editing');
        this.$input.focus();
      },

      // Close the `"editing"` mode, saving changes to the todo.
      close: function() {
        var value = this.$input.val().trim();

        if ( value ) {
          this.model.save({ title: value });
        }

        this.$el.removeClass('editing');
      },

      // If you hit `enter`, we're through editing the item.
      updateOnEnter: function( e ) {
        if ( e.which === ENTER_KEY ) {
          this.close();
        }
      }
    }
  });
```

In the `initialize()` constructor, we set up a listener that monitors a Todo model's change event. As a result, when the todo gets updated, the application will rerender the view and visually reflect its changes. Note that the model passed in the arguments hash by our `AppView` is automatically available to us as `this.model`.

In the `render()` method, we render our Underscore.js `#item-template`, which was previously compiled into `this.template` using Underscore's `_.template()` method. This returns an HTML fragment that replaces the content of the view's element (an `li` element was implicitly created for us based on the `tagName` property). In other words, the rendered template is now present under `this.el` and can be appended to the todo list in the user interface. `render()` finishes by caching the input element within the instantiated template into `this.input`.

Our events hash includes three callbacks:

`edit()`
> Changes the current view into editing mode when a user double-clicks an existing item in the todo list. This allows the user to change the existing value of the item's `title` attribute.

`updateOnEnter()`
> Checks that the user has pressed the Return/Enter key and executes the `close()` function.

```
close()
```
Trims the value of the current text in our `<input/>` field, ensuring that we don't process it further if it does not contain any text (for example, ''). If a valid value has been provided, we save the changes to the current Todo model and close editing mode by removing the corresponding CSS class.

Startup

So now we have two views: `AppView` and `TodoView`. The former needs to be instantiated on page load so its code gets executed. We can accomplish this through jQuery's `ready()` utility, which will execute a function when the DOM is loaded.

```
// js/app.js

var app = app || {};
var ENTER_KEY = 13;

$(function() {

  // Kick things off by creating the **App**.
  new app.AppView();

});
```

In Action

Let's pause and ensure that the work we've done so far functions as intended.

If you are following along, open *file://*path*/index.html* in your browser and monitor its console. If all is well, you shouldn't see any JavaScript errors other than regarding the *router.js* file that we haven't created yet. The todo list should be blank as we haven't yet created any todos. Plus, there is some additional work we'll need to do before the user interface fully functions.

However, a few things can be tested through the JavaScript console.

In the console, add a new todo item: `window.app.Todos.create({ title: 'My first Todo items'});` and press return (see Figure 4-2).

Figure 4-2. Adding a new todo item via the JavaScript console

If all is functioning properly, this should log the new todo we've just added to the Todos collection. The newly created todo is also saved to localStorage and will be available on page refresh.

`window.app.Todos.create()` executes a collection method, `Collection.create(at tributes, [options])`, that instantiates a new model item of the type passed into the collection definition—in our case, `app.Todo`:

```
// from our js/collections/todos.js

var TodoList = Backbone.Collection.extend({

    model: app.Todo // the model type used by collection.create() to
// instantiate new model in the collection
    ...
)};
```

Run the following in the console to check it out:

```
var secondTodo = window.app.Todos.create({ title: 'My second Todo item'});
secondTodo instanceof app.Todo // returns true
```

Now refresh the page; we should be able to see the fruits of our labor.

The todos added through the console should still appear in the list since they are populated from the localStorage. Also, we should be able to create a new todo by typing a title and pressing Enter (Figure 4-3).

Figure 4-3. Adding new todo items

Excellent—we're making great progress, but what about completing and deleting todos?

Completing and Deleting Todos

The next part of our tutorial is going to cover completing and deleting todos. These two actions are specific to each todo item, so we need to add this functionality to the Todo View view. We will do so by adding `togglecompleted()` and `clear()` methods along with corresponding entries in the events hash.

```
// js/views/todos.js

var app = app || {};

// Todo Item View
// --------------

// The DOM element for a todo item...
app.TodoView = Backbone.View.extend({

  //... is a list tag.
  tagName: 'li',
```

```javascript
// Cache the template function for a single item.
template: _.template( $('#item-template').html() ),

// The DOM events specific to an item.
events: {
  'click .toggle': 'togglecompleted', // NEW
  'dblclick label': 'edit',
  'click .destroy': 'clear',          // NEW
  'keypress .edit': 'updateOnEnter',
  'blur .edit': 'close'
},

// The TodoView listens for changes to its model, rerendering. Since there's
// a one-to-one correspondence between a **Todo** and a **TodoView** in this
// app, we set a direct reference on the model for convenience.
initialize: function() {
  this.listenTo(this.model, 'change', this.render);
  this.listenTo(this.model, 'destroy', this.remove);        // NEW
  this.listenTo(this.model, 'visible', this.toggleVisible); // NEW
},

// Rerender the titles of the todo item.
render: function() {
  this.$el.html( this.template( this.model.toJSON() ) );

  this.$el.toggleClass( 'completed', this.model.get('completed') ); // NEW
  this.toggleVisible();                                             // NEW

  this.$input = this.$('.edit');
  return this;
},

// NEW - Toggles visibility of item
toggleVisible : function () {
  this.$el.toggleClass( 'hidden',  this.isHidden());
},

// NEW - Determines if item should be hidden
isHidden : function () {
  var isCompleted = this.model.get('completed');
  return ( // hidden cases only
    (!isCompleted && app.TodoFilter === 'completed')
    || (isCompleted && app.TodoFilter === 'active')
  );
},

// NEW - Toggle the `"completed"` state of the model.
togglecompleted: function() {
  this.model.toggle();
},
```

```
// Switch this view into `"editing"` mode, displaying the input field.
edit: function() {
  this.$el.addClass('editing');
  this.$input.focus();
},

// Close the `"editing"` mode, saving changes to the todo.
close: function() {
  var value = this.$input.val().trim();

  if ( value ) {
    this.model.save({ title: value });
  } else {
    this.clear(); // NEW
  }

  this.$el.removeClass('editing');
},

// If you hit `enter`, we're through editing the item.
updateOnEnter: function( e ) {
  if ( e.which === ENTER_KEY ) {
    this.close();
  }
},

// NEW - Remove the item, destroy the model from
// *localStorage* and delete its view.
clear: function() {
  this.model.destroy();
}
});
```

The key part of this is the two event handlers we've added, a `togglecompleted` event on the todo's checkbox, and a `click` event on the todo's `<button class="destroy" />` button.

Let's look at the events that occur when we click the checkbox for a todo item:

1. The `togglecompleted()` function is invoked, which calls `toggle()` on the Todo model.

2. `toggle()` toggles the completed status of the todo and calls `save()` on the model.

3. The save generates a `change` event on the model that is bound to our `TodoView`'s `render()` method. We've added a statement in `render()` that toggles the completed class on the element depending on the model's completed state. The associated CSS changes the color of the title text and strikes a line through it when the todo is completed.

4. The save also results in a `change:completed` event on the model, which is handled by the `AppView`'s `filterOne()` method. If we look back at the `AppView`, we see that `filterOne()` will trigger a `visible` event on the model. This is used in conjunction with the filtering in our routes and collections so that we display an item only if its completed state falls in line with the current filter. In our update to the `TodoView`, we bound the model's visible event to the `toggleVisible()` method. This method uses the new `isHidden()` method to determine if the todo should be visible and updates it accordingly.

Now let's look at what happens when we click on a todo's destroy button:

1. The `clear()` method is invoked, which calls `destroy()` on the Todo model.

2. The todo is deleted from localStorage and a `destroy` event is triggered.

3. In our update to the `TodoView`, we bound the model's `destroy` event to the view's inherited `remove()` method. This method deletes the view and automatically removes the associated element from the DOM. Since we used `listenTo()` to bind the view's listeners to its model, `remove()` also unbinds the listening callbacks from the model, ensuring that a memory leak does not occur.

4. `destroy()` also removes the model from the Todos collection, which triggers a `remove` event on the collection.

5. Since the `AppView` has its `render()` method bound to `all` events on the Todos collection, that view is rendered and the stats in the footer are updated.

That's all there is to it!

If you want to see an example of those, see the complete source (*http://bit.ly/11eV9ir*).

Todo Routing

Finally, we move on to routing, which will allow us to easily filter the list of items that are active as well as those that have been completed (shown in Figure 4-4). We'll be supporting the following routes:

```
#/ (all - default)
#/active
#/completed
```

Figure 4-4. A filtered list of completed todo items

When the route changes, the todo list will be filtered on a model level and the selected
class on the filter links in the footer will be toggled as just described. When an item is
updated while a filter is active it will be updated accordingly (e.g., if the filter is active
and the item is checked, it will be hidden). The active filter is persisted on reload.

```
// js/routers/router.js

// Todo Router
// ----------

var Workspace = Backbone.Router.extend({
  routes:{
    '*filter': 'setFilter'
  },

  setFilter: function( param ) {
    // Set the current filter to be used

    // Trigger a collection filter event, causing hiding/unhiding
    // of Todo view items
    window.app.Todos.trigger('filter');
  }
});

app.TodoRouter = new Workspace();
Backbone.history.start();
```

Our router uses a `*splat` to set up a default route that passes the string after `#/` in the URL to `setFilter()`, which sets `window.app.TodoFilter` to that string.

As we can see in the line `window.app.Todos.trigger('filter')`, once the filter has been set, we simply trigger filter on our Todos collection to toggle which items are visible and which are hidden. Recall that our `AppView`'s `filterAll()` method is bound to the collection's filter event and that any event on the collection will cause the `AppView` to rerender.

Finally, we create an instance of our router and call `Backbone.history.start()` to route the initial URL during page load.

Summary

We've now built our first complete Backbone.js application. You can view the latest version of the full app online at any time, and the sources are readily available via TodoMVC (*http://www.todomvc.com*).

In Chapter 8, we'll learn how to further modularize this application using RequireJS, swap out our persistence layer to a database backend, and finally unit-test the application with a few different testing frameworks.

CHAPTER 5

Exercise 2: Book Library—Your First RESTful Backbone.js App

While our first application gave us a good taste of how Backbone.js applications are made, most real-world applications will want to communicate with a backend of some sort. Let's reinforce what we have already learned with another example, but this time we will also create a RESTful API for our application to talk to.

In this exercise we will build a library application for managing digital books using Backbone. For each book we will store the title, author, date of release, and some keywords. We'll also show a picture of the cover.

Setting Up

First we need to create a folder structure for our project. To keep the frontend and backend separate, we will create a folder called *site* for our client in the project root. Within it we will create *css*, *img*, and *js* directories.

As with the last example, we will split our JavaScript files by their function, so under the *js* directory create folders named *lib*, *models*, *collections*, and *views*. Your directory hierarchy should look like this:

```
site/
    css/
    img/
    js/
        collections/
        lib/
        models/
        views/
```

Download the Backbone, Underscore, and jQuery libraries and copy them to your *js/lib* folder. We need a placeholder image for the book covers. Save this image, shown in Figure 5-1, to your *site/img* folder.

Figure 5-1. Eloquent JavaScript—our placeholder image for book covers

Just like before, we need to load all of our dependencies in the *site/index.html* file:

```
<!DOCTYPE html>
<html lang="en">
    <head>
        <meta charset="UTF-8"/>
        <title>Backbone.js Library</title>
        <link rel="stylesheet" href="css/screen.css">
    </head>
    <body>
        <script src="js/lib/jquery.min.js"></script>
        <script src="js/lib/underscore-min.js"></script>
        <script src="js/lib/backbone-min.js"></script>
        <script src="js/models/book.js"></script>
        <script src="js/collections/library.js"></script>
        <script src="js/views/book.js"></script>
        <script src="js/views/library.js"></script>
        <script src="js/app.js"></script>
    </body>
</html>
```

We should also add in the HTML for the user interface. We'll want a form for adding a new book, so add the following immediately inside the body element:

```
<div id="books">
    <form id="addBook" action="#">
        <div>
            <label for="coverImage">CoverImage: </label>
            <input id="coverImage" type="file" />
            <label for="title">Title: </label><input id="title" type="text" />
            <label for="author">Author: </label><input id="author" type="text" />
            <label for="releaseDate">Release date: </label>
            <input id="releaseDate" type="text" />
            <label for="keywords">Keywords: </label>
            <input id="keywords" type="text" />
            <button id="add">Add</button>
        </div>
    </form>
</div>
```

We'll also need a template for displaying each book, which should be placed before the
<script> tags:

```
<script id="bookTemplate" type="text/template">
    <img src="<%= coverImage %>"/>
    <ul>
        <li><%= title %></li>
        <li><%= author %></li>
        <li><%= releaseDate %></li>
        <li><%= keywords %></li>
    </ul>

    <button class="delete">Delete</button>
</script>
```

To see what this will look like with some data in it, go ahead and add a manually filled-in book to the *books* div.

```
<div class="bookContainer">
    <img src="img/placeholder.png"/>
    <ul>
        <li>Title</li>
        <li>Author</li>
        <li>Release Date</li>
        <li>Keywords</li>
    </ul>

    <button class="delete">Delete</button>
</div>
```

When you open this file in a browser, it should look something like Figure 5-2.

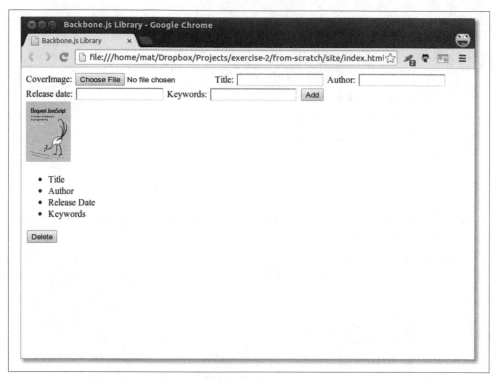

Figure 5-2. The initial application layout

Not so great. This is not a CSS tutorial, but we still need to do some formatting. Create a file named *screen.css* in your *site/css* folder:

```
body {
    background-color: #eee;
}

.bookContainer {
    outline: 1px solid #aaa;
    width: 350px;
    height: 130px;
    background-color: #fff;
    float: left;
    margin: 5px;
}

.bookContainer img {
    float: left;
    margin: 10px;
}

.bookContainer ul {
    list-style-type: none;
```

```
        margin-bottom: 0;
    }

    .bookContainer button {
        float: right;
        margin: 10px;
    }

    #addBook label {
        width: 100px;
        margin-right: 10px;
        text-align: right;
        line-height: 25px;
    }

    #addBook label, #addBook input {
        display: block;
        margin-bottom: 10px;
        float: left;
    }

    #addBook label[for="title"], #addBook label[for="releaseDate"] {
        clear: both;
    }

    #addBook button {
        display: block;
        margin: 5px 20px 10px 10px;
        float: right;
        clear: both;
    }

    #addBook div {
        width: 550px;
    }

    #addBook div:after {
        content: "";
        display: block;
        height: 0;
        visibility: hidden;
        clear: both;
        font-size: 0;
        line-height: 0;
    }
```

Now it looks a bit better, as you can see in Figure 5-3.

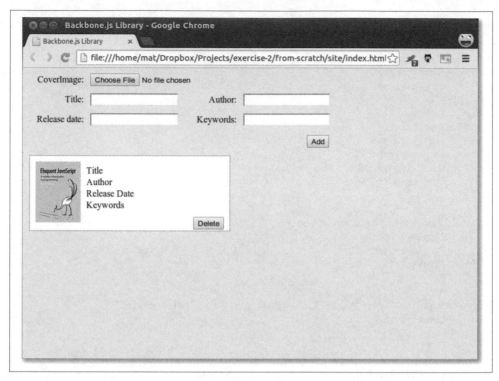

Figure 5-3. An improved user interface for our application

So this is what we want the final result to look like, but with more books. Go ahead and copy the bookContainer div a few more times if you would like to see what it looks like. Now we are ready to start developing the actual application.

Creating the Model, Collection, Views, and App

First, we'll need a model of a book and a collection to hold the list. These are both very simple, with the model only declaring some defaults:

```
// site/js/models/book.js

var app = app || {};

app.Book = Backbone.Model.extend({
    defaults: {
        coverImage: 'img/placeholder.png',
        title: 'No title',
        author: 'Unknown',
        releaseDate: 'Unknown',
        keywords: 'None'
    }
});
```

```
// site/js/collections/library.js

var app = app || {};

app.Library = Backbone.Collection.extend({
    model: app.Book
});
```

Next, in order to display books we'll need a view:

```
// site/js/views/book.js

var app = app || {};

app.BookView = Backbone.View.extend({
    tagName: 'div',
    className: 'bookContainer',
    template: _.template( $('#bookTemplate').html() ),

    render: function() {
        // tmpl is a function that takes a JSON object and returns html

        // this.el is what we defined in tagName. use $el to get access
        // to jQuery html() function
        this.$el.html( this.template( this.model.toJSON() ));

        return this;
    }
});
```

We'll also need a view for the list itself:

```
// site/js/views/library.js

var app = app || {};

app.LibraryView = Backbone.View.extend({
    el: '#books',

    initialize: function( initialBooks ) {
        this.collection = new app.Library( initialBooks );
        this.render();
    },

    // render library by rendering each book in its collection
    render: function() {
        this.collection.each(function( item ) {
            this.renderBook( item );
        }, this );
    },

    // render a book by creating a BookView and appending the
    // element it renders to the library's element
    renderBook: function( item ) {
```

```
        var bookView = new app.BookView({
            model: item
        });
        this.$el.append( bookView.render().el );
    }
});
```

Note that in the `initialize` function we accept an array of data that we pass to the `app.Library` constructor. We'll use this to populate our collection with some sample data so that we can see everything is working correctly. Finally, we have the entry point for our code, along with the sample data:

```
// site/js/app.js

var app = app || {};

$(function() {
    var books = [
        { title: 'JavaScript: The Good Parts', author: 'Douglas Crockford',
          releaseDate: '2008', keywords: 'JavaScript Programming' },
        { title: 'The Little Book on CoffeeScript', author: 'Alex MacCaw',
          releaseDate: '2012', keywords: 'CoffeeScript Programming' },
        { title: 'Scala for the Impatient', author: 'Cay S. Horstmann',
          releaseDate: '2012', keywords: 'Scala Programming' },
        { title: 'American Psycho', author: 'Bret Easton Ellis',
          releaseDate: '1991', keywords: 'Novel Splatter' },
        { title: 'Eloquent JavaScript', author: 'Marijn Haverbeke',
          releaseDate: '2011', keywords: 'JavaScript Programming' }
    ];

    new app.LibraryView( books );
});
```

Our app just passes the sample data to a new instance of `app.LibraryView` that it creates. Since the `initialize()` constructor in `LibraryView` invokes the view's `render()` method, all the books in the library will be displayed. Since we are passing our entry point as a callback to jQuery (in the form of its $ alias), the function will execute when the DOM is ready.

If you view *index.html* in a browser, you should see something like Figure 5-4.

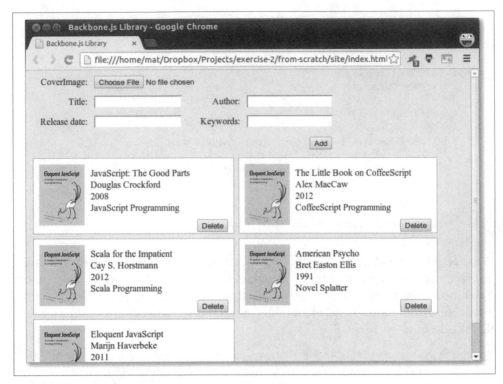

Figure 5-4. Populating our Backbone application with some sample data

This is a complete Backbone application, though it doesn't yet do anything interesting.

Wiring in the Interface

Now we'll add some functionality to the useless form at the top and the delete buttons on each book.

Adding Models

When the user clicks the add button, we want to take the data in the form and use it to create a new model. In the `LibraryView` we need to add an event handler for the click event:

```
events:{
    'click #add':'addBook'
},

addBook: function( e ) {
    e.preventDefault();

    var formData = {};

    $( '#addBook div' ).children( 'input' ).each( function( i, el ) {
        if( $( el ).val() != '' ){
            formData[ el.id ] = $( el ).val();
        }
    });

    this.collection.add( new app.Book( formData ) );
},
```

We select all the input elements of the form that have a value and iterate over them using jQuery's each. Since we used the same names for ids in our form as the keys on our Book model, we can simply store them directly in the formData object. We then create a new book from the data and add it to the collection. We skip fields without a value so that the defaults will be applied.

Backbone passes an event object as a parameter to the event-handling function. This is useful for us in this case since we don't want the form to actually submit and reload the page. Adding a call to preventDefault on the event in the addBook function takes care of this for us.

Now we just need to make the view render again when a new model is added (Figure 5-5). To do this, we put the following in the initialize function of Library View:

```
this.listenTo( this.collection, 'add', this.renderBook );
```

Now you should be ready to take the application for a spin.

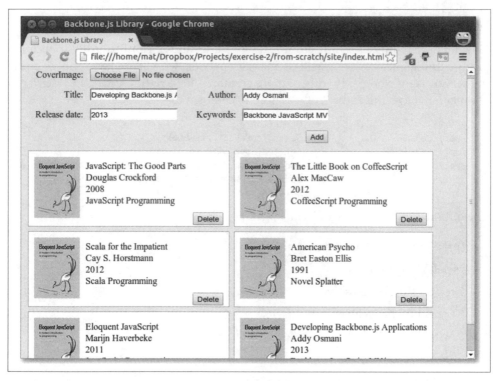

Figure 5-5. The view rendering when a new model is added to the collection

You may notice that the file input for the cover image isn't working, but that is left as an exercise to the reader.

Removing Models

Next, we need to wire up the delete button. Set up the event handler in the `BookView`:

```
events: {
    'click .delete': 'deleteBook'
},

deleteBook: function() {
    // Delete model
    this.model.destroy();

    // Delete view
    this.remove();
},
```

You should now be able to add and remove books from the library.

Creating the Backend

Now we need to make a small detour and set up a server with a REST API (application programming interface). Since this is a JavaScript book, we will use JavaScript to create the server using Node.js. If you are more comfortable in setting up a REST server in another language, this is the API you need to conform to:

```
url              HTTP Method  Operation
/api/books       GET          Get an array of all books
/api/books/:id   GET          Get the book with id of :id
/api/books       POST         Add new book, return the book with id attribute added
/api/books/:id   PUT          Update the book with id of :id
/api/books/:id   DELETE       Delete the book with id of :id
```

The outline for this section looks like this:

- Install Node.js, npm, and MongoDB
- Install node modules
- Create a simple web server
- Connect to the database
- Create the REST API

Install Node.js, npm, and MongoDB

Download and install Node.js from *Nodejs.org*. The node package manager (npm) will be installed as well.

Download and install MongoDB from *mongodb.org*. There are detailed installation guides on the website (*http://docs.mongodb.org/manual/installation/*).

Install Node Modules

Create a file called *package.json* in the root of your project. It should look like the following:

```
{
    "name": "backbone-library",
    "version": "0.0.1",
    "description": "A simple library application using Backbone",
    "dependencies": {
        "express": "~3.1.0",
        "path": "~0.4.9",
        "mongoose": "~3.5.5"
    }
}
```

Among other things, this file tells npm what the dependencies are for our project. On the command line, from the root of your project, type:

```
npm install
```

You should see npm fetch the dependencies that we listed in our *package.json* file and save them within a folder called *node_modules*.

Your folder structure should look something like this:

```
node_modules/
  .bin/
  express/
  mongoose/
  path/
site/
  css/
  img/
  js/
  index.html
package.json
```

Create a Simple Web Server

In the project root, create a file named *server.js* containing the following code:

```
// Module dependencies.
var application_root = __dirname,
    express = require( 'express' ), //Web framework
    path = require( 'path' ), //Utilities for dealing with file paths
    mongoose = require( 'mongoose' ); //MongoDB integration

//Create server
var app = express();

// Configure server
app.configure( function() {
    //parses request body and populates request.body
    app.use( express.bodyParser() );

    //checks request.body for HTTP method overrides
    app.use( express.methodOverride() );

    //perform route lookup based on URL and HTTP method
    app.use( app.router );

    //Where to serve static content
    app.use( express.static( path.join( application_root, 'site') ) );

    //Show all errors in development
    app.use( express.errorHandler({ dumpExceptions: true, showStack: true }));
});
```

```
//Start server
var port = 4711;
app.listen( port, function() {
    console.log( 'Express server listening on port %d in %s mode',
    port, app.settings.env );
});
```

We start off by loading the modules required for this project: Express for creating the HTTP server, Path for dealing with file paths, and mongoose for connecting with the database. We then create an Express server and configure it using an anonymous function. This is a pretty standard configuration, and for our application we don't actually need the methodOverride part. It is used for issuing PUT and DELETE HTTP requests directly from a form, since forms normally only support GET and POST. Finally, we start the server by running the listen function. The port number used—in this case, 4711—could be any free port on your system. I simply used 4711 since it is unlikely to have been used by anything else. We are now ready to run our first server:

```
node server.js
```

If you open a browser on *http://localhost:4711*, you should see something like Figure 5-6.

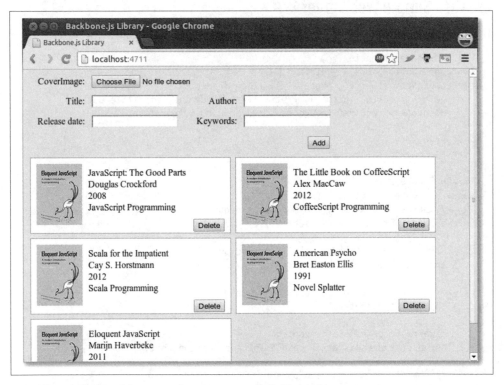

Figure 5-6. Our Backbone application served via Express

We are now running on a server instead of directly from the files. Great job! We can now start defining routes (URLs) that the server should react to. This will be our REST API. We define routes by using app followed by one of the HTTP verbs get, put, post, and delete, which correspond to create, read, update, and delete, respectively. Let's go back to *server.js* and define a simple route:

```
// Routes
app.get( '/api', function( request, response ) {
    response.send( 'Library API is running' );
});
```

The get function takes a URL as the first parameter and a function as the second. The function will be called with request and response objects. Now you can restart Node and go to our specified URL, as shown in Figure 5-7.

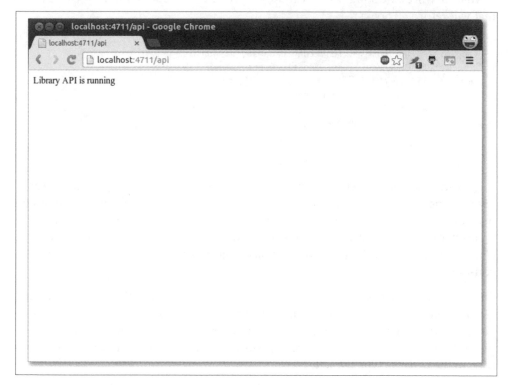

Figure 5-7. An initial response returned from our RESTful API

Connect to the Database

Fantastic. Now, since we want to store our data in MongoDB, we need to define a schema. Add this to *server.js*:

```
//Connect to database
mongoose.connect( 'mongodb://localhost/library_database' );

//Schemas
var Book = new mongoose.Schema({
    title: String,
    author: String,
    releaseDate: Date
});

//Models
var BookModel = mongoose.model( 'Book', Book );
```

As you can see, schema definitions are quite straightforward. They can be more advanced, but this will do for us. I also extracted a model (BookModel) from Mongo. This is what we will be working with. Next up, we define a GET operation for the REST API that will return all books:

```
//Get a list of all books
app.get( '/api/books', function( request, response ) {
    return BookModel.find( function( err, books ) {
        if( !err ) {
            return response.send( books );
        } else {
            return console.log( err );
        }
    });
});
```

The find function of BookModel is defined like this: function find (conditions, fields, options, callback), but since we want a function that returns all books we need only the callback parameter. The callback will be called with an error object and an array of found objects. If there was no error, we return the array of objects to the client using the send function of the response object; otherwise, we log the error to the console.

To test our API, we need to do a little typing in a JavaScript console. Restart Node and go to *localhost:4711* in your browser. Open up the JavaScript console. If you are using Google Chrome, go to View→Developer→JavaScript Console. If you are using Firefox, install Firebug and go to View→Firebug. Most other browsers will have a similar console. In the console, type the following:

```
jQuery.get( '/api/books/', function( data, textStatus, jqXHR ) {
    console.log( 'Get response:' );
    console.dir( data );
    console.log( textStatus );
    console.dir( jqXHR );
});
```

and press Enter. You should see something like Figure 5-8.

Figure 5-8. Making a call to our REST API using jQuery

Here I used jQuery to make the call to our REST API, since it was already loaded on the page. The returned array is obviously empty, since we have not put anything into the database yet. Let's go ahead and create a POST route that enables adding new items in *server.js*:

```
//Insert a new book
app.post( '/api/books', function( request, response ) {
    var book = new BookModel({
        title: request.body.title,
        author: request.body.author,
        releaseDate: request.body.releaseDate
    });
    book.save( function( err ) {
        if( !err ) {
            return console.log( 'created' );
        } else {
            return console.log( err );
        }
    });
    return response.send( book );
});
```

We start by creating a new `BookModel`, passing an object with `title`, `author`, and `releaseDate` attributes. The data is collected from `request.body`. This means that any-one calling this operation in the API needs to supply a JSON object containing the `title`, `author`, and `releaseDate` attributes. Actually, the caller can omit any or all attributes since we have not made any of them mandatory.

We then call the `save` function on the `BookModel`, passing in a callback in the same way as with the previous `get` route. Finally, we return the saved `BookModel`. The reason we return the `BookModel` and not just success or a similar string is that when the `BookModel` is saved it will get an `_id` attribute from MongoDB, which the client needs when updating or deleting a specific book. Let's try it out again. Restart Node and go back to the console and type:

```
jQuery.post( '/api/books', {
    'title': 'JavaScript the good parts',
    'author': 'Douglas Crockford',
    'releaseDate': new Date( 2008, 4, 1 ).getTime()
}, function(data, textStatus, jqXHR) {
    console.log( 'Post response:' );
    console.dir( data );
    console.log( textStatus );
    console.dir( jqXHR );
});
```

and then:

```
jQuery.get( '/api/books/', function( data, textStatus, jqXHR ) {
    console.log( 'Get response:' );
    console.dir( data );
    console.log( textStatus );
    console.dir( jqXHR );
});
```

You should now get a one-element array back from our server. You may wonder about this line:

```
'releaseDate': new Date(2008, 4, 1).getTime()
```

MongoDB expects dates in UNIX time format (milliseconds from the start of January 1, 1970 UTC), so we have to convert dates before posting. The object we get back, however, contains a JavaScript `Date` object. Also note the `_id` attribute of the returned object, shown in Figure 5-9.

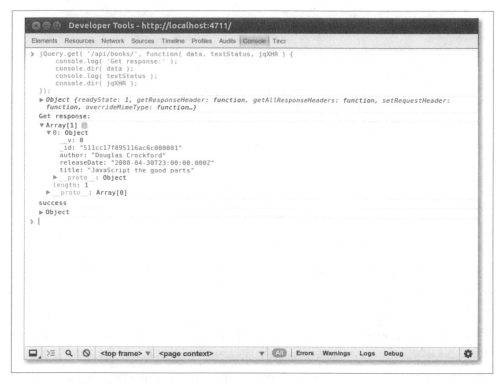

Figure 5-9. Visualizing the structure of our returned BookModel

Let's move on to creating a GET request that retrieves a single book in *server.js*:

```
//Get a single book by id
app.get( '/api/books/:id', function( request, response ) {
    return BookModel.findById( request.params.id, function( err, book ) {
        if( !err ) {
            return response.send( book );
        } else {
            return console.log( err );
        }
    });
});
```

Here we use colon notation (:id) to tell Express that this part of the route is dynamic. We also use the findById function on BookModel to get a single result. If you restart Node, you can get a single book by adding the id previously returned to the URL like this:

```
jQuery.get( '/api/books/4f95a8cb1baa9b8a1b000006',
  function( data, textStatus, jqXHR ) {
    console.log( 'Get response:' );
    console.dir( data );
    console.log( textStatus );
```

```
        console.dir( jqXHR );
    });
```

Let's create the PUT (update) function next:

```
//Update a book
app.put( '/api/books/:id', function( request, response ) {
    console.log( 'Updating book ' + request.body.title );
    return BookModel.findById( request.params.id, function( err, book ) {
        book.title = request.body.title;
        book.author = request.body.author;
        book.releaseDate = request.body.releaseDate;

        return book.save( function( err ) {
            if( !err ) {
                console.log( 'book updated' );
            } else {
                console.log( err );
            }
            return response.send( book );
        });
    });
});
```

This example is a little larger than previous ones, but is also pretty straightforward: we find a book by id, update its properties, save it, and send it back to the client.

To test this, we need to use the more general jQuery ajax function. Again, in these examples you will need to replace the id property with one that matches an item in your own database:

```
jQuery.ajax({
    url: '/api/books/4f95a8cb1baa9b8a1b000006',
    type: 'PUT',
    data: {
        'title': 'JavaScript The good parts',
        'author': 'The Legendary Douglas Crockford',
        'releaseDate': new Date( 2008, 4, 1 ).getTime()
    },
    success: function( data, textStatus, jqXHR ) {
        console.log( 'Post response:' );
        console.dir( data );
        console.log( textStatus );
        console.dir( jqXHR );
    }
});
```

Finally, we create the delete route:

```
//Delete a book
app.delete( '/api/books/:id', function( request, response ) {
    console.log( 'Deleting book with id: ' + request.params.id );
    return BookModel.findById( request.params.id, function( err, book ) {
        return book.remove( function( err ) {
```

```
            if( !err ) {
                console.log( 'Book removed' );
                return response.send( '' );
            } else {
                console.log( err );
            }
        });
    });
});
```

and try it out:

```
jQuery.ajax({
    url: '/api/books/4f95a5251baa9b8a1b000001',
    type: 'DELETE',
    success: function( data, textStatus, jqXHR ) {
        console.log( 'Post response:' );
        console.dir( data );
        console.log( textStatus );
        console.dir( jqXHR );
    }
});
```

So now our REST API is complete—we have support for all four HTTP verbs. What's next? Well, until now I have left out the keywords part of our books. This is a bit more complicated since a book could have several keywords and we don't want to represent them as a string, but rather as an array of strings. To do that, we need another schema. Add a Keywords schema right above our Book schema:

```
//Schemas
var Keywords = new mongoose.Schema({
    keyword: String
});
```

To add a subschema to an existing schema, we use brackets notation like so:

```
var Book = new mongoose.Schema({
    title: String,
    author: String,
    releaseDate: Date,
    keywords: [ Keywords ]                       // NEW
});
```

Also update POST and PUT:

```
//Insert a new book
app.post( '/api/books', function( request, response ) {
    var book = new BookModel({
        title: request.body.title,
        author: request.body.author,
        releaseDate: request.body.releaseDate,
        keywords: request.body.keywords        // NEW
    });
    book.save( function( err ) {
```

```
            if( !err ) {
                return console.log( 'created' );
            } else {
                return console.log( err );
            }
        });
        return response.send( book );
    });

    //Update a book
    app.put( '/api/books/:id', function( request, response ) {
        console.log( 'Updating book ' + request.body.title );
        return BookModel.findById( request.params.id, function( err, book ) {
            book.title = request.body.title;
            book.author = request.body.author;
            book.releaseDate = request.body.releaseDate;
            book.keywords = request.body.keywords; // NEW

            return book.save( function( err ) {
                if( !err ) {
                    console.log( 'book updated' );
                } else {
                    console.log( err );
                }
                return response.send( book );
            });
        });
    });
```

There we are—that should be all we need. Now we can try it out in the console:

```
jQuery.post( '/api/books', {
    'title': 'Secrets of the JavaScript Ninja',
    'author': 'John Resig',
    'releaseDate': new Date( 2008, 3, 12 ).getTime(),
    'keywords':[
        { 'keyword': 'JavaScript' },
        { 'keyword': 'Reference' }
    ]
}, function( data, textStatus, jqXHR ) {
    console.log( 'Post response:' );
    console.dir( data );
    console.log( textStatus );
    console.dir( jqXHR );
});
```

You now have a fully functional REST server that we can hook into from our frontend.

Talking to the Server

In this section, we will cover connecting our Backbone application to the server through the REST API.

As I mentioned in Chapter 3, we can retrieve models from a server using `collec` `tion.fetch()` by setting `collection.url` to be the URL of the API endpoint. Let's update the Library collection to do that now:

```
var app = app || {};

app.Library = Backbone.Collection.extend({
    model: app.Book,
    url: '/api/books'       // NEW
});
```

This results in the default implementation of `Backbone.sync`, assuming that the API looks like this:

```
url              HTTP Method Operation
/api/books       GET         Get an array of all books
/api/books/:id   GET         Get the book with id of :id
/api/books       POST        Add new book, return book with id attribute added
/api/books/:id   PUT         Update the book with id of :id
/api/books/:id   DELETE      Delete the book with id of :id
```

To have our application retrieve the Book models from the server on page load, we need to update the `LibraryView`. The Backbone documentation recommends inserting all models when the page is generated on the server side, rather than fetching them from the client side once the page is loaded. Since this chapter is trying to give you a more complete picture of how to communicate with a server, we will ignore that recommendation. Go to the `LibraryView` declaration and update the `initialize` function as follows:

```
initialize: function() {
    this.collection = new app.Library();
    this.collection.fetch({reset: true}); // NEW
    this.render();

    this.listenTo( this.collection, 'add', this.renderBook );
    this.listenTo( this.collection, 'reset', this.render ); // NEW
},
```

Now that we are populating our library from the database using `this.collec` `tion.fetch()`, the `initialize()` function no longer takes a set of sample data as an argument and doesn't pass anything to the `app.Library` constructor. You can now remove the sample data from *site/js/app.js*, which should reduce it to a single statement that creates the `LibraryView`:

```
// site/js/app.js

var app = app || {};

$(function() {
    new app.LibraryView();
});
```

We have also added a listener on the reset event. We need to do this since the models are fetched asynchronously after the page is rendered. When the fetch completes, Backbone fires the reset event, as requested by the reset: true option, and our listener rerenders the view. If you reload the page now, you should see all books that are stored on the server, as shown in Figure 5-10.

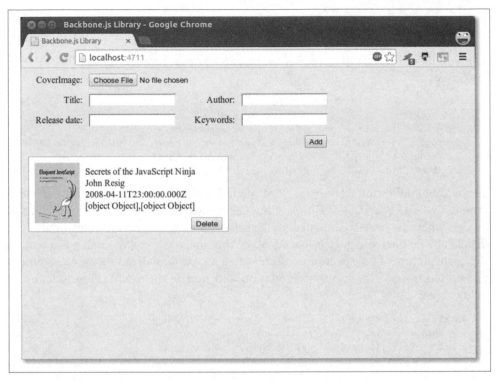

Figure 5-10. Reloading the page displays books stored on the server

As you can see, the date and keywords look a bit weird. The date delivered from the server is converted into a JavaScript Date object, and when applied to the underscore template it will use the toString() function to display it. There isn't very good support for formatting dates in JavaScript, so we will use the dateFormat jQuery plug-in to fix this. Go ahead and download it (*http://github.com/phstc/jquery-dateFormat*) and put it in your *site/js/lib* folder. Update the book template so that the date is displayed with the following:

```
<li><%= $.format.date( new Date( releaseDate ), 'MMMM yyyy' ) %></li>
```

Add a script element for the plug-in:

```
<script src="js/lib/jquery-dateFormat-1.0.js"></script>
```

Now the date on the page should look a bit better. How about the keywords? Since we are receiving the keywords in an array, we need to execute some code that generates a string of separated keywords. To do that we can omit the equals character in the template tag, which will let us execute code that doesn't display anything:

```
<li><% _.each( keywords, function( keyobj ) {%>
    <%= keyobj.keyword %><% } ); %></li>
```

Here I iterate over the keywords array using the Underscore `each` function and print out every single keyword. Note that I display the keyword using Underscore microtemplating syntax. This will display the keywords with spaces between them.

Reloading the page again should result in some visible improvements, as you can see in Figure 5-11.

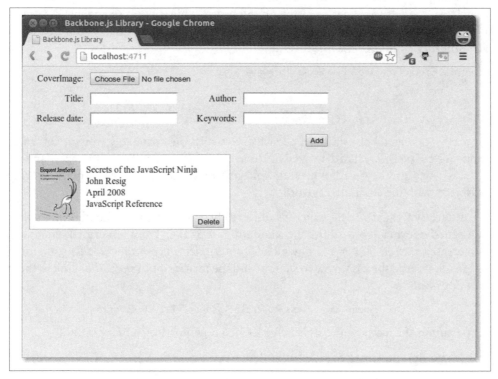

Figure 5-11. Improved date formatting

Now go ahead and delete a book and then reload the page: ta da! the deleted book is back! Not cool; why is this? This happens because when we get the `BookModels` from the server they have an `_id` attribute (notice the underscore), but Backbone expects an `id` attribute (no underscore). Since no `id` attribute is present, Backbone sees this model as new, and deleting a new model doesn't need any synchronization.

To fix this, we can use the `parse` function of `Backbone.Model`. The `parse` function lets you edit the server response before it is passed to the Model constructor. Add a `parse` function to the `BookModel`:

```
parse: function( response ) {
    response.id = response._id;
    return response;
}
```

Simply copy the value of `_id` to the needed `id` attribute. If you reload the page, you will see that models are actually deleted on the server when you press the delete button.

Another, simpler way of making Backbone recognize `_id` as its unique identifier is to set the `idAttribute` of the model to `_id`.

If you now try to add a new book using the form, you'll notice that it is a similar story to delete—models won't get persisted on the server. This is because `Backbone.Collection.add` doesn't automatically sync, but it is easy to fix. In the `LibraryView` we find in *views/library.js*, change the line reading:

```
this.collection.add( new Book( formData ) );
```

to:

```
this.collection.create( formData );
```

Now newly created books will get persisted. Actually, they probably won't if you enter a date. The server expects a date in UNIX timestamp format (milliseconds since January 1, 1970). Also, any keywords you enter won't be stored since the server expects an array of objects with the attribute keyword.

We'll start by fixing the date issue. We don't really want users to manually enter a date in a specific format, so we'll use the standard `datepicker` from jQuery UI. Go ahead and create a custom jQuery UI download (*http://jqueryui.com/download/*) containing `datepicker`. Add the css theme to *site/css/* and the JavaScript to *site/js/lib*. Link to them in *index.html*:

```
<link rel="stylesheet" href="css/cupertino/jquery-ui-1.10.0.custom.css">
```

(cupertino is the name of the style I chose when downloading jQuery UI.)

The JavaScript file must be loaded after jQuery.

```
<script src="js/lib/jquery.min.js"></script>
<script src="js/lib/jquery-ui-1.10.0.custom.min.js"></script>
```

Now, in *app.js*, bind a `datepicker` to our `releaseDate` field:

```
var app = app || {};

$(function() {
    $( '#releaseDate' ).datepicker();
```

```
    new app.LibraryView();
});
```

You should now be able to pick a date when clicking in the releaseDate field, as
Figure 5-12 shows.

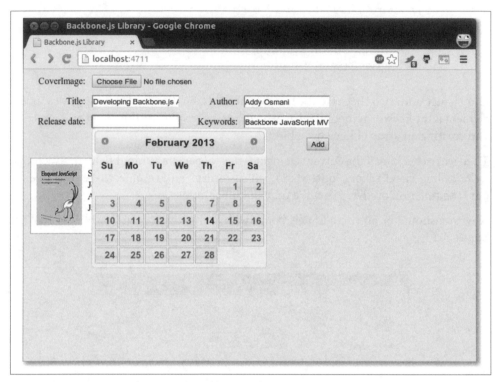

Figure 5-12. Date selection from the releaseDate field in our application

Finally, we have to make sure that the form input is properly transformed into our
storage format. Change the addBook function in LibraryView to:

```
addBook: function( e ) {
    e.preventDefault();

    var formData = {};

    $( '#addBook div' ).children( 'input' ).each( function( i, el ) {
        if( $( el ).val() != '' )
        {
            if( el.id === 'keywords' ) {
                formData[ el.id ] = [];
                _.each( $( el ).val().split( ' ' ), function( keyword ) {
                    formData[ el.id ].push({ 'keyword': keyword });
                });
```

```
        } else if( el.id === 'releaseDate' ) {
            formData[ el.id ] = $( '#releaseDate' ).datepicker( 'getDate' ).getTime();
        } else {
            formData[ el.id ] = $( el ).val();
        }
    }
    // Clear input field value
    $( el ).val('');
});

this.collection.create( formData );
},
```

Our change adds two checks to the form input fields. First, we're checking if the current element is the keywords input field, in which case we're splitting the string on each space and creating an array of keyword objects.

Then we're checking if the current element is the `releaseDate` input field, in which case we're calling `datePicker("getDate")`, which returns a `Date` object. We then use the `getTime` function on that to get the time in milliseconds.

Now you should be able to add new books with both a release date and keywords! See Figure 5-13.

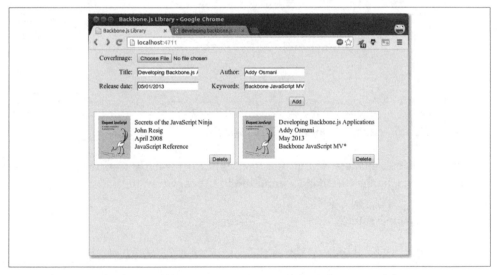

Figure 5-13. Adding new book entries, displaying both a release date and keywords

Summary

In this chapter we made our application persistent by binding it to a server using a REST API. We also looked at some problems that might occur when you are serializing and deserializing data, and their solutions. We looked at the `dateFormat` and the `datepick er` jQuery plug-ins and how to do some more advanced things in our Underscore templates. The code is available from my GitHub page (*http://bit.ly/12C56nH*).

CHAPTER 6

Backbone Extensions

Backbone is flexible, simple, and powerful. However, you may find that the complexity of the application you are working on requires more than what it provides out of the box. There are certain concerns that it just doesn't address directly, as one of its goals is to be minimalist.

Take, for example, views, which provide a default render method that does nothing and produces no real results when called, despite most implementations using it to generate the HTML that the view manages. Also, models and collections have no built-in way of handling nested hierarchies—if you require this functionality, you need to write it yourself or use a plug-in.

In these cases, there are many existing Backbone plug-ins that can provide advanced solutions for large-scale Backbone apps. You can find a fairly complete list of the available plug-ins and frameworks on the Backbone wiki (*https://github.com/document cloud/backbone/wiki/Extensions%2C-Plugins%2C-Resources*). With these add-ons, there is enough for applications of most sizes to be completed successfully.

In this section of the book, we will look at two popular Backbone add-ons: MarionetteJS and Thorax.

MarionetteJS (Backbone.Marionette)

By Derick Bailey and Addy Osmani

As we've seen, Backbone provides a great set of building blocks for our JavaScript applications. It gives us the core constructs that we need to build small to midsize apps, organize jQuery DOM events, or create single-page apps that support mobile devices and large-scale enterprise needs. But Backbone is not a complete framework. It's a set of building blocks that leaves much of the application design, architecture, and scalability to the developer, including memory management, view management, and more.

MarionetteJS (*http://marionettejs.com*), also known as Backbone.Marionette, provides many of the features that the nontrivial application developer needs, above what Backbone itself provides. It is a composite application library that aims to simplify the construction of large-scale applications. It does this by providing a collection of common design and implementation patterns found in the applications that the creator, Derick Bailey (*http://lostechies.com/derickbailey/*), and many other contributors (*http://bit.ly/11PYUWL*) have been using to build Backbone apps.

Marionette's key benefits include:

- Allows you to scale applications out with modular, event-driven architecture
- Provides sensible defaults, such as Underscore templates for view rendering
- Can be easily modified to work with your application's specific needs
- Reduces boilerplate for views, with specialized view types
- Builds on a modular architecture with an application and modules that attach to it
- Allows you to compose your application's visuals at runtime, with region and layout
- Provides nested views and layouts within visual regions
- Includes built-in memory management and zombie killing in views, regions, and layouts
- Provides built-in event cleanup with the EventBinder
- Incorporates event-driven architecture with the EventAggregator
- Offers a flexible, as-needed architecture that allows you to pick and choose what you need

Marionette follows a similar philosophy to Backbone in that it provides a suite of components that can be used independently of one another, or used together to create significant advantages for developers. But it steps above the structural components of Backbone and provides an application layer, with more than a dozen components and building blocks.

Marionette's components range greatly in the features they provide, but they all work together to create a composite application layer that can both reduce boilerplate code and provide a much-needed application structure. Its core components include various and specialized view types that take the boilerplate out of rendering common `Backbone.Model` and `Backbone.Collection` scenarios; an `Application` object and `Module` architecture to scale applications across subapplications, features, and files; integration of a command pattern, event aggregator, and request/response mechanism; and many more object types that can be extended in myriad ways to create an architecture that facilitates an application's specific needs.

In spite of the large number of constructs that Marionette provides, though, you're not required to use all of it just because you want to use some of it. As with Backbone itself, you can pick and choose which features you want to use and when. This allows you to work with other Backbone frameworks and plug-ins very easily. It also means that you are not required to engage in an all-or-nothing migration to begin using Marionette.

Boilerplate Rendering Code

Consider the code that it typically requires to render a view with Backbone and an Underscore template. We need a template to render, which can be placed in the DOM directly, and we need the JavaScript that defines a view that uses the template and populates it with data from a model.

```
<script type="text/html" id="my-view-template">
  <div class="row">
    <label>First Name:</label>
    <span><%= firstName %></span>
  </div>
  <div class="row">
    <label>Last Name:</label>
    <span><%= lastName %></span>
  </div>
  <div class="row">
    <label>Email:</label>
    <span><%= email %></span>
  </div>
</script>
var MyView = Backbone.View.extend({
  template: $('#my-view-template').html(),

  render: function(){

    // compile the Underscore.js template
    var compiledTemplate = _.template(this.template);

    // render the template with the model data
    var data = this.model.toJSON();
    var html = compiledTemplate(data);

    // populate the view with the rendered html
    this.$el.html(html);
  }
});
```

Once this is in place, you need to create an instance of your view and pass your model into it. Then you can take the view's el and append it to the DOM in order to display the view.

```
var Derick = new Person({
  firstName: 'Derick',
```

```
    lastName: 'Bailey',
    email: 'derickbailey@example.com'
});

var myView = new MyView({
    model: Derick
})

myView.render();

$('#content').html(myView.el)
```

This is a standard setup for defining, building, rendering, and displaying a view with Backbone. This is also what we call *boilerplate code*—code that is repeated across every project and every implementation with the same functionality. It gets to be tedious and repetitious very quickly.

Enter Marionette's `ItemView`—a simple way to reduce the boilerplate of defining a view.

Reducing Boilerplate with Marionette.ItemView

All of Marionette's view types—with the exception of `Marionette.View`—include a built-in `render` method that handles the core rendering logic for you. We can take advantage of this by changing the `MyView` instance to inherit from one of these rather than `Backbone.View`. Instead of having to provide our own `render` method for the view, we can let Marionette render it for us. We'll still use the same Underscore.js template and rendering mechanism, but its implementation is hidden behind the scenes. Thus, we can reduce the amount of code needed for this view.

```
var MyView = Marionette.ItemView.extend({
    template: '#my-view-template'
});
```

And that's it—that's all you need to get the exact same behavior as the previous view implementation. Just replace `Backbone.View.extend` with `Marionette.ItemView.ex tend`, then get rid of the `render` method. You can still create the view instance with a `model`, call the `render` method on the view instance, and display the view in the DOM the same way that we did before. But the view definition has been reduced to a single line of configuration for the template.

Memory Management

In addition to reducing code needed to define a view, Marionette includes some advanced memory management in all of its views, making the job of cleaning up a view instance and its event handlers easy.

Consider the following view implementation:

```
var ZombieView = Backbone.View.extend({
  template: '#my-view-template',

  initialize: function(){

    // bind the model change to rerender this view
    this.model.on('change', this.render, this);

  },

  render: function(){

    // This alert is going to demonstrate a problem
    alert('We`re rendering the view');

  }
});
```

If we create two instances of this view using the same variable name for both instances, and then change a value in the model, how many times will we see the alert box?

```
var Person = Backbone.Model.extend({
  defaults: {
    "firstName": "Jeremy",
    "lastName": "Ashkenas",
    "email":    "jeremy@example.com"
  }
});
var Derick = new Person({
  firstName: 'Derick',
  lastName: 'Bailey',
  email: 'derick@example.com'
});


// create the first view instance
var zombieView = new ZombieView({
  model: Derick
});

// create a second view instance, reusing
// the same variable name to store it
zombieView = new ZombieView({
  model: Derick
});

Derick.set('email', 'derickbailey@example.com');
```

Since we're reusing the same zombieView variable for both instances, the first instance of the view will fall out of scope immediately after the second is created. This allows the JavaScript garbage collector to come along and clean it up, which should mean the first view instance is no longer active and no longer going to respond to the model's change event.

But when we run this code, we end up with the alert box showing up twice!

The problem is caused by the model event binding in the view's `initialize` method. Whenever we pass `this.render` as the callback method to the model's on event binding, the model itself is being given a direct reference to the view instance. Since the model is now holding a reference to the view instance, replacing the `zombieView` variable with a new view instance is not going to let the original view fall out of scope. The model still has a reference; therefore, the view is still in scope.

Since the original view is still in scope, and the second view instance is also in scope, changing data on the model will cause both view instances to respond.

Fixing this is easy, though. You just need to call `stopListening` when the view is done with its work and ready to be closed. To do this, add a `close` method to the view.

```
var ZombieView = Backbone.View.extend({
  template: '#my-view-template',

  initialize: function(){
    // bind the model change to rerender this view
    this.listenTo(this.model, 'change', this.render);
  },

  close: function(){
    // unbind the events that this view is listening to
    this.stopListening();
  },

  render: function(){

    // This alert is going to demonstrate a problem
    alert('We`re rendering the view');

  }
});
```

Then call `close` on the first instance when it is no longer needed, and only one view instance will remain alive. For more information about the `listenTo` and `stopListen ing` functions, see Chapter 3 and Derick's post "Managing Events As Relationships, Not Just References" (*http://lostechies.com/derickbailey/2013/02/06/managing-events-as-relationships-not-just-references/*).

```
var Jeremy = new Person({
  firstName: 'Jeremy',
  lastName: 'Ashkenas',
  email: 'jeremy@example.com'
});
```

```
// create the first view instance
var zombieView = new ZombieView({
  model: Person
})
zombieView.close(); // double-tap the zombie

// create a second view instance, reusing
// the same variable name to store it
zombieView = new ZombieView({
  model: Person
})

Person.set('email', 'jeremyashkenas@example.com');
```

Now we see only one alert box when this code runs.

Rather than having to manually remove these event handlers, though, we can let Marionette do it for us.

```
var ZombieView = Marionette.ItemView.extend({
  template: '#my-view-template',

  initialize: function(){

    // bind the model change to rerender this view
    this.listenTo(this.model, 'change', this.render);

  },

  render: function(){

    // This alert is going to demonstrate a problem
    alert('We`re rendering the view');

  }
});
```

Notice in this case we are using a method called listenTo. This method comes from Backbone.Events, and is available in all objects that mix in Backbone.Events—including most Marionette objects. The listenTo method signature is similar to that of the on method, with the exception of passing the object that triggers the event as the first parameter.

Marionette's views also provide a close event, in which the event bindings that are set up with the listenTo are automatically removed. This means we no longer need to define a close method directly, and when we use the listenTo method, we know that our events will be removed and our views will not turn into zombies.

But how do we automate the call to close on a view, in the real application? When and where do we call that? Enter the Marionette.Region—an object that manages the life-cycle of an individual view.

Region Management

After a view is created, it typically needs to be placed in the DOM so that it becomes visible. We usually do this with a jQuery selector and by setting the html() of the resulting object:

```
var Joe = new Person({
  firstName: 'Joe',
  lastName: 'Bob',
  email: 'joebob@example.com'
});

var myView = new MyView({
  model: Joe
})

myView.render();

// show the view in the DOM
$('#content').html(myView.el)
```

This, again, is boilerplate code. We shouldn't have to manually call render and manually select the DOM elements to show the view. Furthermore, this code doesn't lend itself to closing any previous view instance that might be attached to the DOM element we want to populate. And we've seen the danger of zombie views already.

To solve these problems, Marionette provides a Region object—an object that manages the lifecycle of individual views, displayed in a particular DOM element.

```
// create a region instance, telling it which DOM element to manage
var myRegion = new Marionette.Region({
  el: '#content'
});

// show a view in the region
var view1 = new MyView({ /* ... */ });
myRegion.show(view1);

// somewhere else in the code,
// show a different view
var view2 = new MyView({ /* ... */ });
myRegion.show(view2);
```

There are several things to note here. First, we're telling the region what DOM element to manage by specifying an el in the region instance. Second, we're no longer calling the render method on our views. And lastly, we're not calling close on our view, either, though this is getting called for us.

When we use a region to manage the lifecycle of our views, and display the views in the DOM, the region itself handles these concerns. When we pass a view instance into the show method of the region, the region will call the render method on the view for us. It will then take the resulting el of the view and populate the DOM element.

The next time we call the show method of the region, the region remembers that it is currently displaying a view. The region calls the close method on the view, removes it from the DOM, and then proceeds to run the render and display code for the new view that was passed in.

Since the region handles calling close for us, and we're using the listenTo event binder in our view instance, we no longer have to worry about zombie views in our application.

Regions are not limited to just Marionette views, though. Any valid Backbone.View can be managed by a Marionette.Region. If your view happens to have a close method, it will be called when the view is closed. If not, the Backbone.View built-in method re move will be called instead.

Marionette Todo App

Having learned about Marionette's high-level concepts, let's now explore refactoring the Todo application we created in our first exercise to use it. You can find the complete code for this application in Derick's TodoMVC fork (*http://bit.ly/16dXF9x*).

Our final implementation will be visually and functionally equivalent to the original app, as shown in Figure 6-1.

Figure 6-1. The Marionette Todo application we will be authoring

First, we define an application object representing our base TodoMVC app. This will contain initialization code and define the default layout regions for our app.

TodoMVC.js

```
var TodoMVC = new Marionette.Application();

TodoMVC.addRegions({
  header : '#header',
  main   : '#main',
  footer : '#footer'
});

TodoMVC.on('initialize:after', function(){
  Backbone.history.start();
});
```

Regions are used to manage the content that's displayed within specific elements, and the addRegions method on the TodoMVC object is just a shortcut for creating Region objects. We supply a jQuery selector for each region to manage (e.g., #header, #main, and #footer) and then tell the region to show various Backbone views within that region.

Once the application object has been initialized, we call Backbone.history.start() to route the initial URL.

Next, we define our *layouts*. A layout is a specialized type of view that directly extends Marionette.ItemView. This means it's intended to render a single template and may or may not have a model (or item) associated with the template.

One of the main differences between a layout and an ItemView is that the layout contains regions. When defining a layout, we supply it with both a template and the regions that the template contains. After rendering the layout, we can display other views within the layout using the regions that were defined.

In our TodoMVC layout module, we define layouts for:

Header
　　Where we can create new todos

Footer
　　Where we summarize how many todos are remaining or have been completed

This captures some of the view logic that was previously in our AppView and TodoView.

Note that Marionette modules (such as the following) offer a simple module system that is used to create privacy and encapsulation in Marionette apps. These certainly don't have to be used, however, and in "Marionette and Flexibility" on page 144, we'll provide links to alternative implementations using RequireJS + AMD (asynchronous module definition) instead.

TodoMVC.Layout.js

```javascript
TodoMVC.module('Layout', function(Layout, App, Backbone, Marionette, $, _){

  // Layout Header View
  // ------------------

  Layout.Header = Marionette.ItemView.extend({
    template : '#template-header',

    // UI bindings create cached attributes that
    // point to jQuery selected objects
    ui : {
      input : '#new-todo'
    },

    events : {
      'keypress #new-todo':   'onInputKeypress'
    },

    onInputKeypress : function(evt) {
      var ENTER_KEY = 13;
      var todoText = this.ui.input.val().trim();

      if ( evt.which === ENTER_KEY && todoText ) {
        this.collection.create({
          title : todoText
        });
        this.ui.input.val('');
      }
    }
  });

  // Layout Footer View
  // ------------------


  Layout.Footer = Marionette.Layout.extend({
    template : '#template-footer',

    // UI bindings create cached attributes that
    // point to jQuery selected objects
    ui : {
      count   : '#todo-count strong',
      filters : '#filters a'
    },

    events : {
      'click #clear-completed' : 'onClearClick'
    },

    initialize : function() {
      this.listenTo(App.vent, 'todoList:filter', this.updateFilterSelection);
```

```
        this.listenTo(this.collection, 'all', this.updateCount);
      },

      onRender : function() {
        this.updateCount();
      },

      updateCount : function() {
        var count = this.collection.getActive().length;
        this.ui.count.html(count);

        if (count === 0) {
          this.$el.parent().hide();
        } else {
          this.$el.parent().show();
        }
      },

      updateFilterSelection : function(filter) {
        this.ui.filters
          .removeClass('selected')
          .filter('[href="#' + filter + '"]')
          .addClass('selected');
      },

      onClearClick : function() {
        var completed = this.collection.getCompleted();
        completed.forEach(function destroy(todo) {
          todo.destroy();
        });
      }
    });

  });
```

Next, we tackle application routing and workflow, such as controlling layouts in the page that can be shown or hidden.

Recall how Backbone routes trigger methods within the router, as shown here in our original workspace router from our first exercise:

```
var Workspace = Backbone.Router.extend({
  routes:{
    '*filter': 'setFilter'
  },

  setFilter: function( param ) {
    // Set the current filter to be used
    if (param){ param = param.trim()
    }
    app.TodoFilter = param ||";

    // Trigger a collection filter event, causing hiding/unhiding
```

```
      // of Todo view items
      app.Todos.trigger('filter');
    }
  });
```

Marionette uses the concept of an `AppRouter` to simplify routing. This reduces the boilerplate for handling route events and allows routers to be configured to call methods on an object directly. We configure our `AppRouter` using `appRoutes`, which replaces the `'*filter': 'setFilter'` route defined in our original router and invokes a method on our controller.

The TodoList controller, also found in this next code block, handles some of the remaining visibility logic originally found in `AppView` and `TodoView`, albeit using very readable layouts.

TodoMVC.TodoList.js

```
TodoMVC.module('TodoList', function(TodoList, App, Backbone, Marionette, $, _){

  // TodoList Router
  // ---------------
  //
  // Handle routes to show the active versus complete todo items

  TodoList.Router = Marionette.AppRouter.extend({
    appRoutes : {
      '*filter': 'filterItems'
    }
  });

  // TodoList Controller (Mediator)
  // ------------------------------
  //
  // Control the workflow and logic that exists at the application
  // level, above the implementation detail of views and models

  TodoList.Controller = function(){
    this.todoList = new App.Todos.TodoList();
  };

  _.extend(TodoList.Controller.prototype, {

    // Start the app by showing the appropriate views
    // and fetching the list of todo items, if there are any
    start: function(){
      this.showHeader(this.todoList);
      this.showFooter(this.todoList);
      this.showTodoList(this.todoList);

      this.todoList.fetch();
    },
```

```
    showHeader: function(todoList){
      var header = new App.Layout.Header({
        collection: todoList
      });
      App.header.show(header);
    },

    showFooter: function(todoList){
      var footer = new App.Layout.Footer({
        collection: todoList
      });
      App.footer.show(footer);
    },

    showTodoList: function(todoList){
      App.main.show(new TodoList.Views.ListView({
        collection : todoList
      }));
    },

    // Set the filter to show complete or all items
    filterItems: function(filter){
      App.vent.trigger('todoList:filter', filter.trim() || '');
    }
  });

  // TodoList Initializer
  // -------------------
  //
  // Get the TodoList up and running by initializing the mediator
  // when the application is started, pulling in all of the
  // existing todo items and displaying them.

  TodoList.addInitializer(function(){

    var controller = new TodoList.Controller();
    new TodoList.Router({
      controller: controller
    });

    controller.start();

  });

});
```

Controllers

In this particular app, note that controllers don't add a great deal to the overall workflow. In general, Marionette's philosophy on routers is that they should be an afterthought in the implementation of applications. Quite often, we've seen developers abuse Backbone's routing system by making it the sole controller of the entire application workflow and logic.

This inevitably leads to mashing every possible combination of code into the router methods—view creation, model loading, coordinating different parts of the app, and so on. Developers such as Derick view this as a violation of the single-responsibility principle (*http://bit.ly/15y3IpT*), or SRP, and separation of concerns.

Backbone's router and history exist to deal with a specific aspect of browsers—managing the forward and back buttons. Marionette's philosophy is that it should be limited to that, with the code that gets executed by the navigation being somewhere else. This allows the application to be used with or without a router. We can call a controller's show method from a button click, from an application event handler, or from a router, and we will end up with the same application state no matter how we called that method.

Derick has written extensively about his thoughts on this topic, which you can read more about on his blog, Lostechies:

- The Responsibilities Of The Various Pieces Of Backbone.js (*http://bit.ly/11VHN7p*)
- Reducing Backbone Routers To Nothing More Than Configuration (*http://bit.ly/16o8Egn*)
- 3 Stages Of A Backbone Application's Startup (*http://bit.ly/130cGbS*)

CompositeView

Our next task is defining the actual views for individual todo items and lists of items in our TodoMVC application. For this, we make use of Marionette's `CompositeViews`. The idea behind a `CompositeView` is that it represents a visualization of a composite or hierarchical structure of leaves (or nodes) and branches.

Think of these views as being a hierarchy of parent-child models, and recursive by default. The same `CompositeView` type will be used to render each item in a collection that is handled by the composite view. For nonrecursive hierarchies, we are able to override the item view by defining an `itemView` attribute.

For our todo list item view, we define it as an `ItemView`; then, our todo list view is a `CompositeView` where we override the `itemView` setting and tell it to use the todo list item view for each item in the collection.

TodoMVC.TodoList.Views.js

```
TodoMVC.module('TodoList.Views', function
              (Views, App, Backbone, Marionette, $, _){

  // Todo List Item View
  // -------------------
```

```
//
// Display an individual todo item, and respond to changes
// that are made to the item, including marking completed.

Views.ItemView = Marionette.ItemView.extend({
    tagName : 'li',
    template : '#template-todoItemView',

    ui : {
      edit : '.edit'
    },

    events : {
      'click .destroy' : 'destroy',
      'dblclick label' : 'onEditClick',
      'keypress .edit' : 'onEditKeypress',
      'click .toggle'  : 'toggle'
    },

    initialize : function() {
      this.listenTo(this.model, 'change', this.render);
    },

    onRender : function() {
      this.$el.removeClass('active completed');
      if (this.model.get('completed')) this.$el.addClass('completed');
      else this.$el.addClass('active');
    },

    destroy : function() {
      this.model.destroy();
    },

    toggle  : function() {
      this.model.toggle().save();
    },

    onEditClick : function() {
      this.$el.addClass('editing');
      this.ui.edit.focus();
    },

    onEditKeypress : function(evt) {
      var ENTER_KEY = 13;
      var todoText = this.ui.edit.val().trim();

      if ( evt.which === ENTER_KEY && todoText ) {
        this.model.set('title', todoText).save();
        this.$el.removeClass('editing');
      }
    }
});
```

```
// Item List View
// --------------
//
// Controls the rendering of the list of items, including the
// filtering of active versus completed items for display.

Views.ListView = Marionette.CompositeView.extend({
    template : '#template-todoListCompositeView',
    itemView : Views.ItemView,
    itemViewContainer : '#todo-list',

    ui : {
      toggle : '#toggle-all'
    },

    events : {
      'click #toggle-all' : 'onToggleAllClick'
    },

    initialize : function() {
      this.listenTo(this.collection, 'all', this.update);
    },

    onRender : function() {
      this.update();
    },

    update : function() {
      function reduceCompleted(left, right)
      { return left && right.get('completed'); }
      var allCompleted = this.collection.reduce(reduceCompleted,true);
      this.ui.toggle.prop('checked', allCompleted);

      if (this.collection.length === 0) {
        this.$el.parent().hide();
      } else {
        this.$el.parent().show();
      }
    },

    onToggleAllClick : function(evt) {
      var isChecked = evt.currentTarget.checked;
      this.collection.each(function(todo){
        todo.save({'completed': isChecked});
      });
    }
});

// Application Event Handlers
// --------------------------
//
```

```
// Handler for filtering the list of items by showing and
// hiding through the use of various CSS classes

App.vent.on('todoList:filter',function(filter) {
  filter = filter || 'all';
  $('#todoapp').attr('class', 'filter-' + filter);
});

});
```

At the end of the last code block, you will also notice an event handler using vent. This is an event aggregator that allows us to handle filterItem triggers from our TodoList controller.

Finally, we define the model and collection for representing our todo items. These are semantically not very different from the original versions we used in our first exercise and have been rewritten to better fit in with Derick's preferred style of coding.

Todos.js

```
TodoMVC.module('Todos', function(Todos, App, Backbone, Marionette, $, _){

  // Todo Model
  // ----------

  Todos.Todo = Backbone.Model.extend({
    localStorage: new Backbone.LocalStorage('todos-backbone'),

    defaults: {
      title     : '',
      completed : false,
      created   : 0
    },

    initialize : function() {
      if (this.isNew()) this.set('created', Date.now());
    },

    toggle  : function() {
      return this.set('completed', !this.isCompleted());
    },

    isCompleted: function() {
      return this.get('completed');
    }
  });

  // Todo Collection
  // ---------------

  Todos.TodoList = Backbone.Collection.extend({
    model: Todos.Todo,
```

```
      localStorage: new Backbone.LocalStorage('todos-backbone'),

      getCompleted: function() {
        return this.filter(this._isCompleted);
      },

      getActive: function() {
        return this.reject(this._isCompleted);
      },

      comparator: function( todo ) {
        return todo.get('created');
      },

      _isCompleted: function(todo){
        return todo.isCompleted();
      }
    });

  });
```

We finally kick everything off in our application index file by calling `start` on our main application object. Initialization is as follows:

```
$(function(){
  // Start the TodoMVC app (defined in js/TodoMVC.js)
  TodoMVC.start();
});
```

And that's it!

Is the Marionette Implementation of the Todo App More Maintainable?

Derick feels that maintainability largely comes down to modularity, separating responsibilities (single responsibility principle and separation of concerns) by using patterns to keep concerns from being mixed together. It can, however, be difficult to simply extract things into separate modules for the sake of extraction, abstraction, or dividing the concept down into its simplest parts.

The SRP tells us quite the opposite—that we need to understand the context in which things change. What parts always change together, in *this* system? What parts can change independently? Without knowing this, we won't know what pieces should be broken out into separate components and modules versus put together into the same module or object.

The way Derick organizes his apps into modules is by creating a breakdown of concepts at each level. A higher level module is a higher level of concern—an aggregation of responsibilities. Each responsibility is broken down into an expressive API set that is implemented by lower level modules (this is known as the dependency inversion principle). These are coordinated through a mediator, which he typically refers to as the controller in a module.

The way Derick organizes his files also plays directly into maintainability. He has written posts about the importance of keeping a sane application folder structure that I recommend reading:

- JavaScript File & Folder Structures: Just Pick One (*http://bit.ly/ZVp25q*)
- How to organize and structure the files and folders of HiloJS (*http://bit.ly/ 18pzBwN*)

Marionette and Flexibility

Marionette is a flexible framework, much like Backbone itself. It offers a wide variety of tools to help you create and organize an application architecture on top of Backbone, but like Backbone itself, it doesn't dictate that you have to use all of its pieces in order to use any of them.

You'll find the flexibility and versatility in Marionette easiest to understand by examining three variations of TodoMVC implemented with it that have been created for comparison purposes:

Simple (http://bit.ly/15mNsIq), by Jarrod Overson
   This version of TodoMVC shows some raw use of Marionette's various view types, an application object, and the event aggregator. The objects that are created are added directly to the global namespace and are fairly straightforward. This is a great example of how you can use Marionette to augment existing code without having to rewrite everything around Marionette.

RequireJS (http://bit.ly/11eW1DT), also by Jarrod
   Using Marionette with RequireJS helps to create a modularized application architecture—a tremendously important concept in scaling JavaScript applications. RequireJS provides a powerful set of tools that can be leveraged to great advantage, making Marionette even more flexible than it already is.

Marionette modules (http://bit.ly/16dXF9x), by Derick Bailey
   RequireJS isn't the only way to create a modularized application architecture. For those who wish to build applications in modules and namespaces, Marionette provides a built-in module and namespacing structure. This example application takes the simple version of the application and rewrites it into a namespaced application architecture, with an application controller (mediator/workflow object) that brings all of the pieces together.

Marionette certainly provides its share of opinions on how a Backbone application should be architected. The combination of modules, view types, event aggregator, application objects, and more can be used to create a very powerful and flexible architecture based on these opinions.

But as you can see, Marionette isn't a completely rigid, "my way or the highway" framework. It provides many elements of an application foundation that you can mix and match with other architectural styles, such as AMD or namespacing, or you can use it to augment existing projects by reducing boilerplate code for rendering views.

This flexibility creates a much greater opportunity for Marionette to provide value to you and your projects, as it allows you to scale the use of Marionette with your application's needs.

And So Much More

This is just the tip of the proverbial iceberg for Marionette, even for the `ItemView` and `Region` objects that we've explored. There is far more functionality, more features, and more flexibility and customizability that can be put to use in both of these objects. Then we have the other dozen or so components that Marionette provides, each with its own set of behaviors built in, customization and extension points, and more.

To learn more about Marionette's components, the features they provide, and how to use them, check out the Marionette documentation, links to the wiki, links to the source code, the project core contributors, and much more at *http://marionettejs.com.*

Thorax

By Ryan Eastridge and Addy Osmani

Part of Backbone's appeal is that it provides structure but is generally unopinionated, in particular when it comes to views. Thorax makes an opinionated decision to use Handlebars as its templating solution. Some of the patterns found in Marionette are found in Thorax as well. Marionette exposes most of these patterns as JavaScript APIs, whereas in Thorax they are often exposed as template helpers. This chapter assumes the reader has knowledge of Handlebars.

Ryan Eastridge and Kevin Decker developed Thorax to create Walmart's mobile web application. This chapter is limited to Thorax's templating features and patterns implemented in it that you can utilize in your application regardless of whether you choose to adopt Thorax. To learn more about other features implemented in Thorax and to download boilerplate projects, visit the Thorax website (*http://thoraxjs.org*).

Hello World

In Backbone, when you create a new view, options passed are merged into any default options already present on a view and are exposed via `this.options` for later reference.

`Thorax.View` differs from `Backbone.View` in that there is no `options` object. All arguments passed to the constructor become properties of the view, which in turn become available to the template:

```
var view = new Thorax.View({
    greeting: 'Hello',
    template: Handlebars.compile('{{greeting}} World!')
});
view.appendTo('body');
```

In most examples in this chapter, a `template` property will be specified. In larger projects —including the boilerplate projects provided on the Thorax website—a `name` property would instead be used and a template of the same filename in your project would automatically be assigned to the view.

If a `model` is set on a view, its attributes also become available to the template:

```
var view = new Thorax.View({
    model: new Thorax.Model({key: 'value'}),
    template: Handlebars.compile('{{key}}')
});
```

Embedding Child Views

The view helper allows you to embed other views within a view. Child views can be specified as properties of the view:

```
var parent = new Thorax.View({
    child: new Thorax.View(...),
    template: Handlebars.compile('{{view child}}')
});
```

Or the name of a child view to initialize as well as any optional properties you wish to pass. In this case, the child view must have previously been created with `extend` and given a `name` property:

```
var ChildView = Thorax.View.extend({
    name: 'child',
    template: ...
});

var parent = new Thorax.View({
    template: Handlebars.compile('{{view "child" key="value"}}')
});
```

The view helper may also be used as a block helper, in which case the block will be assigned as the `template` property of the child view:

```
{{#view child}}
    child will have this block
    set as its template property
{{/view}}
```

Handlebars is string-based, while Backbone.View instances have a DOM el. Since we are mixing metaphors, the embedding of views works via a placeholder mechanism where the view helper in this case adds the view passed to the helper to a hash of children, then injects placeholder HTML into the template, such as:

```
<div data-view-placeholder-cid="view2"></div>
```

Then, once the parent view is rendered, we walk the DOM in search of all the place-holders we created, replacing them with the child views' els:

```
this.$el.find('[data-view-placeholder-cid]').forEach(function(el) {
    var cid = el.getAttribute('data-view-placeholder-cid'),
        view = this.children[cid];
    view.render();
    $(el).replaceWith(view.el);
}, this);
```

View Helpers

One of the most useful constructs in Thorax is Handlebars.registerViewHelper (not to be confused with Handlebars.registerHelper). This method will register a new block helper that will create and embed a HelperView instance with its template property set to the captured block. A HelperView instance is different from that of a regular child view in that its context will be that of the parent's in the template. Like other child views, it will have a parent property set to that of the declaring view. Many of the built-in helpers in Thorax, including the collection helper, are created in this manner.

A simple example would be an on helper that rerendered the generated HelperView instance each time an event was triggered on the declaring/parent view:

```
Handlebars.registerViewHelper('on', function(eventName, helperView) {
    helperView.parent.on(eventName, function() {
        helperView.render();
    });
});
```

An example use of this would be to have a counter that would increment each time a button was clicked. This example makes use of Thorax's button helper, which simply makes a button that calls a method when clicked:

```
{{#on "incremented"}}{{i}}{/on}}
{{#button trigger="incremented"}}Add{{/button}}
```

And the corresponding view class:

```
new Thorax.View({
    events: {
```

```
        incremented: function() {
            ++this.i;
        }
    },
    initialize: function() {
        this.i = 0;
    },
    template: ...
});
```

collection Helper

The `collection` helper creates and embeds a `CollectionView` instance, creating a view for each item in a collection, and updating when items are added, removed, or changed in the collection. The simplest usage of the helper would look like:

```
{{#collection kittens}}
  <li>{{name}}</li>
{{/collection}}
```

And the corresponding view:

```
new Thorax.View({
  kittens: new Thorax.Collection(...),
  template: ...
});
```

The block in this case will be assigned as the `template` for each item view created, and the context will be the `attributes` of the given model. This helper accepts options that can be arbitrary HTML attributes, a `tag` option to specify the type of tag containing the collection, or any of the following:

`item-template`
  A template to display for each model. If a block is specified, it will become the `item-template`.

`item-view`
  A view class to use when each item view is created.

`empty-template`
  A template to display when the collection is empty. If an `inverse/else` block is specified, it will become the empty-template.

`empty-view`
  A view to display when the collection is empty.

Options and blocks can be used in combination, in this case creating a `KittenView` class with a `template` set to the captured block for each kitten in the collection:

```
{{#collection kittens item-view="KittenView" tag="ul"}}
  <li>{{name}}</li>
{{else}}
```

```
  <li>No kittens!</li>
{{/collection}}
```

Note that multiple collections can be used per view, and collections can be nested. This is useful when there are models that contain collections that contain models that contain:

```
{{#collection kittens}}
  <h2>{{name}}</h2>
  <p>Kills:</p>
  {{#collection miceKilled tag="ul"}}
    <li>{{name}}</li>
  {{/collection}}
{{/collection}}
```

Custom HTML Data Attributes

Thorax makes heavy use of custom HTML data attributes to operate. While some make sense only within the context of Thorax, several are quite useful to have in any Backbone project for writing other functions against, or for general debugging. To add some to your views in non-Thorax projects, override the setElement method in your base view class:

```
MyApplication.View = Backbone.View.extend({
  setElement: function() {
      var response = Backbone.View.prototype.setElement.apply(this, arguments);
      this.name && this.$el.attr('data-view-name', this.name);
      this.$el.attr('data-view-cid', this.cid);
      this.collection && this.$el.attr('data-collection-cid',
      this.collection.cid);
      this.model && this.$el.attr('data-model-cid', this.model.cid);
      return response;
  }
});
```

In addition to making your application more immediately comprehensible in the inspector, it's now possible to extend jQuery/Zepto with functions to look up the closest view, model, or collection to a given element. To make it work, you have to save references to each view created in your base view class by overriding the _configure method:

```
MyApplication.View = Backbone.View.extend({
  _configure: function() {
      Backbone.View.prototype._configure.apply(this, arguments);
      Thorax._viewsIndexedByCid[this.cid] = this;
  },
  dispose: function() {
      Backbone.View.prototype.dispose.apply(this, arguments);
      delete Thorax._viewsIndexedByCid[this.cid];
  }
});
```

Then we can extend jQuery/Zepto:

```
$.fn.view = function() {
    var el = $(this).closest('[data-view-cid]');
    return el && Thorax._viewsIndexedByCid[el.attr('data-view-cid')];
};

$.fn.model = function(view) {
    var $this = $(this),
        modelElement = $this.closest('[data-model-cid]'),
        modelCid = modelElement && modelElement.attr('[data-model-cid]');
    if (modelCid) {
        var view = $this.view();
        return view && view.model;
    }
    return false;
};
```

Now instead of storing references to models randomly throughout your application to look up when a given DOM event occurs, you can use `$(element).model()`. In Thorax, this can be particularly useful in conjunction with the `collection` helper, which generates a view class (with a `model` property) for each `model` in the collection. Here's an example template:

```
{{#collection kittens tag="ul"}}
  <li>{{name}}</li>
{{/collection}}
```

And the corresponding view class:

```
Thorax.View.extend({
  events: {
    'click li': function(event) {
      var kitten = $(event.target).model();
      console.log('Clicked on ' + kitten.get('name'));
    }
  },
  kittens: new Thorax.Collection(...),
  template: ...
});
```

A common antipattern in Backbone applications is to assign a `className` to a single view class. Consider using the `data-view-name` attribute as a CSS selector instead, saving CSS classes for things that will be used multiple times:

```
[data-view-name="child"] {

}
```

Thorax Resources

No Backbone-related tutorial would be complete without a Todo application. A Thorax implementation of TodoMVC (*http://bit.ly/10g3paK*) is available, in addition to this far simpler example composed of this single Handlebars template:

```
{{#collection todos tag="ul"}}
  <li{{#if done}} class="done"{{/if}}>
    <input type="checkbox" name="done"{{#if done}} checked="checked"{{/if}}>
    <span>{{item}}</span>
  </li>
{{/collection}}
<form>
  <input type="text">
  <input type="submit" value="Add">
</form>
```

Here is the corresponding JavaScript:

```
var todosView = Thorax.View({
    todos: new Thorax.Collection(),
    events: {
        'change input[type="checkbox"]': function(event) {
            var target = $(event.target);
            target.model().set({done: !!target.attr('checked')});
        },
        'submit form': function(event) {
            event.preventDefault();
            var input = this.$('input[type="text"]');
            this.todos.add({item: input.val()});
            input.val('');
        }
    },
    template: '...'
});
todosView.appendTo('body');
```

To see Thorax in action on a large-scale website, visit *walmart.com* on any Android or iOS device. For a complete list of resources, visit the Thorax website (*http://thoraxjs.org*).

Summary

While Backbone is a popular choice for building modern client-side applications, some projects require more decisions made right out of the box. Thorax provides a Rails-like development experience for working with Backbone, tackling many of these decisions for you. Thorax answers questions such as "What should a Backbone project look like?", "What kind of directory structure should you use?", and "How do you build your client-side app into deployable pieces for each platform you're targeting?" While Thorax may not be for everyone, it offers some nice sugar for those looking to build more complex applications.

CHAPTER 7

Common Problems and Solutions

In this section, we will review a number of common problems developers often experience once they've started to work on relatively nontrivial projects using Backbone.js, as well as present potential solutions.

Perhaps the most frequent of these questions surround how to do more with views. If you are interested in discovering how to work with nested views, and learn about view disposal and inheritance, this section will hopefully have you covered.

Working with Nested Views

Problem

What is the best approach for rendering and appending nested views (or subviews) in Backbone.js?

Solution 1

Since pages are composed of nested elements and Backbone views correspond to elements within the page, nesting views is an intuitive approach to managing a hierarchy of elements.

The best way to combine views is simply using:

```
this.$('.someContainer').append(innerView.el);
```

which just relies on jQuery. We could use this in a real example as follows:

```
...
initialize : function () {
    //...
},
```

```
render : function () {

    this.$el.empty();

    this.innerView1 = new Subview({options});
    this.innerView2 = new Subview({options});

    this.$('.inner-view-container')
        .append(this.innerView1.el)
        .append(this.innerView2.el);
}
```

Solution 2

Beginners sometimes also try using setElement to solve this problem; however, keep in mind that using this method is an easy way to shoot yourself in the foot. Avoid using this approach when the first solution is a viable option:

```
// Where we have previously defined a View, SubView
// in a parent View we could do:

...
initialize : function () {

    this.innerView1 = new Subview({options});
    this.innerView2 = new Subview({options});
},

render : function () {

    this.$el.html(this.template());

    this.innerView1.setElement('.some-element1').render();
    this.innerView2.setElement('.some-element2').render();
}
```

Here we are creating subviews in the parent view's initialize() method and rendering the subviews in the parent's render() method. The elements managed by the subviews exist in the parent's template, and the View.setElement() method is used to reassign the element associated with each subview.

setElement() changes a view's element, including redelegating event handlers by removing them from the old element and binding them to the new element. Note that setElement() returns the view, allowing us to chain the call to render().

This works and has some positive qualities: you don't need to worry about maintaining the order of your DOM elements when appending, views are initialized early, and the render() method doesn't need to take on too many responsibilities at once.

Unfortunately, downsides are that you can't set the tagName property of subviews and events need to be redelegated. The first solution doesn't suffer from this problem.

Solution 3

One more possible solution to this problem could be written:

```
var OuterView = Backbone.View.extend({
    initialize: function() {
        this.inner = new InnerView();
    },

    render: function() {
        this.$el.html(template); // or this.$el.empty() if you have no template
        this.$el.append(this.inner.$el);
        this.inner.render();
    }
});

var InnerView = Backbone.View.extend({
    render: function() {
        this.$el.html(template);
        this.delegateEvents();
    }
});
```

This tackles a few specific design decisions:

- The order in which you append the subelements matters.
- The OuterView doesn't contain the HTML elements to be set in the InnerView(s), meaning that we can still specify tagName in the InnerView.
- render() is called after the InnerView element has been placed into the DOM. This is useful if your InnerView's render() method is sizing itself on the page based on the dimensions of another element. This is a common use case.

Note that InnerView needs to call View.delegateEvents() to bind its event handlers to its new DOM since it is replacing the content of its element.

Solution 4

A better solution, which is cleaner but has the potential to affect performance, is:

```
var OuterView = Backbone.View.extend({
    initialize: function() {
        this.render();
    },

    render: function() {
        this.$el.html(template); // or this.$el.empty() if you have no template
        this.inner = new InnerView();
        this.$el.append(this.inner.$el);
    }
});
```

```
var InnerView = Backbone.View.extend({
    initialize: function() {
        this.render();
    },

    render: function() {
        this.$el.html(template);
    }
});
```

If multiple views need to be nested at particular locations in a template, you should create a hash of child views indexed by client IDs (cids). In the template, use a custom HTML attribute named data-view-cid to create placeholder elements for each view to embed. Once the template has been rendered and its output appended to the parent view's $el, each placeholder can be queried for and replaced with the child view's el.

A sample implementation containing a single child view could be written as:

```
var OuterView = Backbone.View.extend({
    initialize: function() {
        this.children = {};
        this.child = new Backbone.View();
        this.children[this.child.cid] = this.child;
    },

    render: function() {
        this.$el.html('<div data-view-cid="' + this.child.cid + '"></div>');
        _.each(this.children, function(view, cid) {
            this.$('[data-view-cid="' + cid + '"]').replaceWith(view.el);
        }, this);
    }
};
```

The inclusion of cids here is useful because it illustrates separating a model and its views by having views referenced by their instances and not their attributes. It's quite common to ask for all views that satisfy an attribute on their models, but if you have recursive subviews or repeated views (a common occurrence), you can't simply ask for views by attributes—that is, unless you specify additional attributes that separate duplicates. Using cids solves this problem as it allows for direct references to views.

Generally speaking, more developers opt for Solution 1 or 5 because:

- The majority of their views may already rely on being in the DOM in their ren der() method

- When the OuterView is rerendered, views don't have to be reinitialized where re-initialization has the potential to cause memory leaks and issues with existing bindings

The Backbone extensions Marionette and Thorax provide logic for nesting views, and rendering collections where each item has an associated view. Marionette provides APIs in JavaScript, while Thorax provides APIs via Handlebars template helpers.

Thanks to Lukas (*http://bit.ly/10mhg06*) and Ian Taylor (*http://bit.ly/YCvyOL*) for these tips.

Managing Models in Nested Views

Problem

What is the best way to manage models in nested views?

Solution

In order to reach attributes on related models in a nested setup, models require some prior knowledge of each other, something that Backbone doesn't implicitly handle out of the box.

One approach is to make sure each child model has a parent attribute. This way, you can traverse the nesting first up to the parent and then down to any siblings that you know of. So, assuming we have models modelA, modelB, and modelC:

```
// When initializing modelA, I would suggest setting a link to the parent
// model when doing this, like this:

ModelA = Backbone.Model.extend({

    initialize: function(){
        this.modelB = new modelB();
        this.modelB.parent = this;
        this.modelC = new modelC();
        this.modelC.parent = this;
    }
}
```

This allows you to reach the parent model in any child model function through this.parent.

Now, we have already discussed a few options for how to construct nested views using Backbone. For the sake of simplicity, let us imagine that we are creating a new child view ViewB from within the initialize() method of ViewA below. ViewB can reach out over the ViewA model and listen for changes on any of its nested models.

See inline for comments on exactly what each step is enabling:

```
// Define View A
ViewA = Backbone.View.extend({
```

```
    initialize: function(){
        // Create an instance of View B
        this.viewB = new ViewB();

        // Create a reference back to this (parent) view
        this.viewB.parentView = this;

        // Append ViewB to ViewA
        $(this.el).append(this.viewB.el);
    }
});

// Define View B
ViewB = Backbone.View.extend({

    //...,

    initialize: function(){
        // Listen for changes to the nested models in our parent ViewA
        this.listenTo(this.model.parent.modelB, "change", this.render);
        this.listenTo(this.model.parent.modelC, "change", this.render);

        // We can also call any method on our parent view if it is defined
        // $(this.parentView.el).shake();
    }

});

// Create an instance of ViewA with ModelA
// viewA will create its own instance of ViewB
// from inside the initialize() method
var viewA = new ViewA({ model: ModelA });
```

Rendering a Parent View from a Child View

Problem

How would one render a parent view from one of its children?

Solution

In a scenario where you have a view containing another view, such as a photo gallery containing a larger view model, you may find that you need to render or rerender the parent view from the child. The good news is that solving this problem is quite straightforward.

The simplest solution is to just use `this.parentView.render();`.

If, however, inversion of control is desired, events may be used to provide an equally valid solution.

Say we wish to begin rendering when a particular event has occurred. For the sake of example, let us call this event somethingHappened. The parent view can bind notifications on the child view to know when the event has occurred. It can then render itself.

In the parent view:

```
// Parent initialize
this.listenTo(this.childView, 'somethingHappened', this.render);

// Parent removal
this.stopListening(this.childView, 'somethingHappened');
```

In the child view:

```
// After the event has occurred
this.trigger('somethingHappened');
```

The child will trigger a somethingHappened event and the parent's render function will be called.

Thanks to Tal Bereznitskey (*http://bit.ly/12PdwVl*) for this tip.

Disposing View Hierarchies

Problem

Where your application is set up with multiple parent and child views, you'll probably want to remove any DOM elements associated with such views as well as unbind any event handlers tied to child elements when you no longer require them.

Solution

The solution in the last question should be enough to handle this use case, but if you require a more explicit example that handles children, you can see one here:

```
Backbone.View.prototype.close = function() {
    if (this.onClose) {
        this.onClose();
    }
    this.remove();
};

NewView = Backbone.View.extend({
    initialize: function() {
        this.childViews = [];
    },
    renderChildren: function(item) {
        var itemView = new NewChildView({ model: item });
        $(this.el).prepend(itemView.render());
        this.childViews.push(itemView);
```

```
    },
    onClose: function() {
      _(this.childViews).each(function(view) {
        view.close();
      });
    }
});

NewChildView = Backbone.View.extend({
    tagName: 'li',
    render: function() {
    }
});
```

Here, we implement a `close()` method for views that disposes of a view when it is no longer needed or needs to be reset.

In most cases, the view removal should not affect any associated models. For example, if you are working on a blogging application and you remove a view with comments, perhaps another view in your app shows a selection of comments and resetting the collection would affect those views as well.

Thanks to dira (*http://bit.ly/YCvvm8*) for this tip.

 You may also be interested in reading about the Marionette composite views in Chapter 6.

Rendering View Hierarchies

Problem

Say you have a collection, where each item in the collection could itself be a collection. You can render each item in the collection, and indeed can render any items that themselves are collections. The problem you might have is how to render HTML that reflects the hierarchical nature of the data structure.

Solution

The most straightforward way to approach this problem is to use a framework like Derick Bailey's `Backbone.Marionette` (*http://bit.ly/17zlpCV*). This framework contains a type of view called a `CompositeView`.

The basic idea of a `CompositeView` is that it can render a model and a collection within the same view. It can render a single model with a template. It can also take a collection from that model and for each model in that collection, render a view. By default it uses the same composite view type that you've defined to render each of the models in the collection. All you have to do is tell the view instance where the collection is, via the `initialize` method, and you'll get a recursive hierarchy rendered.

There is a working demo of this in action available online (*http://bit.ly/YCvEWF*).

And you can also get the source code and documentation for Marionette (*http://bit.ly/ 17zlpCV*).

Working with Nested Models or Collections

Problem

Backbone doesn't include support for nested models or collections out of the box, favoring the use of good patterns for modeling your structured data on the client side. How do we work around this?

Solution

As we've seen, it's common to create collections representing groups of models using Backbone. It's also common, however, to wish to nest collections within models, depending on the type of application you are working on.

Take, for example, a Building model that contains many Room models that could sit in a Rooms collection.

You could expose a `this.rooms` collection for each building, allowing you to lazy-load rooms once a building has been opened.

```
var Building = Backbone.Model.extend({

    initialize: function(){
        this.rooms = new Rooms;
        this.rooms.url = '/building/' + this.id + '/rooms';
        this.rooms.on("reset", this.updateCounts);
    },

    // ...

});

// Create a new building model
var townHall = new Building;

// once opened, lazy-load the rooms
townHall.rooms.fetch({reset: true});
```

There are also a number of Backbone plug-ins that can help with nested data structures, such as Backbone Relational (*http://bit.ly/15FQOVY*). This plug-in handles one-to-one,

one-to-many, and many-to-one relations between models for Backbone and has some excellent documentation (*http://backbonerelational.org/*).

Better Model Property Validation

Problem

As we learned earlier in the book, the `validate` method on a model is called by `set` (when the `validate` option is set) and `save`. It is passed the model attributes updated with the values passed to these methods.

By default, when we define a custom `validate` method, Backbone passes all of a model's attributes through this validation each time, regardless of which model attributes are being set.

This means that it can be a challenge to determine which specific fields are being set or validated without being concerned about the others that aren't being set at the same time.

Solution

To illustrate this problem better, let's look at a typical registration form use case that:

- Validates form fields using the blur event
- Validates each field regardless of whether other model attributes (i.e., other form data) are valid or not

Here is one example of a desired use case: say we have a form where a user focuses and blurs first name, last name, and email HTML input boxes without entering any data. A "This field is required" message should be presented next to each form field.

HTML:

```
<!doctype html>
<html>
<head>
  <meta charset=utf-8>
  <title>Form Validation - Model#validate</title>
  <script src='http://code.jquery.com/jquery.js'></script>
  <script src='http://underscorejs.org/underscore.js'></script>
  <script src='http://backbonejs.org/backbone.js'></script>
</head>
<body>
  <form>
    <label>First Name</label>
    <input name='firstname'>
    <span data-msg='firstname'></span>
```

```
    <br>
    <label>Last Name</label>
    <input name='lastname'>
    <span data-msg='lastname'></span>
    <br>
    <label>Email</label>
    <input name='email'>
    <span data-msg='email'></span>
  </form>
</body>
</html>
```

You could write basic validation using the current Backbone `validate` method to work with this form and implement it using something like:

```
validate: function(attrs) {

    if(!attrs.firstname) return 'first name is empty';
    if(!attrs.lastname) return 'last name is empty';
    if(!attrs.email) return 'email is empty';

}
```

Unfortunately, this method would trigger a `firstname` error each time any of the fields were blurred, and the error message would appear only next to the first name field.

One potential solution to the problem is to validate all fields and return all of the errors:

```
validate: function(attrs) {
  var errors = {};

  if (!attrs.firstname) errors.firstname = 'first name is empty';
  if (!attrs.lastname) errors.lastname = 'last name is empty';
  if (!attrs.email) errors.email = 'email is empty';

  if (!_.isEmpty(errors)) return errors;
}
```

We can adapt this into a solution that defines a Field model for each input in our form and works within the parameters of our use case as follows:

```
$(function($) {

  var User = Backbone.Model.extend({
    validate: function(attrs) {
      var errors = this.errors = {};

      if (!attrs.firstname) errors.firstname = 'firstname is required';
      if (!attrs.lastname) errors.lastname = 'lastname is required';
      if (!attrs.email) errors.email = 'email is required';

      if (!_.isEmpty(errors)) return errors;
    }
  });
```

```
var Field = Backbone.View.extend({
  events: {blur: 'validate'},
  initialize: function() {
    this.name = this.$el.attr('name');
    this.$msg = $('[data-msg=' + this.name + ']');
  },
  validate: function() {
    this.model.set(this.name, this.$el.val(), {validate:true});
    this.$msg.text(this.model.errors[this.name] || '');
  }
});

var user = new User;

$('input').each(function() {
  new Field({el: this, model: user});
});

});
```

This works fine, as the solution checks the validation for each attribute individually and sets the message for the correct blurred field. A demo of the preceding example by @braddunbar (*http://github.com/braddunbar*) is available at *http://jsbin.com/afetez/2/ edit*.

Unfortunately, this solution does perform validation on all fields every time, even though we are displaying errors only for the field that has changed. If we have multiple client-side validation methods, we may not want to have to call each validation method on every attribute every time, so this solution might not be ideal for everyone.

Backbone.validateAll

A potentially better alternative to the preceding scenario is to use the `Backbone.vali dateAll` plug-in (*https://github.com/gfranko/Backbone.validateAll*) from @gfranko (*http://github.com/gfranko*), which was created to validate specific model properties (or form fields) without worrying about the validation of any other model properties (or form fields).

Here is how we would set up a partial user model and `validate` method using this plug-in for our use case:

```
// Create a new User Model
var User = Backbone.Model.extend({

    // RegEx Patterns
    patterns: {

        specialCharacters: '[^a-zA-Z 0-9]+',
```

```
        digits: '[0-9]',

        email: '^[a-zA-Z0-9._-]+@[a-zA-Z0-9][a-zA-Z0-9.-]*[.]{1}[a-zA-Z]{2,6}$'
    },

// Validators
  validators: {

      minLength: function(value, minLength) {
        return value.length >= minLength;

      },

      maxLength: function(value, maxLength) {
        return value.length <= maxLength;

      },

      isEmail: function(value) {
        return User.prototype.validators.pattern(value,
        User.prototype.patterns.email);

      },

      hasSpecialCharacter: function(value) {
        return User.prototype.validators.pattern(value,
        User.prototype.patterns.specialCharacters);

      },
      ...

// We can determine which properties are getting validated by
// checking to see if properties are equal to null

    validate: function(attrs) {

      var errors = this.errors = {};

      if(attrs.firstname != null) {
          if (!attrs.firstname) {
              errors.firstname = 'firstname is required';
              console.log('first name isEmpty validation called');
          }

          else if(!this.validators.minLength(attrs.firstname, 2))
            errors.firstname = 'firstname is too short';
          else if(!this.validators.maxLength(attrs.firstname, 15))
            errors.firstname = 'firstname is too large';
          else if(this.validators.hasSpecialCharacter(attrs.firstname))
            errors.firstname = 'firstname cannot contain special characters';
      }
```

```
if(attrs.lastname != null) {

    if (!attrs.lastname) {
        errors.lastname = 'lastname is required';
        console.log('last name isEmpty validation called');
    }

    else if(!this.validators.minLength(attrs.lastname, 2))
        errors.lastname = 'lastname is too short';
    else if(!this.validators.maxLength(attrs.lastname, 15))
        errors.lastname = 'lastname is too large';
    else if(this.validators.hasSpecialCharacter(attrs.lastname))
        errors.lastname = 'lastname cannot contain special characters';

}
```

This allows the logic inside of our `validate` methods to determine which form fields are currently being set/validated, and ignore the model properties that are not being set.

It's fairly straightforward to use as well. We can simply define a new model instance and then set the data on our model via the `validateAll` option to use the behavior defined by the plug-in:

```
var user = new User();
user.set({ 'firstname': 'Greg' }, {validate: true, validateAll: false});
```

That's it. The `Backbone.validateAll` logic doesn't override the default Backbone logic by default, so it's perfectly capable of being used for scenarios where you might care more about field-validation performance (*http://jsperf.com/backbone-validateall*) as well as those where you don't. Both solutions presented in this section should work fine, however.

Backbone.Validation

As we've seen, the `validate` method Backbone offers is `undefined` by default, and you need to override it with your own custom validation logic to get model validation in place. Often developers run into the issue of implementing this validation as nested `if`s and `else`s, which can become unmaintainable when things get complicated.

Another helpful plug-in for Backbone called `Backbone.Validation` (*http://bit.ly/ 12P0JCu*) attempts to solve this problem by offering an extensible way to declare validation rules on the model and overrides the `validate` method behind the scenes.

One of the useful methods this plug-in includes is (pseudo) live validation via a `preVa lidate` method. This can be used to check on keypress whether the input for a model is valid without changing the model itself. You can run any validators for a model attribute by calling the `preValidate` method, passing it the name of the attribute along with the value you would like validated.

```
// If the value of the attribute is invalid, a truthy error message is returned
// if not, it returns a falsy value

var errorMsg = user.preValidate('firstname', 'Greg');
```

Form-Specific Validation Classes

That said, the most optimal solution to this problem may not be to stick validation in
your model attributes. Instead, you could have a function specifically designed for val-
idating a specific form, and there are many good JavaScript form validation libraries
out there that can help with this.

If you want to stick it on your model, you can also make it a class function:

```
User.validate = function(formElement) {
  //...
};
```

For more information on validation plug-ins available for Backbone, see the Backbone
wiki (*http://bit.ly/12r6feb*).

Avoiding Conflicts with Multiple Backbone Versions

Problem

In instances out of your control, you may have to work around having more than one
version of Backbone in the same page. How do you work around this without causing
conflicts?

Solution

Like most client-side projects, Backbone's code is wrapped in an immediately invoked
function expression:

```
(function(){
  // Backbone.js
}).call(this);
```

Several things happen during this configuration stage. A Backbone namespace is created,
and multiple versions of Backbone on the same page are supported through the
noConflict mode:

```
var root = this;
var previousBackbone = root.Backbone;

Backbone.noConflict = function() {
  root.Backbone = previousBackbone;
  return this;
};
```

You can use multiple versions of Backbone on the same page by calling noConflict like this:

```
var Backbone19 = Backbone.noConflict();
// Backbone19 refers to the most recently loaded version,
// and `window.Backbone` will be restored to the previously
// loaded version
```

Building Model and View Hierarchies

Problem

How does inheritance work with Backbone? How can we share code between similar models and views? How can we call methods that have been overridden?

Solution

For its inheritance, Backbone internally uses an inherits function inspired by goog.in herits, Google's implementation from the Closure library. It's basically a function to correctly set up the prototype chain.

```
var inherits = function(parent, protoProps, staticProps) {
    ...
```

The only major difference here is that Backbone's API accepts two objects containing instance and static methods.

Following on from this, for inheritance purposes all of Backbone's objects contain an extend method as follows:

```
Model.extend = Collection.extend = Router.extend = View.extend = extend;
```

Most development with Backbone is based around inheriting from these objects, and they're designed to mimic a classical object-oriented implementation.

The preceding isn't quite the same as ECMAScript 5's Object.create, as it's actually copying properties (methods and values) from one object to another. As this isn't enough to support Backbone's inheritance and class model, the following steps are performed:

1. The instance methods are checked to see if there's a constructor property. If so, the class's constructor is used; otherwise, the parent's constructor is used (such as Back bone.Model).

2. Underscore's extend method is called to add the parent class's methods to the new child class.

3. The prototype property of a blank constructor function is assigned with the parent's prototype, and a new instance of this is set to the child's prototype property.

4. Underscore's extend method is called twice to add the static and instance methods to the child class.

5. The child's prototype's constructor and a __super__ property are assigned.

6. This pattern is also used for classes in CoffeeScript, so Backbone classes are compatible with CoffeeScript classes.

extend can be used for a great deal more, and developers who are fans of mixins will like that it can be used for this too. You can define functionality on any custom object, and then quite literally copy and paste all of the methods and attributes from that object to a Backbone one:

For example:

```
var MyMixin = {
  foo: 'bar',
  sayFoo: function(){alert(this.foo);}
};

var MyView = Backbone.View.extend({
  // ...
});

_.extend(MyView.prototype, MyMixin);

var myView = new MyView();
myView.sayFoo(); //=> 'bar'
```

We can take this further and also apply it to view inheritance. The following is an example of how to extend one view using another:

```
var Panel = Backbone.View.extend({
});

var PanelAdvanced = Panel.extend({
});
```

Calling Overridden Methods

However, if you have an initialize() method in Panel, then it won't be called if you also have an initialize() method in PanelAdvanced, so you would have to call Panel's initialize method explicitly:

```
var Panel = Backbone.View.extend({
  initialize: function(options){
    console.log('Panel initialized');
    this.foo = 'bar';
  }
});

var PanelAdvanced = Panel.extend({
```

```
    initialize: function(options){
      Panel.prototype.initialize.call(this, [options]);
      console.log('PanelAdvanced initialized');
      console.log(this.foo); // Log: bar
    }
});

// We can also inherit PanelAdvaned if needed
var PanelAdvancedExtra = PanelAdvanced.extend({
    initialize: function(options){
      PanelAdvanced.prototype.initialize.call(this, [options]);
      console.log('PanelAdvancedExtra initialized');
    }
});

new Panel();
new PanelAdvanced();
new PanelAdvancedExtra();
```

This isn't the most elegant of solutions because if you have a lot of views that inherit from Panel, then you'll have to remember to call Panel's initialize from all of them.

It's worth noting that if Panel doesn't have an initialize method now but you choose to add it in the future, then you'll need to go to all of the inherited classes in the future and make sure they call Panel's initialize.

So here's an alternative way to define Panel so that your inherited views don't need to call Panel's initialize method:

```
var Panel = function (options) {
  // put all of Panel's initialization code here
  console.log('Panel initialized');
  this.foo = 'bar';

  Backbone.View.apply(this, [options]);
};

_.extend(Panel.prototype, Backbone.View.prototype, {
  // put all of Panel's methods here. For example:
  sayHi: function () {
    console.log('hello from Panel');
  }
});

Panel.extend = Backbone.View.extend;

// other classes then inherit from Panel like this:
var PanelAdvanced = Panel.extend({
  initialize: function (options) {
    console.log('PanelAdvanced initialized');
    console.log(this.foo);
  }
```

```
  });

  var panelAdvanced = new PanelAdvanced();
  // Logs: Panel initialized, PanelAdvanced initialized, bar
  panelAdvanced.sayHi(); // Logs: hello from Panel
```

When used appropriately, Underscore's extend method can save you a great deal of time and effort writing redundant code.

Thanks to Alex Young (*http://dailyjs.com*), Derick Bailey (*http://bit.ly/15y70t6*), and JohnnyO (*http://bit.ly/12PecKA*) for the heads up about these tips.

Backbone-Super

Backbone-Super (*http://bit.ly/15mOdRT*) by Lukas Olson adds a _super method to Backbone.Model using John Resig's Inheritance script (*http://bit.ly/ZN2nr2*). Rather than using Backbone.Model.prototype.set.call as per the Backbone.js documentation, _super can be called instead:

```
// This is how we normally do it
var OldFashionedNote = Backbone.Model.extend({
  set: function(attributes, options) {
    // Call parent's method
    Backbone.Model.prototype.set.call(this, attributes, options);
    // some custom code here
    // ...
  }
});
```

After including this plug-in, you can do the same thing with the following syntax:

```
// This is how we can do it after using the Backbone-super plug-in
var Note = Backbone.Model.extend({
  set: function(attributes, options) {
    // Call parent's method
    this._super(attributes, options);
    // some custom code here
    // ...
  }
});
```

Event Aggregators and Mediators

Problem

How do we channel multiple event sources through a single object?

Solution

Using an event aggregator. It's common for developers to think of mediators when faced with this problem, so let's explore what an event aggregator is, what a mediator is, and how they differ.

Design patterns often differ only in semantics and intent—that is, the language used to describe the pattern is what sets it apart, more than an implementation of that specific pattern. It often comes down to squares versus rectangles versus polygons. You can create the same end result with all three, given the constraints of a square are still met, or you can use polygons to create an infinitely larger and more complex set of things.

When it comes to the mediator and event aggregator patterns, there are some times where it may look like the patterns are interchangeable due to implementation similarities. However, the semantics and intent of these patterns are very different. And even if the implementations both use some of the same core constructs, I believe there is a distinct difference between them. I also believe they should not be interchanged or confused in communication because of the differences.

Event Aggregator

The core idea of the event aggregator, according to Martin Fowler, is to channel multiple event sources through a single object so that other objects needing to subscribe to the events don't need to know about every event source.

Backbone's event aggregator

The easiest event aggregator to show is that of Backbone.js—it's built into the Backbone object directly.

```
var View1 = Backbone.View.extend({
  // ...

  events: {
    "click .foo": "doIt"
  },

  doIt: function(){
    // trigger an event through the event aggregator
    Backbone.trigger("some:event");
  }
});

var View2 = Backbone.View.extend({
  // ...

  initialize: function(){
    // subscribe to the event aggregator's event
    Backbone.on("some:event", this.doStuff, this);
```

```
  },

  doStuff: function(){
    // ...
  }
})
```

In this example, the first view is triggering an event when a DOM element is clicked. The event is triggered through Backbone's built-in event aggregator—the Backbone object. Of course, it's trivial to create your own event aggregator in Backbone, and there are some key things that we need to keep in mind when using an event aggregator, to keep our code simple.

jQuery's event aggregator

Did you know that jQuery has a built-in event aggregator? jQuery doesn't call it this, but it's in there and it's scoped to DOM events. It also happens to look like Backbone's event aggregator:

```
$("#mainArticle").on("click", function(e){

  // handle click event on any element underneath our #mainArticle element

});
```

This code sets up an event handler function that waits for an unknown number of event sources to trigger a click event, and it allows any number of listeners to attach to the events of those event publishers. jQuery just happens to scope this event aggregator to the DOM.

Mediator

A mediator is an object that coordinates interactions (logic and behavior) between multiple objects. It makes decisions on when to call which objects, based on the actions (or inaction) of other objects and input.

A mediator for Backbone

Backbone doesn't have the idea of a mediator built into it like a lot of other MV* frameworks do. But that doesn't mean you can't write one using a single line of code:

```
var mediator = {};
```

Yes, of course this is just an object literal in JavaScript. Once again, we're talking about semantics here. The purpose of the mediator is to control the workflow between objects, and we really don't need anything more than an object literal to do this.

```
var orgChart = {

  addNewEmployee: function(){
```

```
// getEmployeeDetail provides a view that users interact with
var employeeDetail = this.getEmployeeDetail();

// when the employee detail is complete, the mediator (the 'orgchart' object)
// decides what should happen next
employeeDetail.on("complete", function(employee){

  // set up additional objects that have additional events, which are used
  // by the mediator to do additional things
  var managerSelector = this.selectManager(employee);
  managerSelector.on("save", function(employee){
    employee.save();
  });

});
},

// ...
}
```

This example shows a very basic implementation of a mediator object with Backbone-based objects that can trigger and subscribe to events. I've often referred to this type of object as a workflow object in the past, but the truth is that it is a mediator. It is an object that handles the workflow between many other objects, aggregating the responsibility of that workflow knowledge into a single object. The result is a workflow that is easier to understand and maintain.

Similarities and Differences

There are, without a doubt, similarities between the event aggregator and mediator examples that I've shown here. The similarities boil down to two primary items: events and third-party objects. These differences are superficial at best, though. When we dig into the intent of the pattern and see that the implementations can be dramatically different, the nature of the patterns becomes more apparent.

Events

Both the event aggregator and mediator use events in the previous examples. An event aggregator obviously deals with events; it's in the name, after all. The mediator only uses events because it makes life easy when dealing with Backbone, though. There is nothing that says a mediator must be built with events. You can build a mediator with callback methods, by handing the mediator reference to the child object, or by any of a number of other means.

The difference, then, is why these two patterns are both using events. The event aggregator, as a pattern, is designed to deal with events. The mediator, though, only uses them because it's convenient.

Third-party objects

Both the event aggregator and mediator, by design, use a third party object to facilitate things. The event aggregator itself is a third party to the event publisher and the event subscriber. It acts as a central hub for events to pass through. The mediator is also a third party to other objects, though. So where is the difference? Why don't we call an event aggregator a mediator? The answer largely comes down to where the application logic and workflow are coded.

In the case of an event aggregator, the third-party object is there only to facilitate the pass-through of events from an unknown number of sources to an unknown number of handlers. All workflow and business logic that needs to be kicked off is put directly into the object that triggers the events and the objects that handle the events.

In the case of the mediator, though, the business logic and workflow are aggregated into the mediator itself. The mediator decides when an object should have its methods called and attributes updated based on factors that the mediator knows about. It encapsulates the workflow and process, coordinating multiple objects to produce the desired system behavior. The individual objects involved in this workflow each know how to perform their own task. But it's the mediator that tells the objects when to perform the tasks by making decisions at a higher level than the individual objects.

An event aggregator facilitates a fire-and-forget model of communication. The object triggering the event doesn't care if there are any subscribers. It just fires the event and moves on. A mediator, though, might use events to make decisions, but it is definitely not fire and forget. A mediator pays attention to a known set of input or activities so that it can facilitate and coordinate additional behavior with a known set of actors (objects).

Relationships: When to Use Which

Understanding the similarities and differences between an event aggregator and mediator is important for semantic reasons. It's equally important to understand when to use which pattern, though. The basic semantics and intent of the patterns does inform the question of when, but actual experience in using the patterns will help you understand the more subtle points and nuanced decisions that have to be made.

Event aggregator use

In general, an event aggregator is used when you either have too many objects to listen to directly, or you have objects that are entirely unrelated.

When two objects have a direct relationship already—say, a parent view and child view —then there might be little benefit in using an event aggregator. Have the child view trigger an event and the parent view can handle the event. This is most commonly seen in Backbone's collection and model, where all model events are bubbled up to and through its parent collection. A collection often uses model events to modify the state of itself or other models. Handling selected items in a collection is a good example of this.

jQuery's on method as an event aggregator is a great example of too many objects to listen to. If you have 10, 20, or 200 DOM elements that can trigger a click event, it might be a bad idea to set up a listener on all of them individually. This could quickly deteriorate performance of the application and user experience. Instead, using jQuery's on method allows us to aggregate all of the events and reduce the overhead of 10, 20, or 200 event handlers down to 1.

Indirect relationships are also a great time to use event aggregators. In Backbone applications, it is very common to have multiple view objects that need to communicate, but have no direct relationship. For example, a menu system might have a view that handles the menu item clicks. But we don't want the menu to be directly tied to the content views that show all of the details and information when a menu item is clicked. Having the content and menu coupled together would make the code very difficult to maintain, in the long run. Instead, we can use an event aggregator to trigger menu:click:foo events, and have a foo object handle the click event to show its content on the screen.

Mediator use

A mediator is best applied when two or more objects have an indirect working relationship, and business logic or workflow needs to dictate the interactions and coordination of these objects.

A wizard interface is a good example of this, as shown with the orgChart example, in "Mediator" on page 173. There are multiple views that facilitate the entire workflow of the wizard. Rather than tightly coupling the view together by having them reference each other directly, we can decouple them and more explicitly model the workflow between them by introducing a mediator.

The mediator extracts the workflow from the implementation details and creates a more natural abstraction at a higher level, showing us much more quickly what that workflow is. We no longer have to dig into the details of each view in the workflow to see what the workflow actually is.

Event Aggregator and Mediator Together

The crux of the difference between an event aggregator and a mediator, and why these pattern names should not be interchanged, is illustrated best by a demonstration of how they can be used together. The menu example for an event aggregator is the perfect place to introduce a mediator as well.

Clicking a menu item may trigger a series of changes throughout an application. Some of these changes will be independent of others, and using an event aggregator for this makes sense. Some of these changes may be internally related to each other, though, and may use a mediator to enact those changes. A mediator, then, could be set up to listen to the event aggregator. It could run its logic and process to facilitate and coordinate many objects that are related to each other, but unrelated to the original event source.

```
var MenuItem = Backbone.View.extend({

  events: {
    "click .thatThing": "clickedIt"
  },

  clickedIt: function(e){
    e.preventDefault();

    // assume this triggers "menu:click:foo"
    Backbone.trigger("menu:click:" + this.model.get("name"));
  }

});

// ... somewhere else in the app

var MyWorkflow = function(){
  Backbone.on("menu:click:foo", this.doStuff, this);
};

MyWorkflow.prototype.doStuff = function(){
  // instantiate multiple objects here.
  // set up event handlers for those objects.
  // coordinate all of the objects into a meaningful workflow.
};
```

In this example, when the MenuItem with the right model is clicked, the "menu:click:foo" event will be triggered. An instance of the MyWorkflow object, assuming one is already instantiated, will handle this specific event and will coordinate all of the objects that it knows about, to create the desired user experience and workflow.

An event aggregator and a mediator have been combined to create a much more meaningful experience in both the code and the application itself. We now have a clean separation between the menu and the workflow through an event aggregator, and we are still keeping the workflow itself clean and maintainable through the use of a mediator.

Pattern Language: Semantics

There is one overriding point to make in all of this discussion: semantics. Communicating intent and semantics through the use of named patterns is viable and valid only when all parties in a communication medium understand the language in the same way.

If I say "apple," what am I talking about? Am I talking about a fruit? Or am I talking about a technology and consumer products company? As Sharon Cichelli says, "Semantics will continue to be important until we learn how to communicate in something other than language."

CHAPTER 8

Modular Development

When we say an application is *modular*, we generally mean it's composed of a set of highly decoupled, distinct pieces of functionality stored in modules. As you probably know, loose coupling facilitates easier maintainability of apps by removing dependencies where possible. When this is implemented efficiently, it's quite easy to see how changes to one part of a system may affect another.

Unlike some more traditional programming languages, the current iteration of JavaScript (ECMA-262) doesn't provide developers with the means to import such modules of code in a clean, organized manner.

Instead, developers are left to fall back on variations of the module or object literal patterns combined with `<script>` tags or a script loader. With many of these, module scripts are strung together in the DOM with namespaces being described by a single global object where it's still possible to have name collisions. There's also no clean way to handle dependency management without some manual effort or third-party tools.

Whilst native solutions to these problems may be arriving via the ES6 (*http://bit.ly/10utREz*) (the next version of the official JavaScript specification) modules proposal (*http://bit.ly/11yzZHc*), the good news is that writing modular JavaScript has never been easier and you can start doing it today.

In this next part of the book, we're going to look at how to use AMD (asynchronous module definition) modules and RequireJS to cleanly wrap units of code in your application into manageable modules. We'll also cover an alternate approach called Lumbar, which uses routes to determine when modules are loaded.

Organizing Modules with RequireJS and AMD

Partly contributed by Jack Franklin (https://
github.com/jackfranklin)

RequireJS (*http://requirejs.org*) is a popular script loader written by James Burke, a developer who has been quite instrumental in helping shape the AMD module format, which we'll discuss shortly. Among other things, RequireJS helps you to load multiple script files, define modules with or without dependencies, and load in nonscript dependencies such as text files.

Maintainability Problems with Multiple Script Files

You might be thinking that there is little benefit to RequireJS. After all, you can simply load in your JavaScript files through multiple `<script>` tags, which is very straightforward. However, doing it that way has a lot of drawbacks, including increasing the HTTP overhead.

Every time the browser loads in a file you've referenced in a `<script>` tag, it makes an HTTP request to load the file's contents. It has to make a new HTTP request for each file you want to load, which causes problems.

- Browsers are limited in how many parallel requests they can make, so often it's slow to load multiple files, as it can only do a certain number at a time. This number depends on the user's settings and browser, but is usually around four to eight. When you're working on Backbone applications, it's good to split your app into multiple JS files, so it's easy to hit that limit quickly. This can be negated by minifying your code into one file as part of a build process, but does not help with the next point.
- Scripts are loaded *synchronously*. This means that the browser cannot continue page rendering while the script is loading.

What tools like RequireJS do is load scripts asynchronously. This means we have to adjust our code slightly—you can't just swap out `<script>` elements for a small piece of RequireJS code—but the benefits are very worthwhile:

- Loading the scripts asynchronously means the load process is nonblocking. The browser can continue to render the rest of the page as the scripts are being loaded, speeding up the initial load time.
- We can load modules in more intelligently, having more control over when they are loaded and ensuring that modules with dependencies are loaded in the right order.

Need for Better Dependency Management

Dependency management is a challenging subject, in particular when you're writing JavaScript in the browser. The closest thing we have to dependency management by default is simply making sure we order our <script> tags such that code that depends on code in another file is loaded after the file it depends on. This is not a good approach. As I've already discussed, loading multiple files in that way is bad for performance; needing them to be loaded in a certain order is very brittle.

Being able to load code on an as-needed basis is something RequireJS is very good at. Rather than load all our JavaScript code in during initial page load, a better approach is to dynamically load modules when that code is required. This avoids loading all the code when the user first hits your application, consequently speeding up initial load times.

Think about the Gmail web client for a moment. When a user initially loads the page on the first visit, Google can simply hide widgets such as the chat module until the user indicates (by clicking expand) the desire to use it. Through dynamic dependency loading, Google could load up the chat module at that time, rather than forcing all users to load it when the page first initializes. This can improve performance and load times and can definitely prove useful when you're building larger applications. As the codebase for an application grows, this becomes even more important.

The important thing to note here is that while it's absolutely fine to develop applications without a script loader, there are significant benefits to utilizing tools like RequireJS in your application.

Asynchronous Module Definition (AMD)

RequireJS implements the AMD Specification (*https://github.com/amdjs/amdjs-api/wiki/AMD*), which defines a method for writing modular code and managing dependencies. The RequireJS website also has a section documenting the reasons behind implementing AMD (*http://requirejs.org/docs/whyamd.html*):

> The AMD format comes from wanting a module format that was better than today's "write a bunch of <script> tags with implicit dependencies that you have to manually order" and something that was easy to use directly in the browser. Something with good debugging characteristics that did not require server-specific tooling to get started.

Writing AMD Modules with RequireJS

As previously discussed, the overall goal for the AMD format is to provide a solution for modular JavaScript that developers can use today. The two key concepts you need to be aware of when using it with a script loader are the define() method for defining modules and the `require()` method for loading dependencies. `define()` is used to define named or unnamed modules using the following signature:

```
define(
    module_id /*optional*/,
    [dependencies] /*optional*/,
    definition function /*function for instantiating the module or object*/
);
```

As you can tell by the inline comments, the `module_id` is an optional argument that is typically only required when non-AMD concatenation tools are being used (there may be some other edge cases where it's useful, too). When this argument is left out, we call the module *anonymous*. When working with anonymous modules, RequireJS will use a module's filepath as its module id, so you should apply the adage Don't Repeat Yourself (DRY) by omitting the module id in the `define()` invocation.

The `dependencies` argument is an array representing all of the other modules that this module depends on, and the third argument is a factory that can either be a function that should be executed to instantiate the module or an object.

We could define a barebones module (compatible with RequireJS) using `define()` as follows:

```
// A module ID has been omitted here to make the module anonymous

define(['foo', 'bar'],
    // module definition function
    // dependencies (foo and bar) are mapped to function parameters
    function ( foo, bar ) {
        // return a value that defines the module export
        // (i.e the functionality we want to expose for consumption)

        // create your module here
        var myModule = {
            doStuff:function(){
                console.log('Yay! Stuff');
            }
        }

        return myModule;
});
```

 RequireJS is intelligent enough to automatically infer the *.js* extension to your script filenames. Thus, you generally omit this extension when specifying dependencies.

Alternate syntax

There is also a sugared version (*http://requirejs.org/docs/whyamd.html#sugar*) of `define()` available that allows you to declare your dependencies as local variables using `require()`. This will feel familiar to anyone who's used Node, and can be easier to add or remove dependencies. Here is the previous snippet using the alternate syntax:

```
// A module ID has been omitted here to make the module anonymous

define(function(require){
        // module definition function
    // dependencies (foo and bar) are defined as local vars
    var foo = require('foo'),
        bar = require('bar');

    // return a value that defines the module export
    // (i.e., the functionality we want to expose for consumption)

    // create your module here
    var myModule = {
        doStuff:function(){
            console.log('Yay! Stuff');
        }
    }

    return myModule;
});
```

The `require()` method is typically used to load code in a top-level JavaScript file or within a module should you wish to dynamically fetch dependencies. Here's an example of its usage:

```
// Consider 'foo' and 'bar' are two external modules
// In this example, the 'exports' from the two modules loaded are passed as
// function arguments to the callback (foo and bar)
// so that they can similarly be accessed

require( ['foo', 'bar'], function ( foo, bar ) {
    // rest of your code here
    foo.doSomething();
});
```

My post "Writing Modular JS" (*http://addyosmani.com/writing-modular-js/*) covers the AMD specification in much more detail. Defining and using modules will be covered in this book shortly when we look at more structured examples of using RequireJS.

Getting Started with RequireJS

Before using RequireJS and Backbone, we will first set up a very basic RequireJS project to demonstrate how it works. The first thing to do is to download RequireJS (*http://requirejs.org/docs/download.html#requirejs*). When you load in the RequireJS script in your HTML file, you need to also tell it where your main JavaScript file is located. (Typically this will be called something like *app.js*, and is the main entry point for your application.) You do this by adding in a `data-main` attribute to the `<script>` tag:

```
<script data-main="app.js" src="lib/require.js"></script>
```

Now, RequireJS will automatically load *app.js* for you.

RequireJS configuration

In the main JavaScript file that you load with the `data-main` attribute you can configure how RequireJS loads the rest of your application. You do so by calling `require.con fig`, and passing in an object:

```
require.config({
    // your configuration key/values here
    baseUrl: "app",
    // generally the same directory as the script used in a data-main attribute
    // for the top level script
    paths: {},
    // set up custom paths to libraries, or paths to RequireJS plug-ins
    shim: {}, // used for setting up all Shims (see below for more detail)
});
```

The main reason you'd want to configure RequireJS is to add shims, which we'll cover next. To see other configuration options available to you, I recommend checking out the RequireJS documentation (*http://requirejs.org/docs/api.html#config*).

RequireJS Shims. Ideally, each library that we use with RequireJS will come with AMD support—that is, it uses the `define` method to define the library as a module. However, some libraries—including Backbone and one of its dependencies, Underscore—don't do this. Fortunately, RequireJS comes with a way to work around this.

To demonstrate this, first let's shim Underscore, and then we'll shim Backbone too. Shims are very simple to implement:

```
require.config({
    shim: {
        'lib/underscore': {
            exports: '_'
        }
    }
});
```

Note that when specifying paths for RequireJS, you should omit the `.js` from the end of script names.

The important line here is `exports: '_'`. This line tells RequireJS that the script in `'lib/underscore.js'` creates a global variable called _ instead of defining a module. Now when we list Underscore as a dependency, RequireJS will know to give us the

_ global variable as though it were the module defined by that script. We can set up a shim for Backbone too:

```
require.config({
    shim: {
        'lib/underscore': {
          exports: '_'
        },
        'lib/backbone': {
            deps: ['lib/underscore', 'jquery'],
            exports: 'Backbone'
        }
    }
});
```

Again, that configuration tells RequireJS to return the global Backbone variable that Backbone exports, but this time you'll notice that Backbone's dependencies are defined. This means whenever the following code is run, it will first make sure the dependencies are met, and then pass the global Backbone object into the callback function:

```
require( 'lib/backbone', function( Backbone ) {...} );
```

You don't need to do this with every library, only the ones that don't support AMD. For example, jQuery does support it, as of jQuery 1.7.

If you'd like to read more about general RequireJS usage, the RequireJS API docs (*http://requirejs.org/docs/api.html*) are incredibly thorough and easy to read.

Custom paths

Typing long paths to filenames like *lib/backbone* can get tedious. RequireJS lets us set up custom paths in our configuration object. Here, whenever I refer to underscore, RequireJS will look for the file *lib/underscore.js*:

```
require.config({
    paths: {
        'underscore': 'lib/underscore'
    }
});
```

Of course, this can be combined with a shim:

```
require.config({
    paths: {
        'underscore': 'lib/underscore'
    },
    shim: {
        'underscore': {
          exports: '_'
        }
    }
});
```

Just make sure that you refer to the custom path in your shim settings, too. Now you can do the following the shim Underscore but still use a custom path:

```
require( ['underscore'], function(_) {
// code here
});
```

Require.js and Backbone Examples

Now that we've taken a look at how to define AMD modules, let's review how to go about wrapping components like views and collections so that they can also be easily loaded as dependencies for any parts of your application that require them. At its simplest, a Backbone model may just require Backbone and Underscore.js. These are dependencies, so we can define those when defining the new modules. Note that the following examples presume you have configured RequireJS to shim Backbone and Underscore, as discussed previously.

Wrapping models, views, and other components with AMD

For example, here is how a model is defined:

```
define(['underscore', 'backbone'], function(_, Backbone) {
  var myModel = Backbone.Model.extend({

    // Default attributes
    defaults: {
      content: 'hello world',
    },

    // A dummy initialization method
    initialize: function() {
    },

    clear: function() {
      this.destroy();
      this.view.remove();
    }

  });
  return myModel;
});
```

Note how we alias Underscore.js's instance to _ and Backbone to just Backbone, making it very trivial to convert non-AMD code over to using this module format. For a view that might require other dependencies such as jQuery, we can do this similarly as follows:

```
define([
  'jquery',
  'underscore',
  'backbone',
  'collections/mycollection',
```

```
'views/myview'
], function($, _, Backbone, myCollection, myView){

    var AppView = Backbone.View.extend({
    ...
```

Aliasing to the dollar sign ($) once again makes it very easy to encapsulate any part of an application you wish using AMD.

Doing it this way makes it easy to organize your Backbone application as you like. It's recommended to separate modules into folders—for example, individual folders for models, collections, views, and so on. RequireJS doesn't care about what folder structure you use; as long as you use the correct path when using `require`, it will happily pull in the file.

As part of this chapter I've made a very simple Backbone application with RequireJS that you can find on GitHub (*http://bit.ly/17elTOK*). It is a stock application for a manager of a shop. The manager can add new items and filter down the items based on price, but nothing more. Because it's so simple, it's easier to focus purely on the RequireJS part of the implementation, rather than deal with complex JavaScript and Backbone logic, too.

At the base of this application is the `Item` model, which describes a single item in the stock. Its implementation is very straightforward:

```
define( ["lib/backbone"], function ( Backbone ) {
  var Item = Backbone.Model.extend({
    defaults: {
      price: 35,
      photo: "http://www.placedog.com/100/100"
    }
  });
  return Item;
});
```

Converting an individual model, collection, view, or similar into an AMD, RequireJS-compliant one is typically very straightforward. Usually all that's needed is the first line, calling `define`, and to make sure that once you've defined your object—in this case, the `Item` model—you return it.

Let's now set up a view for that individual item:

```
define( ["lib/backbone"], function ( Backbone ) {
  var ItemView = Backbone.View.extend({
    tagName: "div",
    className: "item-wrap",
    template: _.template($("#itemTemplate").html()),

    render: function() {
      this.$el.html(this.template(this.model.toJSON()));
      return this;
```

```
      }
    });
    return ItemView;
  });
```

This view doesn't actually depend on the model it will be used with, so again the only dependency is Backbone. Other than that, it's just a regular Backbone view. There's nothing special going on here, other than returning the object and using `define` so RequireJS can pick it up. Now let's make a collection to view a list of items. This time we will need to reference the `Item` model, so we add it as a dependency:

```
define(["lib/backbone", "models/item"], function(Backbone, Item) {
  var Cart = Backbone.Collection.extend({
    model: Item,
    initialize: function() {
      this.on("add", this.updateSet, this);
    },
    updateSet: function() {
      items = this.models;
    }
  });
  return Cart;
});
```

I've called this collection `Cart`, as it's a group of items. As the `Item` model is the second dependency, I can bind the variable `Item` to it by declaring it as the second argument to the callback function. I can then refer to this within my collection implementation.

Finally, let's have a look at the view for this collection. (This file is much bigger in the application, but I've taken some bits out so it's easier to examine.)

```
define(["lib/backbone", "models/item", "views/itemview"],
  function(Backbone, Item, ItemView) {
  var ItemCollectionView = Backbone.View.extend({
    el: '#yourcart',
    initialize: function(collection) {
      this.collection = collection;
      this.render();
      this.collection.on("reset", this.render, this);
    },
    render: function() {
      this.$el.html("");
      this.collection.each(function(item) {
        this.renderItem(item);
      }, this);
    },
    renderItem: function(item) {
      var itemView = new ItemView({model: item});
      this.$el.append(itemView.render().el);
    },
    // more methods here removed
  });
```

```
        return ItemCollectionView;
    });
```

There really is nothing to it once you've got the general pattern. Define each object (a model, view, collection, router, or otherwise) through RequireJS, and then specify them as dependencies to other objects that need them. Again, you can find this entire application on GitHub (*http://bit.ly/17elTOK*).

If you'd like to take a look at how others do it, Pete Hawkins' Backbone Stack repository (*http://bit.ly/ZiDaFu*) is a good example of structuring a Backbone application using RequireJS. Greg Franko has also written an overview of how he uses Backbone and Require (*http://bit.ly/105SLUN*), and Jeremy Kahn's post (*http://bit.ly/ZBD8Id*) neatly describes his approach. For a look at a full sample application, the Backbone and Require version (*http://bit.ly/105SVvs*) of the TodoMVC application is a good starting point.

Keeping Your Templates External Using RequireJS and the Text Plug-in

Moving your templates to external files is actually quite straightforward, whether they are Underscore, Mustache, Handlebars, or any other text-based template format. Let's look at how we do that with RequireJS.

RequireJS has a special plug-in called *text.js*, which is used to load in text file dependencies. To use the text plug-in, follow these steps:

1. Download the plug-in (*http://requirejs.org/docs/download.html#text*) and place it in either the same directory as your application's main JS file or a suitable subdirectory.

2. Next, include the *text.js* plug-in in your initial RequireJS configuration options. In the following code snippet, we assume that RequireJS is being included in our page prior to this code snippet being executed.

    ```
    require.config( {
        paths: {
            'text': 'libs/require/text',
        },
        baseUrl: 'app'
    } );
    ```

3. When the `text!` prefix is used for a dependency, RequireJS will automatically load the text plug-in and treat the dependency as a text resource. A typical example of this in action may look like:

    ```
    require(['js/app', 'text!templates/mainView.html'],
        function( app, mainView ) {
            // the contents of the mainView file will be
            // loaded into mainView for usage.
    ```

```
        }
    );
```

4. Finally, we can use the text resource that's been loaded for templating purposes. You're probably used to storing your HTML templates inline using a script with a specific identifier.

With Underscore.js's microtemplating (and jQuery), this would typically be:

- HTML

```
<script type="text/template" id="mainViewTemplate">
    <% _.each( person, function( person_item ){ %>
        <li><%= person_item.get('name') %></li>
    <% }); %>
</script>
```

- JS

```
var compiled_template = _.template( $('#mainViewTemplate').html() );
```

With RequireJS and the text plug-in, however, it's as simple as saving the same template into an external text file (say, *mainView.html*) and doing the following:

```
require(['js/app', 'text!templates/mainView.html'],
    function(app, mainView){
        var compiled_template = _.template( mainView );
    }
);
```

That's it! Now you can apply your template to a view in Backbone with something like:

```
collection.someview.$el.html( compiled_template
                        ( { results: collection.models } ) );
```

All templating solutions will have their own custom methods for handling template compilation, but if you understand the preceding, substituting Underscore's micro-templating for any other solution should be fairly trivial.

Optimizing Backbone Apps for Production with the RequireJS Optimizer

Once you've written your application, the next important step is to prepare it for deployment to production. The majority of nontrivial apps are likely to consist of several scripts and so optimizing, minimizing, and concatenating your scripts prior to pushing can reduce the number of scripts your users need to download.

A command-line optimization tool for RequireJS projects called *r.js* is available to help with this workflow. It offers a number of capabilities, including:

- Concatenating specific scripts and minifying them using external tools such as UglifyJS (which is used by default) or Google's Closure Compiler for optimal browser delivery, while preserving the ability to dynamically load modules

- Optimizing CSS and stylesheets by inlining CSS files imported using @import, stripping out comments, and so on

- The ability to run AMD projects in both Node and Rhino (more on this later)

If you find yourself wanting to ship a single file with all dependencies included, r.js can help with this too. While RequireJS does support lazy loading, your application may be small enough that reducing HTTP requests to a single script file is feasible.

You'll notice that I used the word *specific* in the first bullet point. The RequireJS optimizer concatenates only module scripts that have been specified as string literals in require and define calls (which you've probably used). As clarified by the optimizer docs (*http://requirejs.org/docs/optimization.html*), this means that Backbone modules defined like the following will combine fine:

```
define(['jquery', 'backbone', 'underscore', 'collections/sample', 'views/test'],
    function($, Backbone, _, Sample, Test){
        //...
    });
```

However, dynamic dependencies such as the following code will be ignored:

```
var models = someCondition ? ['models/ab', 'models/ac'] :
['models/ba', 'models/bc'];
define(['jquery', 'backbone', 'underscore'].concat(models),
    function($, Backbone, _, firstModel, secondModel){
        //...
    });
```

This is by design, as it ensures that dynamic dependency/module loading can still take place even after optimization.

Although the RequireJS optimizer works fine in both Node and Java environments, it's strongly recommended to run it under Node because it executes significantly faster there.

To get started with r.js, grab it from the RequireJS download page (*http://bit.ly/11ysb9J*) or through NPM (*http://bit.ly/12EXscc*). To begin getting our project to build with r.js, we will need to create a new build profile.

Assuming the code for our application and external dependencies is in *app/libs*, our *build.js* build profile could simply be:

```
({
  baseUrl: 'app',
  out: 'dist/main.js',
```

The preceding paths are relative to the `baseUrl` for our project, and in our case it would make sense to make this the *app* folder. The `out` parameter informs r.js that we want to concatenate everything into a single file called *main.js* under the *dist/* directory. Note that here we do need to add the *.js* extension to the filename. Earlier, we saw that when referencing modules by filenames, you don't need to use the *.js* extension; however, this is one case in which you do.

Alternatively, we can specify `dir`, which will ensure the contents of our `app` directory are copied into this directory. For example:

```
({
    baseUrl: 'app',
    dir: 'release',
    out: 'dist/main.js'
```

Additional options that can be specified, such as `modules` and `appDir`, are not compatible with `out`, but let's briefly discuss them in case you do wish to use them.

`modules` is an array where we can explicitly specify the module names we would like to have optimized.

```
modules: [
    {
        name: 'app',
        exclude: [
            // If you prefer not to include certain
            // libs exclude them here
        ]
    }
```

When `appDir` is specified, our `baseUrl` is relative to this parameter. If `appDir` is not defined, `baseUrl` is simply relative to the *build.js* file.

```
appDir: './',
```

Back to our build profile, the `main` parameter is used to specify our main module; we are making use of `include` here as we're going to take advantage of Almond (*https://github.com/jrburke/almond*), a stripped-down loader for RequireJS modules that is useful should you not need to load modules in dynamically.

```
include: ['libs/almond', 'main'],
wrap: true,
```

`include` is another array that specifies the modules we want to include in the build. When we specify `main`, r.js will trace over all modules `main` depends on and will include them. `wrap` wraps modules that RequireJS needs into a closure so that only what we export is included in the global environment.

```
paths: { backbone: 'libs/backbone', underscore: 'libs/underscore',
    jquery: 'libs/jquery', text: 'libs/text' } })
```

The remainder of the *build.js* file would be a regular `paths` configuration object. We can compile our project into a target file by running:

```
node r.js -o build.js
```

which should place our compiled project into *dist/main.js*.

The build profile is usually placed inside the *scripts* or *js* directory of your project. As per the docs, however, this file can exist anywhere you wish, but you'll need to edit the contents of your build profile accordingly.

That's it. As long as you have UglifyJS/Closure tools set up correctly, r.js should be able to easily optimize your entire Backbone project in just a few keystrokes.

If you would like to learn more about build profiles, James Burke has a heavily commented sample file (*http://bit.ly/132iVMq*) with all the possible options available.

Summary

Dependency management in JavaScript can be challenging. Once you start thinking about modularity, if you break down your application into several files, you still need to keep track of what each file's dependencies are and ensure they are loaded in the correct order. Without strong namespacing conventions, it is also fairly easy to pollute the global namespace with your own custom objects. AMD (and RequireJS) eases this process, providing syntactic sugar for defining reusable modules and their dependencies without polluting the global namespace. Though AMD may not be for everyone, it can certainly assist with code structure, cleanly modularizing groups of models, views, and collections forming up regions of your page. Be sure to evaluate whether the AMD module style works for you. If it does, you should get some good mileage with it.

CHAPTER 9

Exercise 3: Your First Modular Backbone and RequireJS App

In this chapter, we'll look at our first practical Backbone and RequireJS project—how to build a modular Todo application. Similar to Exercise 1 in Chapter 4, the application will allow us to add new todos, edit new todos, and clear todo items that have been marked as completed. For a more advanced practical, see Chapter 12.

You can find the complete code for the application in the *practicals/modular-todo-app* folder of this repo (thanks to Thomas Davis and Jérôme Gravel-Niquet). Alternatively, grab a copy of my side project TodoMVC (*https://github.com/addyosmani/todomvc*), which contains the sources to both AMD and non-AMD versions.

Overview

Writing a modular Backbone application can be a straightforward process. There are, however, some key conceptual differences to be aware of if you're opting to use AMD as your module format of choice:

- As AMD isn't a standard native to JavaScript or the browser, you must use a script loader (such as RequireJS or curl.js) in order to support defining components and modules using this module format. As we've already reviewed, there are a number of advantages to using the AMD as well as RequireJS to assist here.

- Models, views, controllers, and routers need to be encapsulated *using* the AMD format. This allows each component of our Backbone application to cleanly manage dependencies (for example, collections required by a view) in the same way that AMD allows non-Backbone modules to.

- Non-Backbone components/modules (such as utilities or application helpers) can also be encapsulated using AMD. I encourage you to try developing these modules in such a way that they can both be used and tested independent of your Backbone code, as this will increase reuseability elsewhere.

Now that we've reviewed the basics, let's take a look at developing our application. For reference, the structure of our app is as follows:

```
index.html
...js/
    main.js
    .../models
            todo.js
    .../views
            app.js
            todos.js
    .../collections
            todos.js
    .../templates
            stats.html
            todos.html
    ../libs
        .../backbone
        .../jquery
        .../underscore
        .../require
                require.js
                text.js
...css/
```

Markup

The markup for the application is relatively simple and consists of three primary parts: an input section for entering new todo items (create-todo); a list section to display existing items, which can also be edited in place (todo-list); and finally, a section summarizing how many items are left to be completed (todo-stats).

```html
<div id="todoapp">

    <div class="content">

        <div id="create-todo">
          <input id="new-todo" placeholder="What needs to be done?"
           type="text" />
          <span class="ui-tooltip-top">Press Enter to save this task</span>
        </div>

        <div id="todos">
          <ul id="todo-list"></ul>
        </div>

        <div id="todo-stats"></div>
```

```
    </div>

  </div>
```

The rest of the tutorial will now focus on the JavaScript side of the practical.

Configuration Options

If you've read the earlier chapter on AMD, you may have noticed that explicitly needing to define each dependency that a Backbone module (view, collection, or other module) may require with it can get a little tedious. This can, however, be improved.

To simplify referencing common paths the modules in our application may use, we use a RequireJS configuration object (*http://requirejs.org/docs/api.html#config*), which is typically defined as a top-level script file. Configuration objects have a number of useful capabilities, the most useful being mode *name mapping*. Name maps are basically a key/value pair, where the key defines the alias you wish to use for a path and the value represents the true location of the path.

In the following code sample, *main.js*, you can see some typical examples of common name maps, including `backbone`, `underscore`, `jquery`, and depending on your choice, the RequireJS `text` plug-in, which assists with loading text assets like templates.

```
require.config({
  baseUrl:'..//',
  paths: {
    jquery: 'libs/jquery/jquery-min',
    underscore: 'libs/underscore/underscore-min',
    backbone: 'libs/backbone/backbone-optamd3-min',
    text: 'libs/require/text'
  }
});

require(['views/app'], function(AppView){
  var app_view = new AppView;
});
```

The `require()` at the end of our *main.js* file is simply there so we can load and instantiate the primary view for our application (*views/app.js*). You'll commonly see both this and the configuration object included in most top-level script files for a project.

In addition to offering name mapping, the configuration object can be used to define additional properties such as `waitSeconds` (the number of seconds to wait before script loading times out) and `locale` (should you wish to load up i18n bundles for custom languages). The `baseUrl` is simply the path to use for module lookups.

For more information on configuration objects, please feel free to check out the excellent guide to them in the RequireJS docs (*http://requirejs.org/docs/api.html#config*).

Modularizing Our Models, Views, and Collections

Before we dive into AMD-wrapped versions of our Backbone components, let's review a sample of a non-AMD view. The following view listens for changes to its model (a todo item) and rerenders if a user edits the value of the item.

```
var TodoView = Backbone.View.extend({

    //... is a list tag.
    tagName: 'li',

    // Cache the template function for a single item.
    template: _.template($('#item-template').html()),

    // The DOM events specific to an item.
    events: {
      'click .check'               : 'toggleDone',
      'dblclick div.todo-content' : 'edit',
      'click span.todo-destroy'   : 'clear',
      'keypress .todo-input'       : 'updateOnEnter'
    },

    // The TodoView listens for changes to its model, rerendering. Since there's
    // a one-to-one correspondence between a **Todo** and a **TodoView** in this
    // app, we set a direct reference on the model for convenience.
    initialize: function() {
      this.model.on('change', this.render, this);
      this.model.view = this;
    },
    ...
```

Note how for templating we use the common practice of referencing a script by an id (or other selector) and obtaining its value. This, of course, requires that the template being accessed is implicitly defined in our markup. The following is the embedded version of the template we just referenced:

```
<script type="text/template" id="item-template">
    <div class="todo <%= done ? 'done' : '' %>">
      <div class="display">
        <input class="check" type="checkbox" <%= done ?
         'checked="checked"' : '' %> />
        <div class="todo-content"></div>
        <span class="todo-destroy"></span>
      </div>
      <div class="edit">
        <input class="todo-input" type="text" value="" />
      </div>
    </div>
</script>
```

Though there is nothing wrong with the template itself, once we begin to develop larger applications requiring multiple templates, including them all in our markup on page load can quickly become unmanageable and negatively impact performance. We'll look at solving this problem in a minute.

Let's now take a look at the AMD version of our view, *views/todo.js*. As discussed earlier, the module is wrapped using AMD's define(), which allows us to specify the dependencies our view requires. Using the mapped paths simplifies referencing common dependencies, and instances of dependencies are themselves mapped to local variables that we can access (for example, jquery is mapped to $).

```
define([
  'jquery',
  'underscore',
  'backbone',
  'text!templates/todos.html'
], function($, _, Backbone, todosTemplate){
var TodoView = Backbone.View.extend({

  //... is a list tag.
  tagName: 'li',

  // Cache the template function for a single item.
  template: _.template(todosTemplate),

  // The DOM events specific to an item.
  events: {
    'click .check'              : 'toggleDone',
    'dblclick div.todo-content' : 'edit',
    'click span.todo-destroy'   : 'clear',
    'keypress .todo-input'      : 'updateOnEnter'
  },

  // The TodoView listens for changes to its model, rerendering. Since there's
  // a one-to-one correspondence between a **Todo** and a **TodoView** in this
  // app, we set a direct reference on the model for convenience.
  initialize: function() {
    this.model.on('change', this.render, this);
    this.model.view = this;
  },

  // Rerender the contents of the todo item.
  render: function() {
    this.$el.html(this.template(this.model.toJSON()));
    this.setContent();
    return this;
  },

  // Use `jQuery.text` to set the contents of the todo item.
  setContent: function() {
    var content = this.model.get('content');
```

```
    this.$('.todo-content').text(content);
    this.input = this.$('.todo-input');
    this.input.on('blur', this.close);
    this.input.val(content);
},
...
```

From a maintenance perspective, there's nothing logically different in this version of our view, except for how we approach templating.

Using the RequireJS text plug-in (the dependency marked `text`), we can actually store all of the contents for the template we looked at earlier in an external file (*templates/todos.html*).

```
<div class="todo <%= done ? 'done' : '' %>">
    <div class="display">
      <input class="check" type="checkbox" <%= done ?
       'checked="checked"' : '' %> />
      <div class="todo-content"></div>
      <span class="todo-destroy"></span>
    </div>
    <div class="edit">
      <input class="todo-input" type="text" value="" />
    </div>
</div>
```

We no longer need to be concerned with `ids` for the template, as we can map its contents to a local variable (in this case, `todosTemplate`). We then simply pass this to the Underscore.js templating function `_.template()` the same way we normally would have the value of our template script.

Next, let's look at how to define models as dependencies which can be pulled into collections. The following, *models/todo.js*, is an AMD-compatible model module, which has two default values: a `content` attribute for the content of a todo item, and a Boolean done state that allows us to trigger whether the item has been completed or not.

```
define(['underscore', 'backbone'], function(_, Backbone) {
  var TodoModel = Backbone.Model.extend({

    // Default attributes for the todo.
    defaults: {
      // Ensure that each todo created has `content`.
      content: 'empty todo...',
      done: false
    },

    initialize: function() {
    },

    // Toggle the `done` state of this todo item.
    toggle: function() {
      this.save({done: !this.get('done')});
```

```
  },

  // Remove this Todo from *localStorage* and delete its view.
  clear: function() {
    this.destroy();
    this.view.remove();
  }

});
return TodoModel;
});
```

As per other types of dependencies, we can easily map our model module to a local variable (in this case, `Todo`) so it can be referenced as the model to use for our Todo sCollection. This collection, *collections/todos.js*, also supports a simple done() filter for narrowing down todo items that have been completed and a remaining() filter for those that are still outstanding.

```
define([
  'underscore',
  'backbone',
  'libs/backbone/localstorage',
  'models/todo'
], function(_, Backbone, Store, Todo){

  var TodosCollection = Backbone.Collection.extend({

  // Reference to this collection's model.
  model: Todo,

  // Save all of the todo items under the `todos` namespace.
  localStorage: new Store('todos'),

  // Filter down the list of all todo items that are finished.
  done: function() {
    return this.filter(function(todo){ return todo.get('done'); });
  },

  // Filter down the list to only todo items that are still not finished.
  remaining: function() {
    return this.without.apply(this, this.done());
  },
  ...
```

In addition to allowing users to add new todo items from views (which we then insert as models in a collection), we ideally also want to be able to display how many items have been completed and how many are remaining. We've already defined filters that can provide us this information in the preceding collection, so let's use them in our main application view, *views/app.js*.

```
define([
  'jquery',
```

```
  'underscore',
  'backbone',
  'collections/todos',
  'views/todo',
  'text!templates/stats.html'
], function($, _, Backbone, Todos, TodoView, statsTemplate){

var AppView = Backbone.View.extend({

    // Instead of generating a new element, bind to the existing skeleton of
    // the app already present in the HTML.
    el: $('#todoapp'),

    // Our template for the line of statistics at the bottom of the app.
    statsTemplate: _.template(statsTemplate),

    // ...events, initialize() etc. can be seen in the complete file

    // Rerendering the app just means refreshing the statistics—the rest
    // of the app doesn't change.
    render: function() {
      var done = Todos.done().length;
      this.$('#todo-stats').html(this.statsTemplate({
        total:      Todos.length,
        done:       Todos.done().length,
        remaining:  Todos.remaining().length
      }));
    },
    ...
```

Here, we map the second template for this project, *templates/stats.html*, to statsTemplate, which is used for rendering the overall done and remaining states. This works by simply passing our template the length of our overall Todos collection (Todos.length —the number of todo items created so far) and similarly the length (counts) for items that have been completed (Todos.done().length) or are remaining (Todos.remaining().length).

Following are the contents of our statsTemplate. It's nothing too complicated, but does use ternary conditions to evaluate whether we should state that there's one item or two items in a particular state.

```
<% if (total) { %>
    <span class="todo-count">
       <span class="number"><%= remaining %></span>
       <span class="word"><%= remaining == 1 ? 'item' : 'items' %></span>
       </span> left.
    </span>
   <% } %>
   <% if (done) { %>
      <span class="todo-clear">
         <a href="#">
```

```
      Clear <span class="number-done"><%= done %></span>
      completed <span class="word-done"><%= done == 1 ?
      'item' : 'items' %></span>
    </a>
  </span>
<% } %>
```

The rest of the source for the Todo app mainly consists of code for handling user and application events, but that wraps up most of the core concepts for this practical.

To see how everything ties together, feel free to grab the source by cloning this repo or browsing it online (*http://bit.ly/17UyuYC*) to learn more. I hope you find it helpful.

Route-Based Module Loading

This section will discuss a route-based approach to module loading as implemented in Lumbar (*http://walmartlabs.github.com/lumbar*) by Kevin Decker. Like RequireJS, Lumbar is also a modular build system, but the pattern it implements for loading routes may be used with any build system.

The specifics of the Lumbar build tool are not discussed in this book. For a complete Lumbar-based project with the loader and build system, see Thorax (*http://thoraxjs.org*), which provides boilerplate projects for various environments including Lumbar.

JSON-Based Module Configuration

RequireJS defines dependencies per file, while Lumbar defines a list of files for each module in a central JSON configuration file, outputting a single JavaScript file for each defined module. Lumbar requires that each module (except the base module) define a single router and a list of routes. An example file might look like:

```
{
    "modules": {
        "base": {
            "scripts": [
                "js/lib/underscore.js",
                "js/lib/backbone.js",
                "etc"
            ]
        },
        "pages": {
            "scripts": [
                "js/routers/pages.js",
                "js/views/pages/index.js",
                "etc"
            ],
            "routes": {
                "": "index",
```

```
                    "contact": "contact"
                }
            }
        }
    }
```

Every JavaScript file defined in a module will have a `module` object in scope that contains the `name` and `routes` for the module. In *js/routers/pages.js*, we could define a Backbone router for our `pages` module like so:

```
new (Backbone.Router.extend({
    routes: module.routes,
    index: function() {},
    contact: function() {}
}));
```

Module Loader Router

A little-used feature of `Backbone.Router` is its ability to create multiple routers that listen to the same set of routes. Lumbar uses this feature to create a router that listens to all routes in the application. When a route is matched, this master router checks to see if the needed module is loaded. If the module is already loaded, then the master router takes no action and the router defined by the module will handle the route. If the needed module has not yet been loaded, it will be loaded, and then `Backbone.his tory.loadUrl` will be called. This reloads the route, causes the master router to take no further action, and prompts the router defined in the freshly loaded module to respond.

A sample implementation is provided next. The `config` object would need to contain the data from our previously mentioned sample configuration JSON file, and the `load er` object would need to implement `isLoaded` and `loadModule` methods. Note that Lumbar provides all of these implementations; these examples will help you create your own implementation.

```
// Create an object that will be used as the prototype
// for our master router
var handlers = {
    routes: {}
};

_.each(config.modules, function(module, moduleName) {
    if (module.routes) {
        // Generate a loading callback for the module
        var callbackName = "loader_" moduleName;
        handlers[callbackName] = function() {
            if (loader.isLoaded(moduleName)) {
                // Do nothing if the module is loaded
                return;
            } else {
                //the module needs to be loaded
                loader.loadModule(moduleName, function() {
```

```
                        // Module is loaded, reloading the route
                        // will trigger callback in the module's
                        // router
                        Backbone.history.loadUrl();
                    });
                }
            };
            // Each route in the module should trigger the
            // loading callback
            _.each(module.routes, function(methodName, route) {
                handlers.routes[route] = callbackName;
            });
        }
    });

    // Create the master router
    new (Backbone.Router.extend(handlers));
```

Using NodeJS to Handle pushState

`window.history.pushState` support (serving Backbone routes without a hash mark)
requires that the server be aware of what URLs your Backbone application will handle,
since the user should be able to enter the app at any of those routes (or press reload after
navigating to a `pushState` URL).

Another advantage to defining all routes in a single location is that the same JSON
configuration file provided previously could be loaded by the server, listening to each
route. A sample implementation in Node.js and Express:

```
var fs = require('fs'),
    _ = require('underscore'),
    express = require('express'),
    server = express(),
    config = JSON.parse(fs.readFileSync('path/to/config.json'));

_.each(config.modules, function(module, moduleName) {
    if (module.routes) {
        _.each(module.routes, function(methodName, route) {
            server.get(route, function(req, res) {
                res.sendFile('public/index.html');
            });
        });
    }
});
```

This assumes that *index.html* will be serving out your Backbone application. The `Back
bone.History` object can handle the rest of the routing logic as long as a `root` option is
specified. A sample configuration for a simple application that lives at the root might
look like this:

```
Backbone.history || (Backbone.history = new Backbone.History());
Backbone.history.start({
  pushState: true,
  root: '/'
});
```

An Asset Package Alternative for Dependency Management

For more than trivial views, DocumentCloud has a home-built asset packager called Jammit (*https://github.com/documentcloud/jammit*), which is easily integrated with Underscore.js templates and can also be used for dependency management.

Jammit expects your JavaScript templates (JST) to live alongside any ERB templates you're using in the form of *.jst* files. It packages the templates into a global JST object that can be used to render templates into strings. Making Jammit aware of your templates is straightforward—just add an entry for something like `views/**/*.jst` to your app package in *assets.yml*.

To provide Jammit dependencies, you simply write out an *assets.yml* file that either lists the dependencies in order or uses a combination of free capture directories (for example, *//.js, templates/*.js, and specific files).

A template using Jammit can derive its data from the collection object passed to it:

```
this.$el.html(JST.myTemplate({ collection: this.collection }));
```

CHAPTER 10

Paginating Backbone.js Requests and Collections

Pagination is a ubiquitous problem we often find ourselves needing to solve on the Web —perhaps most predominantly when we're working with service APIs and JavaScript-heavy clients that consume them. It's also a problem that is often underrefined because most of us consider pagination relatively easy to get right. This isn't, however, always the case, as pagination tends to get trickier than it initially seems.

Before we dive into solutions for paginating data for your Backbone applications, let's define exactly what we consider pagination to be.

Pagination is a control system allowing users to browse through pages of search results or any type of content that is continued. Search results are the canonical example, but pagination today is found on news sites, blogs, and discussion boards, often in the form of Previous and Next links. More complete pagination systems offer granular control of the specific pages you can navigate to, giving users more power to find what they are looking for.

It isn't a problem limited to pages requiring some visual controls for pagination either —sites like Facebook, Pinterest, and Twitter have demonstrated that there are many contexts where infinite paging is also useful. Infinite paging is, of course, when we prefetch (or appear to prefetch) content from a subsequent page and add it directly to the user's current page, making the experience feel infinite.

Pagination is very context-specific and depends on the content being displayed. In the Google search results, pagination is important because Google wants to offer you the most relevant set of results in the first one or two pages. After that, you might be a little more selective (or random) with the page you choose to navigate to. This differs from cases where you'll want to cycle through consecutive pages (for example, for a news article or blog post).

Pagination is almost certainly content and context-specific, but as Faruk Ates has previously pointed out (*https://gist.github.com/mislav/622561*), the principles of good pagination apply no matter what the content or context is. As with everything extensible when it comes to Backbone, you can write your own pagination to address many of these content-specific types of pagination problems. That said, you'll probably spend quite a bit of time on this, and sometimes you want to use a tried-and-true solution that just works.

On this topic, we're going to go through a set of pagination components that I and a group of contributors (*http://bit.ly/10uKEQH*) wrote for Backbone.js, which should hopefully come in handy if you're working on applications that need to page Backbone collections. These components are part of an extension called Backbone.Paginator (*http://bit.ly/18fe6BF*).

Backbone.Paginator

When working with data on the client side, we are most likely to run into three types of pagination:

Requests to a service layer (API)
>   For example, query for results containing the term *Paul*—if 5,000 results are available, display only 20 results per page (leaving us with 250 possible result pages that can be navigated to).
>
>   This problem actually has quite a great deal more to it, such as maintaining persistence of other URL parameters (such as sort, query, order) that can change based on a user's search configuration in a UI. You also have to think of a clean way to hook up views to this pagination so you can easily navigate between pages (for example, First, Last, Next, Previous, 1, 2, 3), manage the number of results displayed per page, and so on.

Further client-side pagination of data returned
>   For example, we've been returned a JSON response containing 100 results. Rather than displaying all 100 to the user, we display only 20 of these results within a navigable UI in the browser.
>
>   Similar to the request problem, client pagination has its own challenges, like navigation once again (Next, Previous, 1, 2, 3), sorting, order, switching the number of results to display per page, and so on.

Infinite results
>   With services such as Facebook, the concept of numeric pagination is instead replaced with a Load More or View More button. Triggering this normally fetches the next page of *N* results, but rather than replacing entirely the previous set of results loaded, we simply append to them instead.

A request pager, which simply appends results in a view rather than replacing on each new fetch, is effectively an infinite pager.

Let's now take a look at exactly what we're getting out of the box.

Backbone.Paginator, shown in Figure 10-1, is a set of opinionated components for paginating collections of data using Backbone.js. It aims to provide both solutions for assisting with pagination of requests to a server (such as an API) as well as pagination of single loads of data, where we may wish to further paginate a collection of N results into M pages within a view.

Figure 10-1. Backbone.Paginator demonstrating how to visually style the components provided by the project

Backbone.Paginator supports two main pagination components:

`Backbone.Paginator.requestPager`
For pagination of requests between a client and a server-side API

`Backbone.Paginator.clientPager`
For pagination of data returned from a server that you would like to further paginate within the UI (for example, 60 results are returned, paginate into three pages of 20)

Live Examples

If you would like to look at examples built using the components included in the project, links to official demos are included here and use the Netflix API so that you can see them working with an actual data source:

- `Backbone.Paginator.requestPager()` (*http://bit.ly/11J0ZCm*)
- `Backbone.Paginator.clientPager()` (*http://bit.ly/Zimkpv*)
- Infinite pagination (`Backbone.Paginator.requestPager()`) (*http://bit.ly/YKl4b4*)
- `Diacritic plug-in` (*http://bit.ly/10aXFyw*)

Paginator.requestPager

In this section we're going to walk through using the `requestPager` (shown in Figure 10-2). You would use this component when working with a service API that itself supports pagination. This component allows users to control the pagination settings for requests to this API (for example, navigate to the next, previous, *N* pages) via the client side.

The idea is that pagination, searching, and filtering of data can all be done from your Backbone application without the need for a page reload.

Figure 10-2. Using the requestPager component to request paginated results from the Netflix API

1. Create a new Paginated collection.

   First, we define a new Paginated collection using `Backbone.Paginator.request` `Pager()` as follows:

   ```
   var PaginatedCollection = Backbone.Paginator.requestPager.extend({
   ```

2. Set the model for the collection as normal.

   Within our collection, we then (as normal) specify the model to be used with this collection followed by the URL (or base URL) for the service providing our data (such as the Netflix API).

   ```
   model: model,
   ```

3. Configure the base URL and the type of request.

   We need to set a base URL. The `type` of the request is `GET` by default, and the `dataType` is `jsonp` in order to enable cross-domain requests.

   ```
   paginator_core: {
       // the type of the request (GET by default)
   ```

```
type: 'GET',

// the type of reply (jsonp by default)
dataType: 'jsonp',

// the URL (or base URL) for the service
// if you want to have a more dynamic URL, you can make this
// a function that returns a string
url: 'http://odata.netflix.com/Catalog/People(49446)/TitlesActedIn?'
},
```

 If you use dataType *not* jsonp, please remove the callback custom
parameter inside the server_api configuration.

4. Configure how the library will show the results.

   We need to tell the library how many items per page we would like to display, what
   the current page is, what the range of pages should be, and so on.

```
paginator_ui: {
    // the lowest page index your API allows to be accessed
    firstPage: 0,

    // which page should the paginator start from
    // (also, the actual page the paginator is on)
    currentPage: 0,

    // how many items per page should be shown
    perPage: 3,

    // a default number of total pages to query in case the API or
    // service you are using does not support providing the total
    // number of pages for us.
    // 10 as a default in case your service doesn't return the total
    totalPages: 10
},
```

5. Configure the parameters we want to send to the server.

   The base URL won't be enough for most cases, so you can pass more parameters to
   the server. Note how you can use functions instead of hardcoded values, and you
   can also refer to the values you specified in paginator_ui.

```
server_api: {
    // the query field in the request
    '$filter': '',

    // number of items to return per request/page
    '$top': function() { return this.perPage },

    // how many results the request should skip ahead to
```

```
// customize as needed. For the Netflix API, skipping ahead based on
// page * number of results per page was necessary.
'$skip': function() { return this.currentPage * this.perPage },

// field to sort by
'$orderby': 'ReleaseYear',

// what format would you like to request results in?
'$format': 'json',

// custom parameters
'$inlinecount': 'allpages',
'$callback': 'callback'
},
```

 If you use $callback, please ensure that you did use jsonp as a
dataType inside your paginator_core configuration.

6. Finally, configure `Collection.parse()`, and we're done.

   The last thing we need to do is configure our collection's `parse()` method. We want
   to ensure we're returning the correct part of our JSON response containing the data
   our collection will be populated with, which in the following is `response.d.re
   sults` (for the Netflix API).

```
        parse: function (response) {
            // Be sure to change this based on how your results
            // are structured (e.g., d.results is Netflix-specific)
            var tags = response.d.results;
            //Normally this.totalPages would equal response.d.__count
            //but as this particular NetFlix request only returns a
            //total count of items for the search, we divide.
            this.totalPages = Math.ceil(response.d.__count / this.perPage);
            return tags;
        }
    });

});
```

You might also notice that we're setting `this.totalPages` to the total page count
returned by the API. This allows us to define the maximum number of (result)
pages available for the current/last request so that we can clearly display this in the
UI. It also allows us to influence whether clicking, say, a Next button should proceed
with a request or not.

Convenience Methods

For your convenience, the following methods are made available for use in your views to interact with the `requestPager`:

`Collection.goTo( n, options )`
  Go to a specific page

`Collection.nextPage( options )`
  Go to the next page

`Collection.prevPage( options )`
  Go to the previous page

`Collection.howManyPer( n )`
  Set the number of items to display per page

The `requestPager` collection's methods `.goTo()`, `.nextPage()`, and `.prevPage()` are all extensions of the original Backbone `Collection.fetch()` methods (*http://bit.ly/151ku0k*). As such, they all can take the same `option` object as a parameter.

This `option` object can use `success` and `error` parameters to pass a function to be executed after server answers.

```
Collection.goTo(n, {
  success: function( collection, response ) {
    // called if server request success
  },
  error: function( collection, response ) {
    // called if server request fail
  }
});
```

To manage callback, you could also use the jqXHR (*http://bit.ly/12rJmrc*) returned by these methods.

```
Collection
  .requestNextPage()
  .done(function( data, textStatus, jqXHR ) {
    // called if server request success
  })
  .fail(function( data, textStatus, jqXHR ) {
    // called if server request fail
  })
  .always(function( data, textStatus, jqXHR ) {
    // do something after server request is complete
  });
});
```

If you'd like to add the incoming models to the current collection, instead of replacing the collection's contents, pass {`update: true, remove: false`} as options to these methods.

```
Collection.prevPage({ update: true, remove: false });
```

Paginator.clientPager

The clientPager (Figure 10-3) is used to further paginate data that has already been returned by the service API. Say you've requested 100 results from the service and wish to split this into five pages of paginated results, each containing 20 results at a client level—the clientPager makes it trivial to do this.

Figure 10-3. Using the clientPager component to further paginate results returned from the Netflix API

Use the clientPager when you prefer to get results in a single load and thus avoid making additional network requests each time your users want to fetch the next page of items. As the results have all already been requested, it's just a matter of switching between the ranges of data actually presented to the user.

1. Create a new paginated collection with a model and URL.

   As with requestPager, let's first create a new paginated Backbone.Paginator.cli entPager collection, with a model:

   ```
   var PaginatedCollection = Backbone.Paginator.clientPager.extend({

       model: model,
   ```

2. Configure the base URL and the type of request.

We need to set a base URL. The `type` of the request is `GET` by default, and the `dataType` is `jsonp` in order to enable cross-domain requests.

```
paginator_core: {
    // the type of the request (GET by default)
    type: 'GET',

    // the type of reply (jsonp by default)
    dataType: 'jsonp',

    // the URL (or base URL) for the service
    url: 'http://odata.netflix.com/v2/Catalog/Titles?&'
},
```

3. Configure how the library will show the results.

   We need to tell the library how many items per page we would like to display, what the current page is, what the range of pages should be, and so on.

```
paginator_ui: {
    // the lowest page index your API allows to be accessed
    firstPage: 1,

    // which page should the paginator start from
    // (also, the actual page the paginator is on)
    currentPage: 1,

    // how many items per page should be shown
    perPage: 3,

    // a default number of total pages to query in case the API or
    // service you are using does not support providing the total
    // number of pages for us.
    // 10 as a default in case your service doesn't return the total
    totalPages: 10,

    // The total number of pages to be shown as a pagination
    // list is calculated by (pagesInRange * 2) + 1.
    pagesInRange: 4
},
```

4. Configure the parameters we want to send to the server.

   The base URL alone won't be enough for most cases, so you can pass more parameters to the server. Note how you can use functions instead of hardcoded values, and you can also refer to the values you specified in `paginator_ui`.

```
server_api: {
    // the query field in the request
    '$filter': 'substringof(\'america\',Name)',

    // number of items to return per request/page
    '$top': function() { return this.perPage },
```

```
            // how many results the request should skip ahead to
            // customize as needed. For the Netflix API, skipping ahead based on
            // page * number of results per page was necessary.
            '$skip': function() { return this.currentPage * this.perPage },

            // field to sort by
            '$orderby': 'ReleaseYear',

            // what format would you like to request results in?
            '$format': 'json',

            // custom parameters
            '$inlinecount': 'allpages',
            '$callback': 'callback'
        },
```

5. Finally, configure `Collection.parse()`, and we're done.

   And finally we have our `parse()` method, which in this case isn't concerned with
   the total number of result pages available on the server, as we have our own total
   count of pages for the paginated data in the UI.

```
    parse: function (response) {
            var tags = response.d.results;
            return tags;
        }

    });
```

Convenience Methods

As mentioned, your views can hook into a number of convenience methods to navigate
around UI-paginated data. For `clientPager`, these include:

`Collection.goTo( n, options )`
    Go to a specific page.

`Collection.prevPage( options )`
    Go to the previous page.

`Collection.nextPage( options )`
    Go to the next page.

`Collection.howManyPer( n )`
    Set how many items to display per page.

`Collection.setSort( sortBy, sortDirection )`
    Update sort on the current view. Sorting will automatically detect if you're trying
    to sort numbers (even if they're stored as strings) and will do the right thing.

```
Collection.setFilter( filterFields, filterWords )
```
Filter the current view. Filtering supports multiple words without any specific order, so you'll basically get a full-text search ability. Also, you can pass it only one field from the model, or you can pass an array with fields and all of them will get filtered. The last option is to pass it an object containing a comparison method and rules. Currently, only the Levenshtein method is available. The Levenshtein distance is the difference between two strings and is effectively the minimum number of changes required to change one word into another.

The goTo(), prevPage(), and nextPage() functions do not require the options param since they will be executed synchronously. However, when specified, the success callback will be invoked before the function returns. For example:

```
nextPage(); // this works just fine!
nextPage({success: function() { }}); // this will call the success function
```

The options param exists to preserve (some) interface unification between the requestPaginator and clientPaginator so that they may be used interchangeably in your Backbone.Views.

```
this.collection.setFilter(
  {'Name': {cmp_method: 'levenshtein', max_distance: 7}}
  , "American P" // Note the switched 'r' and 'e', and the 'P' from 'Pie'
);
```

Also note that the Levenshtein plug-in should be loaded and enabled via the useLe venshteinPlugin variable. Last but not less important: performing Levenshtein comparison returns the distance between two strings. It won't let you *search* lengthy text. The distance between two strings means the number of characters that should be added, removed, or moved to the left or to the right so the strings get equal. That means that comparing "Something" in "This is a test that could show something" will return 32, which is bigger than comparing "Something" and "ABCDEFG (9)." Use Levenshtein only for short texts (titles, names, and so on).

```
Collection.doFakeFilter( filterFields, filterWords )
```
Returns the models count after fake-applying a call to Collection.setFilter.

```
Collection.setFieldFilter( rules )
```
Filter each value of each model according to rules that you pass as an argument. Say you have a collection of books with release year and author. You can filter only the books that were released between 1999 and 2003. And then you can add another rule that will filter those books only to authors whose name starts with A. Possible rules: function, required, min, max, range, minLength, maxLength, rangeLength, oneOf, equalTo, containsAllOf, pattern. Passing this an empty rules set will remove any FieldFilter rules applied.

```
my_collection.setFieldFilter([
  {field: 'release_year', type: 'range', value:
```

```
              {min: '1999', max: '2003'}},
              {field: 'author', type: 'pattern', value: new RegExp('A*', 'igm')}
          ]);

          //Rules:
          //
          //var my_var = 'green';
          //
          //{field: 'color', type: 'equalTo', value: my_var}
          //{field: 'color', type: 'function', value: function(field_value){
          //  return field_value == my_var; } }
          //{field: 'color', type: 'required'}
          //{field: 'number_of_colors', type: 'min', value: '2'}
          //{field: 'number_of_colors', type: 'max', value: '4'}
          //{field: 'number_of_colors', type: 'range', value: {min: '2', max: '4'} }
          //{field: 'color_name', type: 'minLength', value: '4'}
          //{field: 'color_name', type: 'maxLength', value: '6'}
          //{field: 'color_name', type: 'rangeLength', value: {min: '4', max: '6'}}
          //{field: 'color_name', type: 'oneOf', value: ['green', 'yellow']}
          //{field: 'color_name', type: 'pattern', value: new RegExp('gre*', 'ig')}
          //{field: 'color_name', type: 'containsAllOf', value:
          //  ['green', 'yellow', 'blue']}
```

Collection.doFakeFieldFilter(*rules*)

> Returns the models count after fake-applying a call to Collection
> .setFieldFilter.

Implementation Notes

You can use some variables in your view to represent the actual state of the paginator.

totalUnfilteredRecords

> Contains the number of records, including all records filtered in any way (available only in clientPager).

totalRecords

> Contains the number of records.

currentPage

> The actual page where the paginator is located.

perPage

> The number of records the paginator will show per page.

totalPages

> The number of total pages.

startRecord

> The position of the first record shown in the current page—for example, 41 to 50 from 2,000 records (available only in clientPager).

endRecord

The position of the last record shown in the current page—for example, 41 to 50 from 2,000 records (available only in `clientPager`).

pagesInRange

The number of pages to be drawn on each side of the current page. So, if `pagesIn Range` is 3 and `currentPage` is 13, you will get the numbers 10, 11, 12, 13 (selected), 14, 15, 16.

```html
<!-- sample template for pagination UI -->
<script type="text/html" id="tmpServerPagination">

  <div class="row-fluid">

    <div class="pagination span8">
      <ul>
        <% _.each (pageSet, function (p) { %>
        <% if (currentPage == p) { %>
          <li class="active"><span><%= p %></span></li>
        <% } else { %>
          <li><a href="#" class="page"><%= p %></a></li>
        <% } %>
        <% }); %>
      </ul>
    </div>

    <div class="pagination span4">
      <ul>
        <% if (currentPage > firstPage) { %>
          <li><a href="#" class="serverprevious">Previous</a></li>
        <% }else{ %>
          <li><span>Previous</span></li>
        <% }%>
        <% if (currentPage < totalPages) { %>
          <li><a href="#" class="servernext">Next</a></li>
        <% } else { %>
          <li><span>Next</span></li>
        <% } %>
        <% if (firstPage != currentPage) { %>
          <li><a href="#" class="serverfirst">First</a></li>
        <% } else { %>
          <li><span>First</span></li>
        <% } %>
        <% if (totalPages != currentPage) { %>
          <li><a href="#" class="serverlast">Last</a></li>
        <% } else { %>
          <li><span>Last</span></li>
        <% } %>
      </ul>
    </div>
```

```
    </div>

    <span class="cell serverhowmany"> Show <a href="#"
      class="selected">18</a> | <a href="#" class="">9</a> |
      <a href="#" class="">12</a> per page
    </span>

    <span class="divider">/</span>

    <span class="cell first records">
      Page: <span class="label"><%= currentPage %></span> of
      <span class="label"><%= totalPages %></span> shown
    </span>

  </script>
```

Plug-ins

Diacritic.js is a plug-in for Backbone.Paginator that replaces diacritic characters (´, ˝, ˚, ~, and so on) with characters that match them most closely, as shown in Figure 10-4. This is particularly useful for filtering.

Figure 10-4. The Diacritics plug-in being used to correctly render special characters with the clientPager

To enable the plug-in, set this.useDiacriticsPlugin to true, as shown in this example:

```
Paginator.clientPager = Backbone.Collection.extend({

    // Default values used when sorting and/or filtering.
    initialize: function(){
```

```
    this.useDiacriticsPlugin = true; // use diacritics plug-in if available
    ...
```

Bootstrapping

By default, both the `clientPager` and `requestPager` will make an initial request to the server in order to populate their internal paging data. To avoid this additional request, you may find it beneficial to bootstrap your Backbone.Paginator instance from data that already exists in the DOM, as shown here in `Backbone.Paginator.clientPager`.

```
// Extend the Backbone.Paginator.clientPager with your own configuration options
var MyClientPager = Backbone.Paginator.clientPager.extend({paginator_ui: {}});
// Create an instance of your class and populate with the models of your
// entire collection
var aClientPager = new MyClientPager([{id: 1, title: 'foo'},
{id: 2, title: 'bar'}]);
// Invoke the bootstrap function
aClientPager.bootstrap();
```

 If you intend to bootstrap a `clientPager`, there is no need to specify a `paginator_core` object in your configuration (since you should have already populated the `clientPager` with the entirety of its necessary data), as shown here in `Backbone.Paginator.requestPager`.

```
// Extend the Backbone.Paginator.requestPager with your own configuration options
var MyRequestPager = Backbone.Paginator.requestPager.extend({paginator_ui: {}});
// Create an instance of your class with the first page of data
var aRequestPager = new MyRequestPager([{id: 1, title: 'foo'},
{id: 2, title: 'bar'}]);
// Invoke the bootstrap function and configure requestPager with 'totalRecords'
aRequestPager.bootstrap({totalRecords: 50});
```

 Both the `clientPager` and `requestPager` bootstrap function will accept an `options` parameter that will be extended by your Backbone.Paginator instance. However, the `totalRecords` property will be set implicitly by the `clientPager`.

For more on Backbone bootstrapping, see Rico Sta Cruz's website (*http://bit.ly/ZiqY6T*).

Styling

You're free, of course, to customize the overall look and feel of the paginators as much as you wish. By default, all sample applications make use of the Twitter Bootstrap (*http://twitter.github.com/bootstrap*) for styling links, buttons, and drop-downs.

CSS classes are available to style record counts, filters, sorting, and more, as shown in Figure 10-5.

Figure 10-5. Inspecting the Paginator using the Chrome DevTool console provides insights into some of the classes' support for styling

Classes are also available for styling more granular elements like page counts within breadcrumb > pages (for example, .page, .page selected), as shown in Figure 10-6.

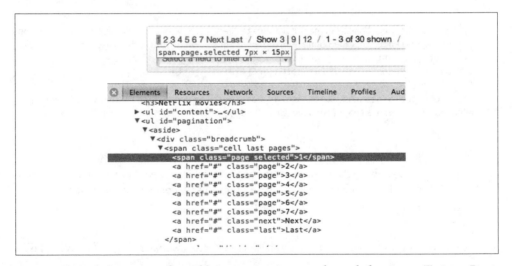

Figure 10-6. A demonstration of how pagination can be styled using a Twitter Bootstrap breadcrumb

There's a tremendous amount of flexibility available for styling, and as you're in control of templating too, your paginators can be made to look as visually simple or complex as needed.

Summary

Although it's certainly possible to write your own custom pagination classes to work with Backbone collections, Backbone.Paginator tries to take care of much of this for you.

It's highly configurable, preventing you from having to write your own paging when working with collections of data sourced from your database or API. Use the plug-in to help tame large lists of data into more manageable, easily navigatable, paginated lists.

Additionally, if you have any questions about Backbone.Paginator (or would like to help improve it), feel free to post to the project issues list (*https://github.com/addyosmani/backbone.paginator*).

CHAPTER 11

Backbone Boilerplate and Grunt-BBB

Boilerplates provide us a starting point for working on projects. They're a base for building upon using the minimum required code to get something functional put together. When you're working on a new Backbone application, a new model typically takes only a few lines of code to get working.

That alone probably isn't enough, however, as you'll need a collection to group those models, a view to render them, and perhaps a router if you're looking to make specific views of your collection data bookmarkable. If you're starting on a completely fresh project, you may also need a build process in place to produce an optimized version of your app that can be pushed to production.

This is where boilerplate solutions are useful. Rather than having to manually write out the initial code for each piece of your Backbone app, a boilerplate could do this for you, also ideally taking care of the build process.

Backbone Boilerplate (*http://bit.ly/11EOXeu*)—or just BB—does exactly this. It is an excellent set of best practices and utilities for building Backbone.js applications, created by Backbone contributor Tim Branyen (*https://github.com/tbranyen*). He took the gotchas, pitfalls, and common tasks he ran into while heavily using Backbone to build apps and crafted BB as a result of his experience.

Grunt-BBB or Boilerplate Build Buddy (*http://bit.ly/106aStC*) is the companion tool to BB, which offers scaffolding, file watcher, and build capabilities. Used together with BB, it provides an excellent base for quickly starting new Backbone applications. See Figure 11-1.

Figure 11-1. The Grunt-BBB authoring tool running at the command line

Out of the box, BB and Grunt-BBB provide us with:

- Backbone; Lo-Dash (*https://github.com/bestiejs/lodash*), an Underscore.js (*http://underscorejs.org/*) alternative; and jQuery (*http://jquery.com*) with an HTML5 Boilerplate (*http://html5boilerplate.com*) foundation.
- Boilerplate and scaffolding support, allowing us to spend minimal time writing boilerplate for modules, collections, and so on.
- A build tool for template precompilation, concatenation and minification of all our libraries, application code, and stylesheets.
- A lightweight Node.js web server.

Notes on build tool steps:

- Template precompilation: using a template library such as Underscore microtemplating or Handlebars.js generally involves three steps: (1) reading a raw template, (2) compiling it into a JavaScript function, and (3) running the compiled template with your desired data. Precompiling eliminates the second step from runtime by moving this process into a build step.
- Concatenation is the process of combining multiple assets (in our case, script files) into a fewer number of files (or a single file) to reduce the number of HTTP requests required to obtain them.

- Minification is the process of removing unnecessary characters (such as whitespace, new lines, comments) from code and compressing it to reduce the overall size of the scripts being served.

Getting Started

To get started we're going to install Grunt-BBB, which will include Backbone Boilerplate and any third-party dependencies it might need such as the Grunt build tool.

We can install Grunt-BBB via npm by running:

```
npm install -g bbb
```

That's it. We should now be good to go.

Here's a typical workflow for using Grunt-BBB, which we will use later:

1. Initialize a new project (`bbb init`).
2. Add new modules and templates (`bbb init:module`).
3. Preview changes using the built-in server (`bbb server.`)
4. Run the build tool (`bbb build`).
5. Link JavaScript, compile templates, build your application using r.js, and minify CSS and JavaScript (using `bbb release`).

Creating a New Project

Let's create a new directory for our project and run `bbb init` to kick things off. A number of project subdirectories and files will be stubbed out for us, as shown here:

```
$ bbb init
Running "init" task
This task will create one or more files in the current directory, based on the
environment and the answers to a few questions. Note that answering "?" to any
question will show question-specific help and answering "none" to most questions
will leave its value blank.

"bbb" template notes:
This tool will help you install, configure, build, and maintain your Backbone
Boilerplate project.
Writing app/app.js...OK
Writing app/config.js...OK
Writing app/main.js...OK
Writing app/router.js...OK
Writing app/styles/index.css...OK
Writing favicon.ico...OK
Writing grunt.js...OK
```

```
Writing index.html...OK
Writing package.json...OK
Writing readme.md...OK
Writing test/jasmine/index.html...OK
Writing test/jasmine/spec/example.js...OK
Writing test/jasmine/vendor/jasmine-html.js...OK
Writing test/jasmine/vendor/jasmine.css...OK
Writing test/jasmine/vendor/jasmine.js...OK
Writing test/jasmine/vendor/jasmine_favicon.png...OK
Writing test/jasmine/vendor/MIT.LICENSE...OK
Writing test/qunit/index.html...OK
Writing test/qunit/tests/example.js...OK
Writing test/qunit/vendor/qunit.css...OK
Writing test/qunit/vendor/qunit.js...OK
Writing vendor/h5bp/css/main.css...OK
Writing vendor/h5bp/css/normalize.css...OK
Writing vendor/jam/backbone/backbone.js...OK
Writing vendor/jam/backbone/package.json...OK
Writing vendor/jam/backbone.layoutmanager/backbone.layoutmanager.js...OK
Writing vendor/jam/backbone.layoutmanager/package.json...OK
Writing vendor/jam/jquery/jquery.js...OK
Writing vendor/jam/jquery/package.json...OK
Writing vendor/jam/lodash/lodash.js...OK
Writing vendor/jam/lodash/lodash.min.js...OK
Writing vendor/jam/lodash/lodash.underscore.min.js...OK
Writing vendor/jam/lodash/package.json...OK
Writing vendor/jam/require.config.js...OK
Writing vendor/jam/require.js...OK
Writing vendor/js/libs/almond.js...OK
Writing vendor/js/libs/require.js...OK

Initialized from template "bbb".

Done, without errors.
```

Let's review what has been generated.

index.html

This is a fairly standard stripped-down HTML5 boilerplate foundation with the notable exception of including RequireJS (*http://requirejs.org*) at the bottom of the page.

```
<!doctype html>
<html lang="en">
<head>
  <meta charset="utf-8">
  <meta http-equiv="X-UA-Compatible" content="IE=edge,chrome=1">
  <meta name="viewport" content="width=device-width,initial-scale=1">

  <title>Backbone Boilerplate</title>

  <!-- Application styles. -->
```

```
<!--(if target dummy)><!-->
<link rel="stylesheet" href="/app/styles/index.css">
<!--<!(endif)-->
</head>
<body>
  <!-- Application container. -->
  <main role="main" id="main"></main>

  <!-- Application source. -->
  <!--(if target dummy)><!-->
  <script data-main="/app/config" src="/vendor/js/libs/require.js"></script>
  <!--<!(endif)-->

</body>
</html>
```

RequireJS—the AMD (*http://bit.ly/Yp9ozD*) module and script loader—will assist us with managing the modules in our application. We've already covered it in Chapter 10, but let's recap what this particular block does in terms of the boilerplate:

```
<script data-main="/app/config" src="/vendor/js/libs/require.js"></script>
```

The `data-main` attribute is used to inform RequireJS to load *app/config.js* (a configuration object) after it has finished loading itself. You'll notice that we've omitted the *.js* extension here because RequireJS can automatically add it for us; however, it will respect your paths if we do choose to include it regardless. Let's now look at the config file being referenced.

config.js

A RequireJS configuration object allows us to specify aliases and paths for dependencies we're likely to reference often (e.g., jQuery), bootstrap properties like our base application URL, and shim libraries that don't support AMD natively. This is what the config file in Backbone Boilerplate looks like:

```
// Set the require.js configuration for your application.
require.config({

  // Initialize the application with the main application file and the JamJS
  // generated configuration file.
  deps: ["../vendor/jam/require.config", "main"],

  paths: {
    // Put paths here.
  },

  shim: {
    // Put shims here.
  }

});
```

The first option defined in the preceding config is deps: ["../vendor/jam/ require.config", "main"]. This informs RequireJS to load up additional RequireJS configuration as well as a *main.js* file, which is considered the entry point for our application.

You may notice that we haven't specified any other path information for main. Require will infer the default baseUrl using the path from our data-main attribute in *index.html*. In other words, our baseUrl is *app/*, and any scripts we require will be loaded relative to this location. We could use the baseUrl option to override this default if we wanted to use a different location.

The next block is paths, which we can use to specify paths relative to the baseUrl as well as the paths/aliases to dependencies we're likely to regularly reference.

After this comes shim, an important part of our RequireJS configuration that allows us to load libraries that are not AMD-compliant. The basic idea here is that rather than requiring all libraries to implement support for AMD, the shim takes care of the hard work for us.

Going back to deps, the contents of our *require.config* file are as follows:

```
var jam = {
    "packages": [
        {
            "name": "backbone",
            "location": "../vendor/jam/backbone",
            "main": "backbone.js"
        },
        {
            "name": "backbone.layoutmanager",
            "location": "../vendor/jam/backbone.layoutmanager",
            "main": "backbone.layoutmanager.js"
        },
        {
            "name": "jquery",
            "location": "../vendor/jam/jquery",
            "main": "jquery.js"
        },
        {
            "name": "lodash",
            "location": "../vendor/jam/lodash",
            "main": "./lodash.js"
        }
    ],
    "version": "0.2.11",
    "shim": {
        "backbone": {
            "deps": [
                "jquery",
                "lodash"
            ],
```

```
            "exports": "Backbone"
        },
        "backbone.layoutmanager": {
            "deps": [
                "jquery",
                "backbone",
                "lodash"
            ],
            "exports": "Backbone.LayoutManager"
        }
    }
};
```

The jam object is to support configuration of Jam (*http://jamjs.org/*), a package manager for the frontend that helps install, upgrade, and configure the dependencies used by your project. It is currently the package manager of choice for Backbone Boilerplate.

Under the packages array, a number of dependencies are specified for inclusion, such as Backbone, the Backbone.LayoutManager plug-in, jQuery, and Lo-Dash.

For those curious about Backbone.LayoutManager (*http://bit.ly/14MJw3n*), it's a Backbone plug-in that provides a foundation for assembling layouts and views within Backbone.

Additional packages you install using Jam will have a corresponding entry added to packages.

main.js

Next, we have *main.js*, which defines the entry point for our application. We use a global require() method to load an array containing any other scripts needed, such as our application *app.js* and our main router *router.js*. Note that most of the time, we will use require() only for bootstrapping an application and a similar method called de fine() for all other purposes.

The function defined after our array of dependencies is a callback that doesn't fire until these scripts have loaded. Notice how we're able to locally alias references to app and router as app and Router for convenience.

```
require([
  // Application.
  "app",

  // Main Router.
  "router"
],

function(app, Router) {

  // Define your master router on the application namespace and trigger all
```

```
    // navigation from this instance.
    app.router = new Router();

    // Trigger the initial route and enable HTML5 History API support, set the
    // root folder to '/' by default.  Change in app.js.
    Backbone.history.start({ pushState: true, root: app.root });

    // All navigation that is relative should be passed through the navigate
    // method, to be processed by the router. If the link has a `data-bypass`
    // attribute, bypass the delegation completely.
    $(document).on("click", "a[href]:not([data-bypass])", function(evt) {
      // Get the absolute anchor href.
      var href = { prop: $(this).prop("href"), attr: $(this).attr("href") };
      // Get the absolute root.
      var root = location.protocol + "//" + location.host + app.root;

      // Ensure the root is part of the anchor href, meaning it's relative.
      if (href.prop.slice(0, root.length) === root) {
        // Stop the default event to ensure the link will not cause a page
        // refresh.
        evt.preventDefault();

        // `Backbone.history.navigate` is sufficient for all Routers and will
        // trigger the correct events. The Router's internal `navigate` method
        // calls this anyways.  The fragment is sliced from the root.
        Backbone.history.navigate(href.attr, true);
      }
    });

  });
```

Inline, Backbone Boilerplate includes boilerplate code for initializing our router with HTML5 History API support and handling other navigation scenarios, so we don't have to.

app.js

Let us now look at our *app.js* module. Typically, in non-Backbone Boilerplate applications, an *app.js* file may contain the core logic or module references needed to kick start an app.

In this case, however, this file is used to define templating and layout configuration options as well as utilities for consuming layouts. To a beginner, this might look like a lot of code to comprehend, but the good news is that for basic apps, you're unlikely to need to heavily modify this. Instead, you'll be more concerned with modules for your app, which we'll look at next.

```
define([
  "backbone.layoutmanager"
], function() {
```

```javascript
// Provide a global location to place configuration settings and module
// creation.
var app = {
  // The root path to run the application.
  root: "/"
};

// Localize or create a new JavaScript Template object.
var JST = window.JST = window.JST || {};

// Configure LayoutManager with Backbone Boilerplate defaults.
Backbone.LayoutManager.configure({
  // Allow LayoutManager to augment Backbone.View.prototype.
  manage: true,

  prefix: "app/templates/",

  fetch: function(path) {
    // Concatenate the file extension.
    path = path + ".html";

    // If cached, use the compiled template.
    if (JST[path]) {
      return JST[path];
    }

    // Put fetch into `async-mode`.
    var done = this.async();

    // Seek out the template asynchronously.
    $.get(app.root + path, function(contents) {
      done(JST[path] = _.template(contents));
    });
  }
});

// Mix Backbone.Events, modules, and layout management into the app object.
return _.extend(app, {
  // Create a custom object with a nested Views object.
  module: function(additionalProps) {
    return _.extend({ Views: {} }, additionalProps);
  },

  // Helper for using layouts.
  useLayout: function(name, options) {
    // Enable variable arity by allowing the first argument to be the options
    // object and omitting the name argument.
    if (_.isObject(name)) {
      options = name;
    }

    // Ensure options is an object.
```

```
        options = options || {};

        // If a name property was specified use that as the template.
        if (_.isString(name)) {
          options.template = name;
        }

        // Create a new Layout with options.
        var layout = new Backbone.Layout(_.extend({
          el: "#main"
        }, options));

        // Cache the refererence.
        return this.layout = layout;
      }
    }, Backbone.Events);

  });
```

 JST stands for *JavaScript templates* and generally refers to templates that have been (or will be) precompiled as part of a build step. When you're running bbb release or bbb debug, Underscore/Lo-dash templates will be precompiled to avoid the need to compile them at runtime within the browser.

Creating Backbone Boilerplate Modules

Not to be confused with simply being an AMD module, a Backbone Boilerplate module is a script composed of a:

- Model
- Collection
- Views (optional)

We can easily create a new Boilerplate module with grunt-bbb, once again using init:

```
# Create a new module
$ bbb init:module

# Grunt prompt
Please answer the following:
[?] Module Name foo
[?] Do you need to make any changes to the above before continuing? (y/N)

Writing app/modules/foo.js...OK
Writing app/styles/foo.styl...OK
Writing app/templates/foo.html...OK
```

```
    Initialized from template "module".

    Done, without errors.
```

This will generate a module *foo.js* as follows:

```javascript
// Foo module
define([
  // Application.
  "app"
],

// Map dependencies from above array.
function(app) {

  // Create a new module.
  var Foo = app.module();

  // Default Model.
  Foo.Model = Backbone.Model.extend({

  });

  // Default Collection.
  Foo.Collection = Backbone.Collection.extend({
    model: Foo.Model
  });

  // Default View.
  Foo.Views.Layout = Backbone.Layout.extend({
    template: "foo"
  });

  // Return the module for AMD compliance.
  return Foo;

});
```

Notice how boilerplate code for a model, collection, and view have been scaffolded out for us.

Optionally, we may also wish to include references to plug-ins such as the Backbone localStorage or Offline adapters. One clean way of including a plug-in in the preceding boilerplate could be:

```javascript
// Foo module
define([
  // Application.
  "app",
  // Plug-ins
  'plugins/backbone-localstorage'
],
```

```
// Map dependencies from above array.
function(app) {

  // Create a new module.
  var Foo = app.module();

  // Default Model.
  Foo.Model = Backbone.Model.extend({
    // Save all of the items under the `"foo"` namespace.
    localStorage: new Store('foo-backbone'),
  });

  // Default Collection.
  Foo.Collection = Backbone.Collection.extend({
    model: Foo.Model
  });

  // Default View.
  Foo.Views.Layout = Backbone.Layout.extend({
    template: "foo"
  });

  // Return the module for AMD compliance.
  return Foo;

});
```

router.js

Finally, let's look at our application router, which is used for handling navigation. The default router Backbone Boilerplate generates for us includes sane defaults out of the box and can be easily extended.

```
define([
  // Application.
  "app"
],

function(app) {

  // Defining the application router, you can attach subrouters here.
  var Router = Backbone.Router.extend({
    routes: {
      "": "index"
    },

    index: function() {

    }
  });

  return Router;
```

```
  });
```

If, however, we would like to execute some module-specific logic, when the page loads (such as when a user hits the default route), we can pull in a module as a dependency and optionally use the Backbone LayoutManager to attach views to our layout as follows:

```
define([
  // Application.
  'app',

  // Modules
  'modules/foo'
],

function(app, Foo) {

  // Defining the application router, you can attach subrouters here.
  var Router = Backbone.Router.extend({
    routes: {
      '': 'index'
    },

    index: function() {
            // Create a new Collection
            var collection = new Foo.Collection();

            // Use and configure a 'main' layout
            app.useLayout('main').setViews({
                    // Attach the bar View into the content View
                    '.bar': new Foo.Views.Bar({
                            collection: collection
                    })
            }).render();
    }
  });

  // Fetch data (e.g., from localStorage)
  collection.fetch();

  return Router;

});
```

Other Useful Tools and Projects

When working with Backbone, you usually need to write a number of different classes and files for your application. Scaffolding tools such as Grunt-BBB can help automate this process by generating basic boilerplates for the files you need.

Yeoman

If you appreciated Grunt-BBB but would like to explore a tool for assisting with your broader development workflow, I'm happy to recommend a tool I helped create called Yeoman (*http://yeoman.io*). See Figure 11-2.

```
              2. /Users/addyo (bash)
   create     app/scripts/vendor/jquery.min.js
   create     app/scripts/vendor/lodash.min.js
   create     app/styles/main.css
   create     Gruntfile.js
   create     package.json
   create     test/index.html
   create     test/lib/chai.js
   create     test/lib/expect.js
   create     test/lib/mocha-1.2.2/mocha.css
   create     test/lib/mocha-1.2.2/mocha.js
   create     test/runner/mocha.js
   invoke     backbone:router:backbone
   create     app/scripts/routes/application-router.js
   invoke     backbone:view:backbone
   create     app/scripts/views/application-view.js
   create     app/scripts/templates/application.ejs
   invoke     backbone:model:backbone
   create     app/scripts/models/application-model.js
   invoke     backbone:collection:backbone
   create     app/scripts/collections/application-collection.js
addyo at addyo-macbookair3 in ~/projects/backbone-app
$
```

Figure 11-2. The Yeoman 'yo' scaffolding tool being used to scaffold a new Backbone application

Yeoman is a workflow comprising a collection of tools and best practices for helping you develop more efficiently. It's composed of yo, a scaffolding tool shown in Figure 11-2; Grunt (*http://gruntjs.com*), a build tool; and Bower (*http://bower.io*), a client-side package manager shown in Figure 11-3.

Where Grunt-BBB focuses on offering an opinionated start for Backbone projects, Yeoman allows you to scaffold apps using Backbone (or other frameworks); get Backbone plug-ins directly from the command line; and compile your CoffeeScript, Sass, or other abstractions without additional effort.

Figure 11-3. A list of Backbone plug-ins and extensions available via the Bower package manager

You may also be interested in Brunch (*http://brunch.io/*), a similar project that uses skeleton boilerplates to generate new applications.

Backbone DevTools

When you're building an application with Backbone, there's some additional tooling available for your day-to-day debugging workflow.

For example, Backbone DevTools is a Chrome DevTools extension that allows you to inspect events, syncs, View-DOM bindings, and what objects have been instantiated (see Figure 11-4).

A useful view hierarchy is displayed in the Elements panel. Also, when you inspect a DOM element, the closest view will be exposed via $view in the console.

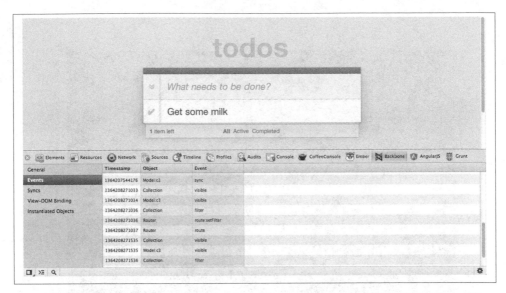

Figure 11-4. The Backbone DevTools extension being used to debug the Todo application we created earlier in the book

At the time of writing, the project is available on GitHub (*http://bit.ly/18ffNPA*).

Summary

In this section we reviewed Backbone Boilerplate and learned how to use the bbb tool to help us scaffold out our application.

If you would like to learn more about how this project helps structure your app, BBB includes some built-in boilerplate sample apps that you can easily generate for review.

These include a boilerplate tutorial project (bbb init:tutorial) and an implementation of my TodoMVC (*http://todomvc.com*) project (bbb init:todomvc). I recommend checking these out, as they'll provide you with a more complete picture of how Backbone Boilerplate and its templates fit into the overall setup for a web app.

For more about Grunt-BBB, remember to take a look at the official project repository (*http://bit.ly/106aStC*). There is also a related slidedeck (*http://bit.ly/10b73lU*) available for those interested in reading more.

CHAPTER 12

Backbone and jQuery Mobile

Mobile App Development with jQuery Mobile

The mobile web is huge and it is continuing to grow at an impressive rate. Along with its massive growth comes a striking diversity of devices and browsers. As a result, making your applications cross-platform and mobile-ready is both important and challenging. Creating native apps is expensive. It is very costly in terms of time, and it usually requires varied experiences in programming languages like Objective C , C#, Java, and JavaScript to support multiple runtime environments.

HTML, CSS, and JavaScript enable you to build a single application targeting a common runtime environment: the browser. This approach supports a broad range of mobile devices such as tablets, smartphones, and notebooks along with traditional PCs.

The challenging task is not only to adapt contents like text and pictures properly to various screen resolutions, but also to offer the same user experience across native apps under different operating systems. Like jQueryUI, jQuery Mobile (or jQMobile) is a user interface framework based on jQuery that works across all popular phone, tablet, eReader, and desktop platforms. It is built with accessibility and universal access in mind.

The main idea of the framework is to enable anyone to create a mobile app using only HTML. Knowledge of a programming language is not required and there is no need to write complex, device-specific CSS. For this reason, jQMobile follows two main principles we first need to understand in order to integrate the framework to Backbone: *progressive enhancement* and *responsive web design*.

The Principle of Progressive Widget Enhancement by jQMobile

jQuery Mobile follows progressive enhancement[1] and responsive web design principles[2] using HTML5 markup-driven definitions and configurations.

A page in jQuery Mobile consists of an element with a `data-role="page"` attribute. Within the `page` container, any valid HTML markup can be used, but for typical pages in jQM, the immediate children are divs with `data-role="header"`, `data-role="content"`, and `data-role="footer"`. The baseline requirement for a page is only a page wrapper to support the navigation system; the rest is optional.

An initial HTML page looks like this:

```
<!DOCTYPE html>
<html>
<head>
    <title>Page Title</title>

    <meta name="viewport" content="width=device-width, initial-scale=1">

    <link rel="stylesheet"
      href="http://code.jquery.com/mobile/1.3.0/jquery.mobile-1.3.0.min.css" />
    <script src="http://code.jquery.com/jquery-1.9.1.min.js"></script>
    <script src="http://code.jquery.com/mobile/1.3.0/jquery.mobile-1.3.0.min.js">
    </script>
</head>
<body>

<div data-role="page">
  <div data-role="header">
    <h1>Page Title</h1>
  </div>
  <div data-role="content">
    <p>Page content goes here.</p>
    <form>
      <label for="slider-1">Slider with tooltip:</label>
      <input type="range" name="slider-1" id="slider-1" min="0"
       max="100" value="50"
       data-popup-enabled="true">
    </form>
  </div>
  <div data-role="footer">
    <h4>Page Footer</h4>
```

1. Progressive enhancement uses web platform features in a layered manner, allowing access to the basic content and functionality of a page, even if JavaScript is turned off or a user is not on a modern browser. An enhanced experience is offered to those with JavaScript turned on or who have a more capable recent browser.

2. Responsive web design (RWD) is an approach to designing pages that adapt the layout of the page to the viewing environment in order to offer a more optimal viewing experience. CSS media queries are often employed to achieve this goal.

```
    </div>
  </div>
  </body>
  </html>
```

jQuery Mobile will transform the written HTML definition to the rendered HTML and CSS using its Progressive Widget Enhancement API. It also executes JavaScript that is conditioned by configurations, attribute properties, and runtime-specific settings. You can see the result in Figure 12-1.

This implies that whenever HTML content is added or changed, it needs to be handled by the progressive widget enhancement of jQuery Mobile.

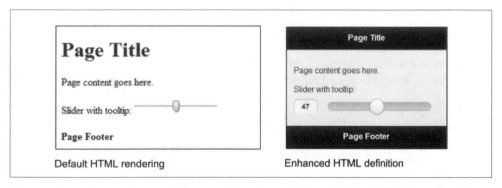

Figure 12-1. Comparison of the user interface of the default HTML to the jQuery Mobile–enhanced version

Understanding jQuery Mobile Navigation

The jQuery Mobile navigation system controls its application's lifecycle by automatically hijacking standard links and form submissions and turning them into AJAX requests. Whenever a link is clicked or a form is submitted, that event is automatically intercepted and used to issue an AJAX request based on the `href` or form action instead of reloading the page.

When the page document is requested, jQuery Mobile searches the document for all elements with the `data-role="page"` attribute, parses its contents, and inserts that code into the DOM of the original page. Once the new page is prepared, jQuery Mobile's JavaScript triggers a transition that shows the new page and hides the HTML of the previous page in the DOM.

Next, any widgets in the incoming page are enhanced to apply all the styles and behavior. The rest of the incoming page is discarded so any scripts, stylesheets, or other information will not be included.

Via the *multipage templating feature*, you can add as many pages as you want to the same HTML file within the <body> tag by defining `div`s with `data-role="page"` or `data-role="dialog"` attributes along with an `id` that can be used in links (preceded by a hashbang):

```html
<html>
  <head>...</head>
  <body>
  ...
  <div data-role="page" id="firstpage">
    ...
   <div data-role="content">
     <a href="#secondpage">go to secondpage</a>
   </div>
  </div>
  <div data-role="page" id="secondpage">
    ...
    <div data-role="content" >
       <a href="#firstdialog" data-rel="dialog" >open a page as a dialog</a>
    </div>
  </div>
  <div data-role="dialog" id="firstdialog">
    ...
    <div data-role="content">
       <a href="#firstpage">leave dialog and go to first page</a>
    </div>
  </div>
 </body>
 </html>
```

To, for example, navigate to `secondpage` and have it appear in a modal dialog using a `fade-transition`, you would just add the `data-rel="dialog"`, `data-transition="fade"`, and `href="index.html#secondpage"` attributes to an anchor tag.

Roughly speaking, having its own event cycle, jQuery Mobile is a tiny MVC framework that includes features like progressive widget enhancement, prefetching, caching, and multipage templating by HTML configurations innately. In general, a Backbone.js developer does not need to know about its internal event workflow, but will need to know how to apply HTML-based configurations that will take action within the event phase. The *Intercepting jQuery Mobile Events* section goes into detail regarding how to handle special scenarios when fine-grained JavaScript adaptions need to be applied.

For further introduction and explanations about jQuery Mobile, visit:

- *http://view.jquerymobile.com/1.3.0/docs/intro/*
- *http://view.jquerymobile.com/1.3.0/docs/widgets/pages/*
- *http://view.jquerymobile.com/1.3.0/docs/intro/rwd.php*

Basic Backbone App Setup for jQuery Mobile

The first major hurdle developers typically run into when building applications with jQuery Mobile and an MV* framework is that both frameworks want to handle application navigation.

To combine Backbone and jQuery Mobile, we first need to disable jQuery Mobile's navigation system and progressive enhancement. The second step will then be to make use of jQM's custom API to apply configurations and enhance components during Backbone's application lifecycle instead.

The mobile app in Figure 12-2 is based on the existing codebase of the TodoMVC *Backbone-Require.js* example, which was discussed in Chapter 8, and is enhanced to support jQuery Mobile.

Figure 12-2. The TodoMVC app with jQuery Mobile

This implementation makes use of Grunt-BBB as well as *Handlebars.js*. Additional utilities useful for mobile applications will be provided, which can be easily combined and extended, as shown in Figure 12-3. (See Chapters 6 and 11.)

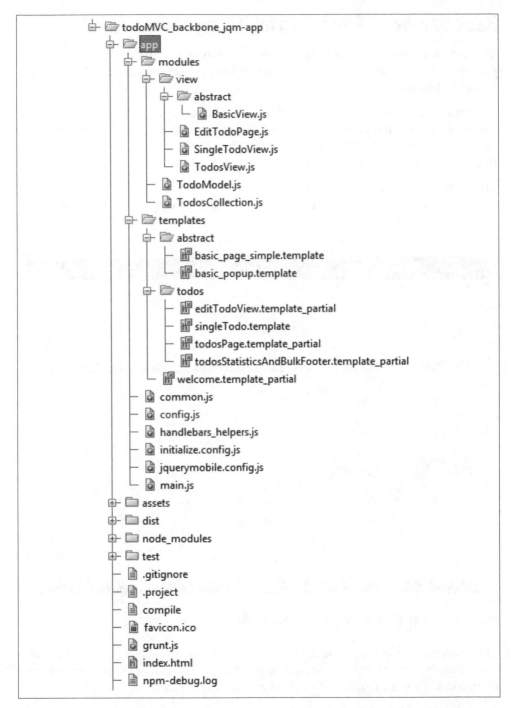

Figure 12-3. Workspace of the TodoMVC app with jQueryMobile and Backbone

The order of the files loaded by *Require.js* is as follows:

1. jQuery
2. Underscore/Lo-Dash
3. handlebars.compiled
4. TodoRouter (instantiates specific views)
5. jQueryMobile
6. jQueryMobileCustomInitConfig
7. Instantiation of the Backbone router

When you open the console in the project directory and then run the Grunt-Backbone command `grunt handlebars` or `grunt watch`, all template files will be combined and compiled to *dist/debug/handlebars_packaged*. To start the application, run `grunt server`.

The files instantiated, when redirected from the Backbone router, are:

BasicView.js and basic_page_simple.template
    The BasicView is responsible for the Handlebars multipage-template processing. Its implementation of `render` calls the jQuery Mobile API `$.mobile.changePage` to handle page navigation and progressive widget enhancement.

Concrete view with its template partial—for example, `EditTodoPage.js` *and* `editTodo View.template_partial`
    The head section of *index.html* needs to load the *jquerymobile.css* as well as the *base.css*, which is used by all Todo-MVC apps, and the *index.css* for some project-specific custom CSS.

```html
<html>
<head>
    <meta charset="utf-8">
    <meta http-equiv="X-UA-Compatible" content="IE=edge,chrome=1">
    <meta name="viewport" content="width=device-width,initial-scale=1">

    <title>TodoMVC Jquery Mobile</title>

<!-- widget and responsive design styles -->
    <link rel="stylesheet" href="/assets/css/jquerymobile.css">
<!-- used by all TodoMVC apps -->
    <link rel="stylesheet" href="/assets/css/base.css">
<!-- custom css -->
    <link rel="stylesheet" href="/assets/css/index.css">
</head>

<body>
    <script data-main="/app/config" src="/assets/js/libs/require.js"></script>
```

```
</body>
</html>
```

Workflow with Backbone and jQueryMobile

By delegating the routing and navigation functions of the jQuery Mobile Framework to Backbone, we can profit from its clear separation of application structure to later easily share application logic between a desktop web page, tablets, and mobile apps.

We now need to contend with the different ways in which Backbone and jQuery Mobile handle requests. `Backbone.Router` offers an explicit way to define custom navigation routes, while jQuery Mobile uses URL hash fragments to reference separate pages or views in the same document.

Some of the ideas that have been previously proposed to work around this problem include manually patching Backbone and jQuery Mobile. The solution demonstrated next will not only simplify the handling of the jQuery Mobile component initialization event cycle, but also enable use of existing Backbone Router handlers.

To adapt the navigation control from jQuery Mobile to Backbone, we first need to apply some specific settings to the `mobileinit` event, which occurs after the framework has loaded in order to let the Backbone Router decide which page to load.

This configuration, *jquerymobile.config.js*, will get jQM to delegate navigation to Backbone and will also enable manual widget creation triggering:

```javascript
$(document).bind("mobileinit", function(){

// Disable jQM routing and component creation events
    // disable hash-routing
    $.mobile.hashListeningEnabled = false;
    // disable anchor-control
    $.mobile.linkBindingEnabled = false;
    // can cause calling object creation twice and back button issues are solved
    $.mobile.ajaxEnabled = false;
    // Otherwise after mobileinit, it tries to load a landing page
    $.mobile.autoInitializePage = false;
    // we want to handle caching and cleaning the DOM ourselves
    $.mobile.page.prototype.options.domCache = false;

// consider due to compatibility issues
    // not supported by all browsers
    $.mobile.pushStateEnabled = false;
    // Solves phonegap issues with the back-button
    $.mobile.phonegapNavigationEnabled = true;
    //no native datepicker will conflict with the jQM component
    $.mobile.page.prototype.options.degradeInputs.date = true;
});
```

The behavior and usage of the new workflow is explained next, grouped by its functionalities:

1. Routing to a concrete view page
2. Management of mobile page templates
3. DOM management
4. `$.mobile.changePage`

In the following discussion, steps 1–11 in the text refer to the new workflow diagram of the mobile application in Figure 12-4.

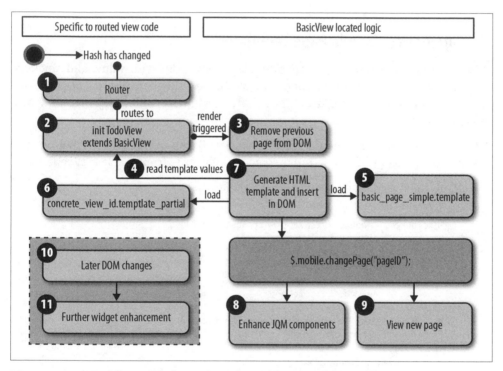

Figure 12-4. Workflow of TodoMVC, with Backbone and jQueryMobile

Routing to a Concrete View Page, Inheriting from BasicView

When the hash URL changes (for example, a link is clicked), the configuration just shown prevents jQM from triggering its events. Instead, the Backbone router listens to the hash changes and decides which view to request.

Experience has shown that, for mobile pages, it is a good practice to create basic prototypes for jQM components such as basic pages, pop ups, and dialogs, as well as for using the jQuery validation plug-in. This makes it much easier to exchange device-specific view logic at runtime and adopt general strategies. This will also help to add syntax and to support multichaining of prototype inheritance with JavaScript and Backbone.

By creating a BasicView superclass, we enable all inheriting view pages to share a common way of handling jQM along with common usage of a template engine and specific view handling.

When building with Grunt/Yeoman, the semantic templates are compiled by Handlebar.js and the AMDs template files are combined into a single file. By merging all page definitions into a single-file app, we make it offline capable, which is important for mobile app.

Management of Mobile Page Templates

Within a concrete view page, you can override properties for static values and functions to return dynamic values of the superclass BasicView. These values will be processed later by the BasicView to construct the HTML of a jQuery Mobile page with the help of Handlebars.

Additional dynamic template parameters (such as Backbone model information) will be taken from the specific view and merged with the ones from the BasicView.

A concrete view might look like this (*EditTodoPage.js*):

```
define([
    "backbone", "modules/view/abstract/BasicView"],
    function (Backbone, BasicView) {
        return BasicView.extend({
            id : "editTodoView",
            getHeaderTitle : function () {
                return "Edit Todo";
            },
            getSpecificTemplateValues : function () {
                return this.model.toJSON();
            },
            events : function () {
                // merged events of BasicView, to add an older fix for
                // back button functionality
                return _.extend({
                    'click #saveDescription' : 'saveDescription'
                }, this.constructor.__super__.events);
            },
            saveDescription : function (clickEvent) {
                this.model.save({
                    title : $("#todoDescription", this.el).val()
                });
                return true;
            }
```

```
      });
    });
```

By default, the BasicView uses *basic_page_simple.template* as the Handlebars template. If you need to use a custom template or want to introduce a new Super abstract view with an alternate template, override the getTemplateID function:

```
getTemplateID : function(){
  return "custom_page_template";
}
```

By convention, the id attribute will be taken as the ID of the jQM page as well as the filename of the corresponding template file to be inserted as a partial in *basic_page_simple.template*. In the case of the EditTodoPage view, the name of the file will be *editTodoPage.template_partial*.

Every concrete page is meant to be a partial, which will be inserted in the data-role="content" element, where the parameter templatePartialPageID is located.

Later on, the result of the getHeaderTitle function from EditTodoPage will replace the headerTitle in the abstract template (*basic_page_simple.template*).

```
<div data-role="header">
        {{whatis "Specific loaded Handlebars parameters:"}}
        {{whatis this}}
        <h2>{{headerTitle}}</h2>
        <a id="backButton" href="href="javascript:history.go(-1);"
         data-icon="star" data-rel="back" >back</a>
    </div>
    <div data-role="content">
        {{whatis "Template page trying to load:"}}
        {{whatis templatePartialPageID}}
        {{> templatePartialPageID}}
    </div>
    <div data-role="footer">
        {{footerContent}}
</div>
```

 The whatis Handlebars view helper does simple logging of parameters.

All the additional parameters being returned by getSpecificTemplateValues will be inserted into the concrete template *editTodoPage.template_partial*.

Because footerContent is expected to be used rarely, its content is returned by getSpecificTemplateValues.

In the case of the EditTodoPage view, all the model information is being returned and `title` is used in the concrete partial page:

```
<div data-role="fieldcontain">
    <label for="todoDescription">Todo Description</label>
    <input type="text" name="todoDescription" id="todoDescription"
     value="{{title}}" />
</div>
    <a id="saveDescription" href="#" data-role="button" data-mini="true">Save</a>
```

When `render` is triggered, the *basic_page_simple.template* and *editTodoView.template_partial* templates will be loaded, and the parameters from `EditTodoPage` and `BasicView` will be combined and generated by Handlebars to generate:

```
<div data-role="header">
    <h2>Edit Todo</h2>
    <a id="backButton" href="href="javascript:history.go(-1);"
     data-icon="star" data-rel="back" >back</a>
</div>
<div data-role="content">
  <div data-role="fieldcontain">
   <label for="todoDescription">Todo Description</label>
   <input type="text" name="todoDescription" id="todoDescription"
    value="Cooking" />
  </div>
  <a id="saveDescription" href="#" data-role="button" data-mini="true">Save
  </a>
</div>
<div data-role="footer">
    Footer
</div>
```

The next section explains how the template parameters are collected by the `Basic View` class and the HTML definition is loaded.

DOM Management and $.mobile.changePage

When `render` is executed (line 29 is the source code listing in the upcoming example), `BasicView` first cleans up the DOM by removing the previous page (line 70). To delete the elements from the DOM, `$.remove` cannot be used, but `$previousEl.detach()` can be since `detach` does not remove the element's attached events and data.

This is important, because jQuery Mobile still needs information (for example, to trigger transition effects when switching to another page). Keep in mind that the DOM data and events should be cleared later on as well to avoid possible performance issues.

Other strategies than the one used in the function `cleanupPossiblePageDuplicatioNInDOM` to clean up the DOM are viable. Removing only the old page having the same `id` as the current from the DOM, when it was already requested before, would also be a working strategy for preventing DOM duplication. Depending on what best fits your application needs, it is also possibly a one-banana problem to exchange it using a caching mechanism.

Next, `BasicView` collects all template parameters from the concrete view implementation and inserts the HTML of the requested page into the body. This is done in steps 4, 5, 6, and 7 in Figure 12-4 (between lines 23 and 51 in the source listing).

Additionally, the `data-role` will be set on the jQuery Mobile page. Commonly used attribute values are `page`, `dialog`, or `popup`.

As you can see in *BasicView.js*, (starting at line 74), the `goBackInHistory` function contains a manual implementation to handle the back button's action. In certain scenarios, the back button navigation functionality of jQuery Mobile was not working with older versions and disabled jQMobile's navigation system.

```
 1 define([
 2      "lodash",
 3      "backbone",
 4      "handlebars",
 5      "handlebars_helpers"
 6 ],
 7
 8 function (_, Backbone, Handlebars) {
 9      var BasicView = Backbone.View.extend({
10          initialize: function () {
11              _.bindAll();
12              this.render();
13          },
14          events: {
15              "click #backButton": "goBackInHistory"
16          },
17          role: "page",
18          attributes: function () {
19              return {
20                  "data-role": this.role
21              };
22          },
23          getHeaderTitle: function () {
24              return this.getSpecificTemplateValues().headerTitle;
25          },
26          getTemplateID: function () {
27              return "basic_page_simple";
28          },
29          render: function () {
30              this.cleanupPossiblePageDuplicationInDOM();
31              $(this.el).html(this.getBasicPageTemplateResult());
32              this.addPageToDOMAndRenderJQM();
33              this.enhanceJQMComponentsAPI();
34          },
35 // Generate HTML using the Handlebars templates
36          getTemplateResult: function (templateDefinitionID, templateValues) {
```

```
37              return window.JST[templateDefinitionID](templateValues);
38          },
39 // Collect all template parameters and merge them
40          getBasicPageTemplateResult: function () {
41              var templateValues = {
42                  templatePartialPageID: this.id,
43                  headerTitle: this.getHeaderTitle()
44              };
45              var specific = this.getSpecificTemplateValues();
46              $.extend(templateValues, this.getSpecificTemplateValues());
47              return this.getTemplateResult(this.getTemplateID(),
                 templateValues);
48          },
49          getRequestedPageTemplateResult: function () {
50              this.getBasicPageTemplateResult();
51          },
52          enhanceJQMComponentsAPI: function () {
53 // changePage
54              $.mobile.changePage("#" + this.id, {
55                  changeHash: false,
56                  role: this.role
57              });
58          },
59 // Add page to DOM
60          addPageToDOMAndRenderJQM: function () {
61              $("body").append($(this.el));
62              $("#" + this.id).page();
63          },
64 // Cleanup DOM strategy
65          cleanupPossiblePageDuplicationInDOM: function () {
66          // Can also be moved to the event "pagehide": or "onPageHide"
67              var $previousEl = $("#" + this.id);
68              var alreadyInDom = $previousEl.length >= 0;
69              if (alreadyInDom) {
70                  $previousEl.detach();
71              }
72          },
73 // Strategy to always support back button with disabled navigation
74          goBackInHistory: function (clickEvent) {
75              history.go(-1);
76              return false;
77          }
78      });
79
80      return BasicView;
81 });
```

After the dynamic HTML is added to the DOM, `$.mobile.changePage` has to be applied at step 8 (code line 54).

This is the most important API call, because it triggers the jQuery Mobile component creation for the current page.

Next, the page will be displayed to the user at step 9 (see Figure 12-5).

```
<a data-mini="true" data-role="button" href="#" id="saveDescription"
 data-corners="true"
 data-shadow="true" data-iconshadow="true" data-wrapperels="span" data-theme="c"
 class="ui-btn ui-shadow ui-btn-corner-all ui-mini ui-btn-up-c">
    <span class="ui-btn-inner">
        <span class="ui-btn-text">Save</span>
    </span>
</a>
```

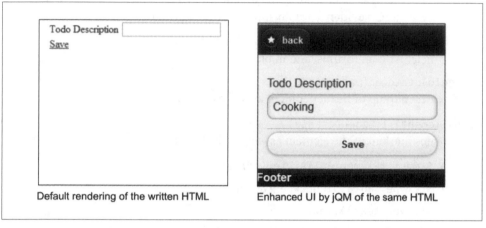

Figure 12-5. Look and feel of the written HTML code and the jQuery Mobile–enhanced
todo description page

UI enhancement is done in the enhanceJQMComponentsAPI function in line 52:

```
$.mobile.changePage("#" + this.id, {
                    changeHash: false,
                    role: this.role
                });
```

To retain control of hash routing, we must set changeHash to false and provide the
proper role parameter to guarantee proper page appearance. Finally, changePage will
show the new page with its defined transition to the user.

For the basic use cases, it is advised to have one view per page, and always render the
complete page again by calling $.mobile.changePage when you need to do widget
enhancement.

To progress component enrichment of a newly added HTML fragment into the DOM,
you need to apply advanced techniques to guarantee correct appearance of the mobile
components. You also need to be very careful when creating partial HTML code and
updating values on UI elements. The next section will explain how to handle these
situations.

Applying Advanced jQM Techniques to Backbone

Dynamic DOM Scripting

The solution previously described solves the issues of handling routing with Backbone by calling `$.mobile.changePage('pageID')`. Additionally, it guarantees that the HTML page will be completely enhanced by the markup for jQuery Mobile.

The second tricky part with jQuery Mobile is to dynamically manipulate specific DOM contents (for example, after loading in content with Ajax). I suggest you use this technique only if there is evidence for an appreciable performance gain.

With the current version (1.3), jQM provides three ways, documented and explained in the official API, on forums, and in blogs.

`$(pageId).trigger(pagecreate)`
> Creates markup of header content as well as footer

`$(anyElement).trigger(create)`
> Creates markup of the element as well as all children:

> - `$(myListElement).listview(refresh)`
> - `$([type=radio]).checkboxradio()`
> - `$([type=text]).textinput()`
> - `$([type=button]).button()`
> - `$([data-role=navbar]).navbar()`
> - `$([type=range]).slider()`
> - `$(select).selectmenu()`

> Every component of jQM offers plug-ins methods that can be invoked to update the state of specific UI elements.

Sometimes, when creating a component from scratch, you might see the following error: "Cannot call methods on ListView prior to initialization." You can avoid this, with component initialization prior to markup enhancement, by calling it in the following way:

```
$('#mylist').listview().listview('refresh')
```

To see more details and enhancements for further scripting pages of JQM, read its API and follow the release notes frequently:

- jQuery Mobile: Page Scripting (*http://bit.ly/11AJsOp*)
- jQuery Mobile: Document Ready vs. Page Events (*http://bit.ly/ZMzkix*)
- StackOverflow: Markup Enhancement of Dynamically Added Content (*http://bit.ly/XTNfHa*)

If you consider using a `Model-Binding Plugin`, you will need to come up with an automated mechanism to enrich single components.

Now that you know more about dynamic DOM scripting, it might not be acceptable to completely recreate a component (such as a Listview) that takes a longer time to load and to reduce the complexity of event delegation. Instead, we should use the component-specific plug-ins, which will only update the needed parts of the HTML and CSS.

In the case of a `ListView`, you would need to call the following function to update the list of added, edited, or removed entries:

```
$('#mylist').listview()
```

You need to come up with a means of detecting the component type in order to decide which plug-in method needs to be called. The jQuery Mobile Angular.js Adapter provides such a strategy and solution as well.

See an example of model binding with jQuery Mobile at GitHub (*http://bit.ly/YrZ2wu*).

Intercepting jQuery Mobile Events

In special situations, you will need to take action on a triggered jQuery Mobile event, which you can do as follows:

```
$('#myPage').live('pagebeforecreate', function(event){
    console.log(page was inserted into the DOM');

    // run your own enhancement scripting here...
    // prevent the page plug-in from making its manipulations
    return false;
});

$('#myPage').live('pagecreate', function(event){
    console.log('page was enhanced by jQM');
});
```

In such scenarios, it is important to know when the jQuery Mobile events occur. Figure 12-6 depicts the event cycle (page A is the outgoing page and page B is the incoming page).

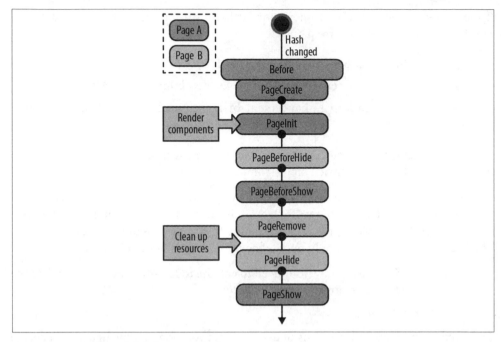

Figure 12-6. jQuery Mobile event cycle

An alternative is the jQuery Mobile Router project, which you might use to replace the Backbone router. With the help of the jQM Router project, you have a powerful way to intercept and route one of the various jQM events. It is an extension to jQuery Mobile, which can be used independently.

Be aware that jQM Router misses some features of Backbone.Router and is tightly coupled with the jQuery Mobile framework. For these reasons, we did not use it for the TodoMVC app. If you intend to use it, consider using a Backbone.js custom build to exclude the router code. This might save around 25% relative to the max compressed size of 17.1 KB.

Check out Backbone's custom builder (*http://gregfranko.com/backbone/customBuild/*).

Performance

Performance is an important topic on mobile devices. jQuery Mobile provides various tools that create performance logs, which can give you a good overview of the actual time spent in routing logic, component enhancement, and visual effects.

Depending on the device, the time spent on transitions can take up to 90% of the load time. To disable all transitions, you can either pass the transition `none` to `$.mo bile.changePage()`, in the configuration code block:

```
$(document).bind("mobileinit", function(){
…
// Otherwise, depending on takes up to 90% of loadtime
  $.mobile.defaultPageTransition = "none";
  $.mobile.defaultDialogTransition = "none";
    });
  })
```

or consider adding device-specific settings; for example:

```
$(document).bind("mobileinit", function(){

  var iosDevice =((navigator.userAgent.match(/iPhone/i))
  || (navigator.userAgent.match(/iPod/i))) ? true : false;

  $.extend( $.mobile , {
    slideText :  (iosDevice) ? "slide" : "none",
    slideUpText :  (iosDevice) ? "slideup" : "none",
    defaultPageTransition:(iosDevice) ? "slide" : "none",
    defaultDialogTransition:(iosDevice) ? "slide" : "none"
  });
```

Also, consider doing your own precaching of enhanced jQuery Mobile pages.

The jQuery Mobile API is frequently enhanced with regards to this topic in each new release. We suggest you take a look at the latest updated API to determine an optimal caching strategy with dynamic scripting that best fits your needs.

For further information on performance, see the following:

- jQuery Mobile profiling tools (*http://bit.ly/YKNm50*)
- Device-specific jQuery Mobile configurations (*http://bit.ly/ZMzTZT*)
- jQuery Mobile debugging tools (*http://bit.ly/17UMba2*)
- jQuery Mobile precaching functionalities (*http://bit.ly/17NGCaz*)

Clever Multiplatform Support Management

Nowadays, a company typically has an existing web page and management decides to provide an additional mobile app to customers. The code of the web page and the code of the mobile app become independent of each other, and the time required for content or feature changes becomes much longer than for the web page alone.

As the trend is toward offering an increasing number of mobile platforms and dimensions, the effort required to support them is only increasing as well. Ultimately, creating per-device experiences is not always viable. However, it is essential that content is available to all users, regardless of their browser and platform. You must keep this principle in mind during the design phase.

Responsive design (http://www.lukew.com/ff/entry.asp?933) and *mobile-first (http://www.abookapart.com/products/mobile-first)* approaches address these challenges.

The mobile app architecture presented in this chapter takes care of a lot of the actual heavy lifting required, as it supports responsive layouts out of the box and even supports browsers that cannot handle media queries. It might not be obvious that jQM is a UI framework not dissimilar to jQuery UI. jQuery Mobile is using the widget factory and can be used for more than just mobile environments.

To support multiplatform browsers using jQuery Mobile and Backbone, you can have, in order of increasing time and effort:

1. Ideally, one code project, where only CSS differs for different devices.

2. Same code project, and at runtime different HTML templates and superclasses are exchanged per device type.

3. Same code project, and the Responsive Design API and most widgets of jQuery Mobile will be reused. For the desktop browser, some components will be added by another widget framework (such as *jQueryUI* or *Twitter Bootstrap*), say, controlled by the HTML templating.

4. Same code project, and at runtime, jQuery Mobile will be completely replaced by another widget framework (such as *jQueryUI* or *Twitter Boostrap*). Superclasses and configurations, as well as concrete `Backbone.View` code snippets, need to be replaced.

5. Different code projects, but common modules are reused.

6. A completely separate code project for the desktop app. Reasons might be the usage of completely different programming languages and/or frameworks, lack of responsive design knowledge, or legacy of pollution.

The ideal solution—to build a nice-looking desktop application with only one mobile framework—sounds crazy, but is feasible.

If you have a look at the jQuery Mobile API page in a desktop browser, it does not look anything like a mobile application (Figure 12-7).

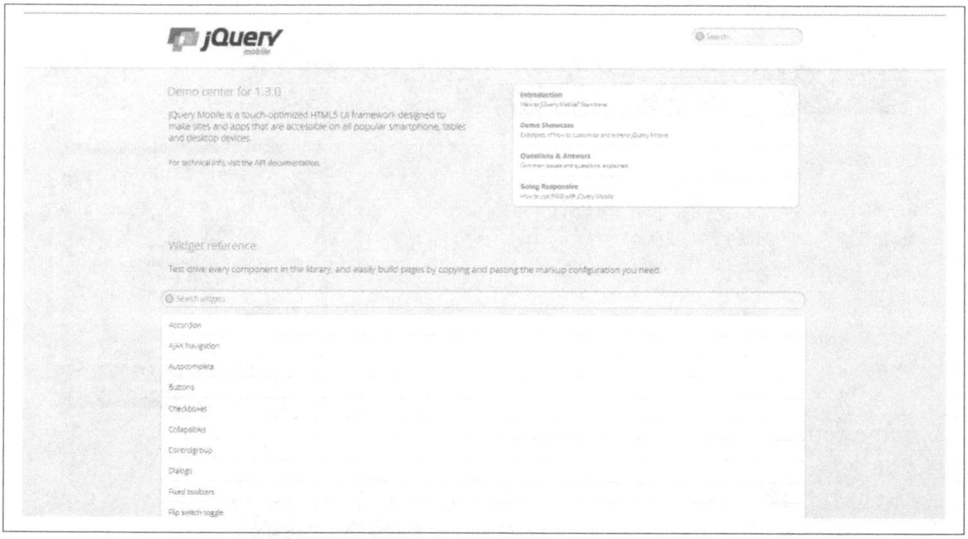

Figure 12-7. Desktop view of the jQuery Mobile API and Docs application (http://view.jquerymobile.com/1.3.0/)

The same goes for the jQuery Mobile design examples, where jQuery Mobile intends to add further user interface experiences (Figure 12-8).

The accordions, datepickers, sliders—everything in the desktop UI—is reusing what jQM would be providing users on mobile devices. By way of example, adding the attribute `data-mini="true"` on components will lose the clumsiness of the mobile widgets on a desktop browser.

See jQuery Mobile (*http://bit.ly/151DdJa*) for more on mini-widgets for desktop applications.

Thanks to some media queries, the desktop UI can make optimal use of whitespace, expanding component blocks out and providing alternative layouts while still making use of jQM as the component framework.

Figure 12-8. Design examples of jQuery Mobile for desktop environments (http://jquery mobile.com/designs/#desktop)

The benefit of this is that you don't need to pull in another widget framework (for example, jQuery UI) separately to be able to take advantage of these features. Thanks to the ThemeRoller, the components can look pretty much exactly how you would like them to and users of the app can get a jQM UI for lower resolutions and a jQM-ish UI for everything else.

The takeaway here is just to remember that if you are not already going through the hassle of conditional script/style loading based on screen resolution (using matchMedia.js, and so on), there are simpler approaches you can take to cross-device component theming. At least the Responsive Design API of jQuery Mobile, which was added since version 1.3.0, is always reasonable because it will work for mobile as well as for desktop. In summary, you can manage jQuery Mobile components to give users a typical desktop appearance, and they will not realize a difference.

For more on responsive design with jQuery Mobile, see *http://view.jquerymobile.com/ 1.3.0/docs/intro/rwd.php*.

Also, if you hit your limits of CSS styling and configurations of your jQuery Mobile application for desktop browsers, the additional effort to use jQuery Mobile and Twitter Bootstrap together can be minimal. In the case that a desktop browser requests the page and Twitter Bootstrap has been loaded, the mobile TodoMVC app would need conditional code to not trigger the jQM widget processive enhancement plug-ins API (demonstrated in "Dynamic DOM Scripting" on page 256) in the `Backbone.View` implementation. Therefore, as explained in the previous sections, we recommend triggering widget enhancements by `$.mobile.changePage` only once to load the complete page.

Figure 12-9 shows an example of such widget hybrid usage.

Twitter Boostrap version   jQuery Mobile version

Figure 12-9. App Engine boilerplate, desktop, and mobile appearance

Although this is using server-side technologies for templating using the programming language Python, the principle of triggering progressive enhancement at page load is the same as $mobile.changePage.

As you can see, the JavaScript and even the CSS stays the same. The only device-specific conditions and differences in implementations are for selecting the appropriate framework imports, which are located in the HTML template:

```
...
{% if is_mobile %}
    <link rel="stylesheet" href="/mobile/jquery.mobile-1.1.0.min.css" />
    {% else %}
      <link rel="apple-touch-icon" href="/apple-touch-icon.png" />
      <link rel="stylesheet" href="/css/style.css" />
      <link rel="stylesheet" href="/css/bootstrap.min.css">
      <link rel="stylesheet" href="/css/bootstrap-responsive.min.css">
    {% endif %}
      <link rel="stylesheet" href="/css/main.css" />

    {% block mediaCSS %}{% endblock %}
...
{% if is_mobile %}
    <script src="/mobile/jquery.mobile-1.1.0.min.js"></script>
    {% else %}
    <script src="/js/libs/bootstrap.min.js"></script>
    {% endif %}
...
```

CHAPTER 13

Jasmine

One definition of *unit testing* is the process of taking the smallest piece of testable code in an application, isolating it from the remainder of your codebase, and determining if it behaves exactly as expected.

For an application to be considered well tested, each function should ideally have its own separate unit tests where it's tested against the different conditions you expect it to handle. All tests must pass before functionality is considered complete. This allows developers to modify a unit of code and its dependencies with a level of confidence about whether these changes have caused any breakage.

A basic example of unit testing is where a developer asserts that passing specific values to a sum function results in the correct value being returned. For an example more relevant to this book, we may wish to assert that adding a new todo item to a list correctly adds a model of a specific type to a Todos collection.

When you are building modern web applications, it's typically considered a best practice to include automated unit testing as a part of your development process. In the following chapters, we are going to look at three different solutions for unit-testing your Backbone.js apps: Jasmine, QUnit, and SinonJS.

Behavior-Driven Development

In this chapter, we'll be taking a look at how to unit-test Backbone applications using a popular JavaScript testing framework called Jasmine (*http://bit.ly/18uX5Rm*) from Pivotal Labs.

Jasmine describes itself as a behavior-driven development, or BDD (*http://bit.ly/1217r9F*), framework for testing JavaScript code. Before we jump into how the framework works, it's useful to understand exactly what BDD is.

BDD is a second-generation testing approach first described by Dan North (*http://dannorth.net/introducing-bdd/*), the authority on BDD, that attempts to test the behavior of software. It's considered second-generation because it came out of merging ideas from domain-driven design (DDD) and lean software development. BDD helps teams deliver high-quality software by answering many of the more confusing questions early on in the agile process. Such questions commonly include those concerning documentation and testing.

If you were to read a book on BDD, it's likely that it would be described as being *outside-in* and *pull-based*. The reason for this is that it borrows the idea of pulling features from lean manufacturing, which effectively ensures that the right software solutions are being written by:

- Focusing on the expected outputs of the system
- Ensuring these outputs are achieved

BDD recognizes that there are usually multiple stakeholders in a project and not a single amorphous user of the system. These different groups will be affected by the software being written in differing ways and will have varying opinions of what quality in the system means to them. It's for this reason that it's important to understand whom the software will be bringing value to and exactly what in it will be valuable to them.

Finally, BDD relies on automation. Once you've defined the quality expected, your team will want to check on the functionality of the solution being built regularly and compare it to the results they expect. In order to facilitate this efficiently, the process has to be automated. BDD relies heavily on the automation of specification testing, and Jasmine is a tool that can assist with this.

BDD helps both developers and nontechnical stakeholders:

- Better understand and represent the models of the problems being solved
- Explain supported test cases in a language that nondevelopers can read
- Focus on minimizing translation of the technical code being written and the domain language spoken by the business

What this means is that developers should be able to show Jasmine unit tests to a project stakeholder and (at a high level, thanks to a common vocabulary being used) that person will ideally be able to understand what the code supports.

Developers often implement BDD in unison with another testing paradigm known as test-driven development, or TDD (*http://bit.ly/10YXfTw*). The main idea behind TDD is using the following development process:

1. Write unit tests that describe the functionality you would like your code to support.

---

2. Watch these tests fail (as the code to support them hasn't yet been written).

3. Write code to make the tests pass.

4. Rinse, repeat, and refactor.

In this chapter we're going to use BDD (with TDD) to write unit tests for a Backbone application.

 I've seen a lot of developers also opt for writing tests to validate behavior of their code after having written it. While this is fine, note that it can come with pitfalls such as only testing for behavior your code currently supports, rather than the behavior needed to fully solve the problem.

Suites, Specs, and Spies

When using Jasmine, you'll be writing suites and specifications (specs). Suites basically describe scenarios, while specs describe what can be done in these scenarios.

Each spec is a JavaScript function, described with a call to it() using a description string and a function. The description should describe the behavior the particular unit of code should exhibit and, keeping in mind BDD, should ideally be meaningful. Here's an example of a basic spec:

```
it('should be incrementing in value', function(){
    var counter = 0;
    counter++;
});
```

On its own, a spec isn't particularly useful until expectations are set about the behavior of the code. You define expectations in specs using the expect() function and an expectation matcher (*http://bit.ly/100yWTt*)—for example, toEqual(), toBeTruthy(), toContain(). A revised example using an expectation matcher would look like:

```
it('should be incrementing in value', function(){
    var counter = 0;
    counter++;
    expect(counter).toEqual(1);
});
```

The preceding code passes our behavioral expectation as counter equals 1. Notice how easy it was to read the expectation on the last line (you probably grokked it without any explanation).

Specs are grouped into suites that we describe using Jasmine's describe() function, again passing a string as a description and a function as we did for it(). The name/description for your suite is typically that of the component or module you're testing.

Jasmine will use the description as the group name when it reports the results of the specs you've asked it to run. A simple suite containing our sample spec could look like:

```
describe('Stats', function(){
    it('can increment a number', function(){
        ...
    });

    it('can subtract a number', function(){
        ...
    });
});
```

Suites also share a functional scope, so it's possible to declare variables and functions inside a `describe` block that are accessible within specs:

```
describe('Stats', function(){
    var counter = 1;

    it('can increment a number', function(){
        // the counter was = 1
        counter = counter + 1;
        expect(counter).toEqual(2);
    });

    it('can subtract a number', function(){
        // the counter was = 2
        counter = counter - 1;
        expect(counter).toEqual(1);
    });
});
```

 Suites are executed in the order in which they are described, which can be useful to know if you would prefer to see test results for specific parts of your application reported first.

Jasmine also supports *spies*—a way to mock, spy, and fake behavior in our unit tests. Spies replace the function they're spying on, allowing us to simulate behavior we would like to mock (i.e., test without using the actual implementation).

In this example, we're spying on the `setComplete` method of a dummy `Todo` function to test that arguments can be passed to it as expected.

```
var Todo = function(){
};

Todo.prototype.setComplete = function (arg){
    return arg;
}
```

```
describe('a simple spy', function(){
    it('should spy on an instance method of a Todo', function(){
        var myTodo = new Todo();
        spyOn(myTodo, 'setComplete');
        myTodo.setComplete('foo bar');

        expect(myTodo.setComplete).toHaveBeenCalledWith('foo bar');

        var myTodo2 = new Todo();
        spyOn(myTodo2, 'setComplete');

        expect(myTodo2.setComplete).not.toHaveBeenCalled();

    });
});
```

You are more likely to use spies for testing asynchronous behavior (*http://bit.ly/ 13PySEx*) in your application such as AJAX requests. Jasmine supports:

- Writing tests that can mock AJAX requests using spies. This allows us to test both the code that initiates the AJAX request and the code executed upon its completion. It's also possible to mock/fake the server responses. The benefit of this type of testing is that it's faster as no real calls are being made to a server. The ability to simulate any response from the server is also of great benefit.
- Asynchronous tests that don't rely on spies.

This example of the first kind of test shows how to fake an AJAX request and verify that the request was both calling the correct URL and executed a callback where one was provided.

```
it('the callback should be executed on success', function () {

    // `andCallFake()` calls a passed function when a spy
    // has been called
    spyOn($, 'ajax').andCallFake(function(options) {
        options.success();
    });

    // Create a new spy
    var callback = jasmine.createSpy();

    // Execute the spy callback if the
    // request for Todo 15 is successful
    getTodo(15, callback);

    // Verify that the URL of the most recent call
    // matches our expected Todo item.
    expect($.ajax.mostRecentCall.args[0]['url']).toEqual('/todos/15');

    // `expect(x).toHaveBeenCalled()` will pass if `x` is a
```

```
        // spy and was called.
        expect(callback).toHaveBeenCalled();
    });

    function getTodo(id, callback) {
        $.ajax({
            type: 'GET',
            url: '/todos/'' + id,
            dataType: 'json',
            success: callback
        });
    }
```

All of these are spy-specific matchers and are documented on the Jasmine wiki (*http:// bit.ly/17zGddr*).

For the second type of test (asynchronous tests), we can take the preceding further by taking advantage of three other methods Jasmine supports (as documented by Git-Hub (*http://bit.ly/ZC0FbX*)):

waits(*timeout*)

A native timeout before the next block is run.

waitsFor(*function, optional message, optional timeout*)

A way to pause specs until some other work has completed. Jasmine waits until the supplied function returns true here before it moves on to the next block.

runs(*function*)

A block that runs as if it were directly called. It exists so that we can test asynchronous processes.

```
it('should make an actual AJAX request to a server', function () {

    // Create a new spy
    var callback = jasmine.createSpy();

    // Execute the spy callback if the
    // request for Todo 16 is successful
    getTodo(16, callback);

    // Pause the spec until the callback count is
    // greater than 0
    waitsFor(function() {
        return callback.callCount > 0;
    });

    // Once the wait is complete, our runs() block
    // will check to ensure our spy callback has been
    // called
    runs(function() {
        expect(callback).toHaveBeenCalled();
    });
```

```
});

function getTodo(id, callback) {
    $.ajax({
        type: 'GET',
        url: 'todos.json',
        dataType: 'json',
        success: callback
    });
}
```

 It's useful to remember that making real requests to a web server in your
unit tests has the potential to massively slow down the speed at which
tests run (due to many factors, including server latency). As this also
introduces an external dependency that can (and should) be minimized
in your unit testing, it is strongly recommended that you opt for spies
to remove the dependency on a web server.

beforeEach() and afterEach()

Jasmine also supports specifying code that can be run before each (beforeEach()) and
after each (afterEach()) test. This is useful for enforcing consistent conditions (such
as resetting variables that may be required by specs). In the following example, be
foreEach() is used to create a new sample Todo model that specs can use for testing
attributes.

```
beforeEach(function(){
    this.todo = new Backbone.Model({
        text: 'Buy some more groceries',
        done: false
    });
});

it('should contain a text value if not the default value', function(){
    expect(this.todo.get('text')).toEqual('Buy some more groceries');
});
```

Each nested describe() in your tests can have its own beforeEach() and after
Each() methods that support including setup and teardown methods relevant to a particular suite.

You can use beforeEach() and afterEach() together to write tests verifying that our
Backbone routes are being correctly triggered when we navigate to the URL. We can
start with the index action:

```
describe('Todo routes', function(){

    beforeEach(function(){
```

```
        // Create a new router
        this.router = new App.TodoRouter();

        // Create a new spy
        this.routerSpy = jasmine.spy();

        // Begin monitoring hashchange events
        try{
            Backbone.history.start({
                silent:true,
                pushState: true
            });
        }catch(e){
            // ...
        }

        // Navigate to a URL
        this.router.navigate('/js/spec/SpecRunner.html');
    });

    afterEach(function(){

        // Navigate back to the URL
        this.router.navigate('/js/spec/SpecRunner.html');

        // Disable Backbone.history temporarily.
        // Note that this is not really useful in real apps but is
        // good for testing routers
        Backbone.history.stop();
    });

    it('should call the index route correctly', function(){
        this.router.bind('route:index', this.routerSpy, this);
        this.router.navigate('', {trigger: true});

        // If everything in our beforeEach() and afterEach()
        // calls has been correctly executed, the following
        // should now pass.
        expect(this.routerSpy).toHaveBeenCalledOnce();
        expect(this.routerSpy).toHaveBeenCalledWith();
    });

});
```

The actual TodoRouter for that would make the preceding test pass look like:

```
var App = App || {};
App.TodoRouter = Backbone.Router.extend({
    routes:{
        '': 'index'
    },
    index: function(){
```

```
        //...
    }
});
```

Shared Scope

Let's imagine we have a suite where we wish to check for the existence of a new todo item instance. We could do this by duplicating the spec as follows:

```
describe("Todo tests", function(){

    // Spec
    it("Should be defined when we create it", function(){
        // A Todo item we are testing
        var todo = new Todo("Get the milk", "Tuesday");
        expect(todo).toBeDefined();
    });

    it("Should have the correct title", function(){
        // Where we introduce code duplication
        var todo = new Todo("Get the milk", "Tuesday");
        expect(todo.title).toBe("Get the milk");
    });

});
```

As you can see, we've introduced duplication that should ideally be refactored into something cleaner. We can do this using Jasmine's *suite (shared) functional scope*.

All of the specs within the same suite share the same functional scope, meaning that variables declared within the suite itself are available to all of the specs in that suite. This gives us a way to work around our duplication problem by moving the creation of our todo objects into the common functional scope:

```
describe("Todo tests", function(){

    // The instance of Todo, the object we wish to test
    // is now in the shared functional scope
    var todo = new Todo("Get the milk", "Tuesday");

    // Spec
    it("should be correctly defined", function(){
        expect(todo).toBeDefined();
    });

    it("should have the correct title", function(){
        expect(todo.title).toBe("Get the milk");
    });

});
```

In the previous section you may have noticed that we initially declared `this.todo` within the scope of our `beforeEach()` call and were then able to continue using this reference in `afterEach()`.

This is again down to shared function scope, which allows such declarations to be common to all blocks (including `runs()`).

Variables declared outside of the shared scope (within the local scope `var todo=...`) will not be shared.

Getting Set Up

Now that we've reviewed some fundamentals, let's go through downloading Jasmine and getting everything set up to write tests.

You can download a standalone release of Jasmine from the official release page (*http://bit.ly/ZXXHOr*).

You'll need a file called *SpecRunner.html* in addition to the release. You can download from GitHub (*http://bit.ly/Y1MttO*) or as part of a download of the complete Jasmine repo (*http://bit.ly/16tRVbx*). Alternatively, you can `git clone` the main Jasmine repository from GitHub (*http://bit.ly/ZC14v4*).

Let's review *SpecRunner.html.jst* (*http://bit.ly/YrZ8EA*).

It first includes both Jasmine and the necessary CSS required for reporting:

```
<link rel="stylesheet" type="text/css"
 href="lib/jasmine-<%= jasmineVersion %>/jasmine.css">
<script src="lib/jasmine-<%= jasmineVersion %>/jasmine.js"></script>
<script src="lib/jasmine-<%= jasmineVersion %>/jasmine-html.js"></script>
<script src="lib/jasmine-<%= jasmineVersion %>/boot.js"></script>
```

Next come the sources being tested:

```
<!-- include source files here... -->
<script src="src/Player.js"></script>
<script src="src/Song.js"></script>
```

Finally, some sample tests are included:

```
<!-- include spec files here... -->
<script src="spec/SpecHelper.js"></script>
<script src="spec/PlayerSpec.js"></script>
```

 Following this section of SpecRunner is code responsible for running the actual tests.

Given that we won't be covering modifying this code, I'm going to skip reviewing it. I do, however, encourage you to take a look through *PlayerSpec.js* (*http://bit.ly/131HS9V*) and *SpecHelper.js* (*http://bit.ly/ZpFOoE*). They're useful basic examples that go through how a minimal set of tests might work.

Also note that for the purposes of introduction, some of the examples in this chapter will be testing aspects of Backbone.js itself, just to give you a feel for how Jasmine works. You generally will not need to write tests ensuring a framework is working as expected.

TDD with Backbone

When developing applications with Backbone, you might have to test both individual modules of code as well as models, views, collections, and routers. Taking a TDD approach to testing, let's review some specs for testing these Backbone components using the popular Backbone Todo application (*http://bit.ly/12OZbs8*).

Models

The complexity of Backbone models can vary greatly depending on what your application is trying to achieve. In the following example, we're going to test default values, attributes, state changes, and validation rules.

First, we begin our suite for model testing using `describe()`:

```
describe('Tests for Todo', function() {
```

Models should ideally have default values for attributes. This helps ensure that when instances are created without a value set for any specific attribute, a default one (e.g., an empty string) is used instead. The idea here is to allow your application to interact with models without any unexpected behavior.

In the following spec, we create a new todo without any attributes passed and then check to find out what the value of the `text` attribute is. As no value has been set, we expect a default value of `''` to be returned.

```
it('Can be created with default values for its attributes.', function() {
    var todo = new Todo();
    expect(todo.get('text')).toBe('');
});
```

If you are testing this spec before your models have been written, you'll incur a failing test, as expected. What's required for the spec to pass is a default value for the attribute `text`. We can set this and some other useful defaults (which we'll be using shortly) in our Todo model as follows:

```
window.Todo = Backbone.Model.extend({

    defaults: {
```

```
        text: '',
        done:  false,
        order: 0
    }
```

Next, it is common to include validation logic in your models to ensure that input passed from users or other modules in the application is valid.

A Todo app may wish to validate the text input supplied in case it contains rude words. Similarly, if we're storing the done state of a todo item using Booleans, we need to validate that truthy/falsy values are passed and not just any arbitrary string.

In the following spec, we take advantage of the fact that validations that fail model.val idate() trigger an invalid event. This allows us to test if validations are correctly failing when invalid input is supplied.

We create an errorCallback spy using Jasmine's built-in createSpy() method, which allows us to spy on the invalid event as follows:

```
it('Can contain custom validation rules, and will trigger an invalid event on
failed validation.', function() {

    var errorCallback = jasmine.createSpy('-invalid event callback-');

    var todo = new Todo();

    todo.on('invalid', errorCallback);

    // What would you need to set on the todo properties to
    // cause validation to fail?

    todo.set({done:'a non-boolean value'});

    var errorArgs = errorCallback.mostRecentCall.args;

    expect(errorArgs).toBeDefined();
    expect(errorArgs[0]).toBe(todo);
    expect(errorArgs[1]).toBe('Todo.done must be a boolean value.');
});
```

The code to make the preceding failing test support validation is relatively simple. In our model, we override the validate() method (as recommended in the Backbone docs), checking to make sure a model has a done property and that its value is a valid Boolean before allowing it to pass.

```
validate: function(attrs) {
    if (attrs.hasOwnProperty('done') && !_.isBoolean(attrs.done)) {
        return 'Todo.done must be a boolean value.';
    }
}
```

If you would like to review the final code for our Todo model, here it is:

```
window.Todo = Backbone.Model.extend({

    defaults: {
      text: '',
      done:  false,
      order: 0
    },

    initialize: function() {
        this.set({text: this.get('text')}, {silent: true});
    },

    validate: function(attrs) {
        if (attrs.hasOwnProperty('done') && !_.isBoolean(attrs.done)) {
            return 'Todo.done must be a boolean value.';
        }
    },

    toggle: function() {
        this.save({done: !this.get('done')});
    }

});
```

Collections

We now need to define specs to test a Backbone collection of Todo models (a Todo List). Collections are responsible for a number of list tasks, including managing order and filtering.

Here are a few specific specs that come to mind when we're working with collections:

- Making sure we can add new Todo models as both objects and arrays
- Attribute testing to make sure attributes such as the base URL of the collection are values we expect
- Purposefully adding items with a status of done:true and checking against how many items the collection thinks have been completed versus those that are remaining

In this section we're going to cover the first two of these with the third left as an extended exercise you can try on your own.

Testing that Todo models can be added to a collection as objects or arrays is relatively trivial. First, we initialize a new TodoList collection and check to make sure its length (such as the number of Todo models it contains) is 0. Next, we add new todos, both as objects and arrays, checking the length property of the collection at each stage to ensure the overall count is what we expect:

```
describe('Tests for TodoList', function() {

    it('Can add Model instances as objects and arrays.', function() {
        var todos = new TodoList();

        expect(todos.length).toBe(0);

        todos.add({ text: 'Clean the kitchen' });

        // how many todos have been added so far?
        expect(todos.length).toBe(1);

        todos.add([
            { text: 'Do the laundry', done: true },
            { text: 'Go to the gym'}
        ]);

        // how many are there in total now?
        expect(todos.length).toBe(3);
    });
    ...
```

Similar to model attributes, it's also quite straightforward to test attributes in collections. Here we have a spec that ensures the collection URL (the URL reference to the collection's location on the server) is what we expect it to be:

```
    it('Can have a url property to define the basic url structure for all contained
            models.', function() {
        var todos = new TodoList();

        // what has been specified as the url base in our model?
        expect(todos.url).toBe('/todos/');
    });
```

For the third spec (which you will write as an exercise), note that the implementation for our collection will have methods for filtering how many todo items are done and how many are remaining; we'll call these done() and remaining(). Consider writing a spec that creates a new collection and adds one new model that has a preset done state of true and two others that have the default done state of false. Testing the length of what's returned using done() and remaining() will tell us whether the state management in our application is working or needs a little tweaking.

The final implementation for our TodoList collection is as follows:

```
    window.TodoList = Backbone.Collection.extend({

        model: Todo,

        url: '/todos/',

        done: function() {
            return this.filter(function(todo) { return todo.get('done'); });
```

```
        },

        remaining: function() {
            return this.without.apply(this, this.done());
        },

        nextOrder: function() {
            if (!this.length) {
                return 1;
            }

            return this.last().get('order') + 1;
        },

        comparator: function(todo) {
            return todo.get('order');
        }

    });
```

Views

Before we take a look at testing Backbone views, let's briefly review a jQuery plug-in that can assist with writing Jasmine specs for them.

As we know our Todo application will be using jQuery for DOM manipulation, there's a useful jQuery plug-in called jasmine-jquery (*http://bit.ly/18fo6e7*) that will help us simplify BDD testing of the rendering performed by our views.

The plug-in provides a number of additional Jasmine matchers (*http://bit.ly/100yWTt*) to help test jQuery-wrapped sets such as:

toBe(jQuerySelector)
    For example, expect($('<div id="some-id"></div>')).toBe('div#some-id')

toBeChecked()
    For example, expect($('<input type="checkbox" checked="checked"/>')).toBeChecked()

toBeSelected()
    For example, expect($('<option selected="selected"></option>')).toBeSelected()

and many others (*https://github.com/velesin/jasmine-jquery*). The complete list of matchers supported can be found on the project home page. It's useful to know that similar to the standard Jasmine matchers, you can invert the custom matchers just listed using the .not prefix (for example, expect(x).not.toBe(y)):

```
expect($('<div>I am an example</div>')).not.toHaveText(/other/)
```

jasmine-jquery also includes a fixtures module that can be used to load arbitrary HTML content we wish to use in our tests.

Include some HTML in an external fixtures file, *some.fixture.html*:

```
<div id="sample-fixture">some HTML content</div>
```

Then, inside our actual test we would load it as follows:

```
loadFixtures('some.fixture.html')
$('some-fixture').myTestedPlugin();
expect($('#some-fixture')).to<the rest of your matcher would go here>
```

The jasmine-jquery plug-in loads fixtures from a directory named *spec/javascripts/ fixtures* by default. If you wish to configure this path, you can do so by initially setting `jasmine.getFixtures().fixturesPath = 'your custom path'`.

Finally, jasmine-jquery includes support for spying on jQuery events without the need for any extra plumbing work. You can do this using the `spyOnEvent()` and `assert(even tName).toHaveBeenTriggered(selector)` functions. For example:

```
spyOnEvent($('#el'), 'click');
$('#el').click();
expect('click').toHaveBeenTriggeredOn($('#el'));
```

View Testing

In this section we will review the three dimensions of specs writing for Backbone views: initial setup, view rendering, and templating. The latter two of these are the most commonly tested, but we'll see shortly why writing specs for the initialization of your views can also be beneficial.

Initial setup

At their most basic, specs for Backbone views should validate that they are being correctly tied to specific DOM elements and are backed by valid data models. The reason for this is that these specs can identify issues that will trip up more complex tests later on. Also, they're fairly simple to write given the overall value offered.

To help ensure a consistent testing setup for our specs, we use `beforeEach()` to append both an empty `<ul>` (#todoList) to the DOM and initialize a new instance of a Todo View using an empty Todo model. `afterEach()` is used to remove the previous #todo List `<ul>` as well as the previous instance of the view.

```
describe('Tests for TodoView', function() {

    beforeEach(function() {
        $('body').append('<ul id="todoList"></ul>');
        this.todoView = new TodoView({ model: new Todo() });
    });
```

```
afterEach(function() {
    this.todoView.remove();
    $('#todoList').remove();
});
```

...

The first spec useful to write is a check that the `TodoView` we've created is using the correct `tagName` (element or class name). The purpose of this test is to make sure it was correctly tied to a DOM element when it was created.

Backbone views typically create empty DOM elements once initialized; however, these elements are not attached to the visible DOM in order to allow them to be constructed without an impact on rendering performance.

```
it('Should be tied to a DOM element when created, based off the property
    provided.', function() {
    //what html element tag name represents this view?
    expect(todoView.el.tagName.toLowerCase()).toBe('li');
});
```

Once again, if the `TodoView` has not already been written, we will experience failing specs. Thankfully, solving this is as simple as creating a new `Backbone.View` with a specific `tagName`.

```
var todoView = Backbone.View.extend({
    tagName:  'li'
});
```

If instead of testing against the `tagName` you would prefer to use a `className` instead, you can take advantage of jasmine-jquery's `toHaveClass()` matcher:

```
it('Should have a class of "todos"'), function(){
    expect(this.view.$el).toHaveClass('todos');
});
```

The `toHaveClass()` matcher operates on jQuery objects and if the plug-in hadn't been used, an exception would have been thrown. It is also possible to test for the `class Name` by accessing `el.className` if you don't use jasmine-jquery.

You may have noticed that in `beforeEach()`, we passed our view an initial (albeit unfilled) Todo model. Views should be backed by a model instance that provides data. As this is quite important to our view's ability to function, we can write a spec to ensure a model is defined (using the `toBeDefined()` matcher) and then test attributes of the model to ensure defaults both exist and are the values we expect them to be.

```
it('Is backed by a model instance, which provides the data.', function() {

    expect(todoView.model).toBeDefined();

    // what's the value for Todo.get('done') here?
```

```
      expect(todoView.model.get('done')).toBe(false); // or toBeFalsy()
    });
```

View rendering

Next we're going to take a look at writing specs for view rendering. Specifically, we want to test that our `TodoView` elements are actually rendering as expected.

In smaller applications, those new to BDD might argue that visual confirmation of view rendering could replace unit testing of views. The reality is that when you're dealing with applications that might grow to a large number of views, it makes sense to automate this process as much as possible from the get-go. There are also aspects of rendering that require verification beyond what is visually presented on screen (which we'll see very shortly).

We're going to begin testing views by writing two specs. The first spec will check that the view's `render()` method is correctly returning the view instance, which is necessary for chaining. Our second spec will check that the HTML produced is exactly what we expect based on the properties of the model instance that's been associated with our `TodoView`.

Unlike some of the previous specs we've covered, this section will make greater use of `beforeEach()` to both demonstrate how to use nested suites and also ensure a consistent set of conditions for our specs. In our first example we're simply going to create a sample model (based on Todo) and instantiate a `TodoView` with it.

```
describe('TodoView', function() {

  beforeEach(function() {
    this.model = new Backbone.Model({
      text: 'My Todo',
      order: 1,
      done: false
    });
    this.view = new TodoView({model:this.model});
  });

  describe('Rendering', function() {

    it('returns the view object', function() {
      expect(this.view.render()).toEqual(this.view);
    });

    it('produces the correct HTML', function() {
      this.view.render();

      // let's use jasmine-jquery's toContain() to avoid
      // testing for the complete content of a todo's markup
      expect(this.view.el.innerHTML)
        .toContain('<label class="todo-content">My Todo</label>');
```

```
  });

 });

});
```

When these specs are run, only the second one (produces the correct HTML) fails. Our first spec (returns the view object), which is testing that the `TodoView` instance is returned from `render()`, passes since this is Backbone's default behavior and we haven't overwritten the `render()` method with our own version yet.

 For the purposes of maintaining readability, all template examples in this section will use a minimal version of the following todo view template. As it's relatively trivial to expand this, please feel free to refer to this sample if needed:

```
<div class="todo <%= done ? 'done' : '' %>">
      <div class="display">
        <input class="check" type="checkbox" <%= done ?
         'checked="checked"' : '' %> />
        <label class="todo-content"><%= text %></label>
        <span class="todo-destroy"></span>
      </div>
      <div class="edit">
        <input class="todo-input" type="text" value="<%= content %>" />
      </div>
    </div>
```

The second spec fails with the following message:

```
Expected '' to contain '<label class="todo-content">My Todo</label>'.
```

The reason for this is that the default behavior for `render()` doesn't create any markup. Let's write a replacement for `render()` that fixes this:

```
render: function() {
  var template = '<label class="todo-content">+++PLACEHOLDER+++</label>';
  var output = template
    .replace('+++PLACEHOLDER+++', this.model.get('text'));
  this.$el.html(output);
  return this;
}
```

The previous code specifies an inline string template and replaces fields found in the template within the +++PLACEHOLDER+++ blocks with their corresponding values from the associated model. As we're also returning the `TodoView` instance from the method, the first spec will still pass.

It would be impossible to discuss unit testing without mentioning fixtures. Fixtures typically contain test data (such as HTML) that is loaded in when needed (either locally or from an external file) for unit testing. So far we've been establishing jQuery expectations based on the view's el property. This works for a number of cases; however, there are instances where it may be necessary to render markup into the document. The optimal way to handle this within specs is through using fixtures (another feature brought to us by the jasmine-jquery plug-in).

Rewriting the last spec to use fixtures would look as follows:

```
describe('TodoView', function() {

  beforeEach(function() {
    ...
    setFixtures('<ul class="todos"></ul>');
  });

  ...

  describe('Template', function() {

    beforeEach(function() {
      $('.todos').append(this.view.render().el);
    });

    it('has the correct text content', function() {
      expect($('.todos').find('.todo-content'))
        .toHaveText('My Todo');
    });

  });

});
```

What we're now doing in this spec is appending the rendered todo item into the fixture. We then set expectations against the fixture, which may be desirable when a view is set up against an element that already exists in the DOM. We'd have to provide both the fixture and test the el property, correctly picking up the expected element when the view is instantiated.

Rendering with a templating system

When a user marks a todo item as complete (done), we may wish to provide visual feedback (such as a line through the text) to differentiate the item from those that are remaining. We can do this by attaching a new class to the item. Let's begin by writing a test:

```
describe('When a todo is done', function() {

  beforeEach(function() {
    this.model.set({done: true}, {silent: true});
    $('.todos').append(this.view.render().el);
  });
```

```
  it('has a done class', function() {
    expect($('.todos .todo-content:first-child'))
      .toHaveClass('done');
  });

});
```

This will fail with the following message:

```
Expected '<label class="todo-content">My Todo</label>' to have class 'done'.
```

which we can fix in the existing `render()` method as follows:

```
render: function() {
  var template = '<label class="todo-content">' +
    '<%= text %></label>';
  var output = template
    .replace('<%= text %>', this.model.get('text'));
  this.$el.html(output);
  if (this.model.get('done')) {
    this.$('.todo-content').addClass('done');
  }
  return this;
}
```

However, this can get unwieldy fairly quickly. As the level of complexity and logic in our templates increases, so do the challenges associated with testing them. We can ease this process by taking advantage of modern templating libraries, many of which have already been demonstrated to work well with testing solutions such as Jasmine.

JavaScript templating systems—such as Handlebars (*http://handlebarsjs.com/*), Mustache (*http://mustache.github.com/*), and Underscore's own microtemplating (*http://underscorejs.org/#template*)—support conditional logic in template strings. What this effectively means is that we can add if/else/ternery expressions inline that can then be evaluated as needed, allowing us to build even more powerful templates.

In our case, we are going to use the microtemplating found in Underscore.js, as no additional files are required to use it and we can easily modify our existing specs to use it without a great deal of effort.

Assuming our template is defined using a `<script>` tag of ID `myTemplate`:

```
<script type="text/template" id="myTemplate">
  <div class="todo <%= done ? 'done' : '' %>">
    <div class="display">
      <input class="check" type="checkbox"
      <%= done ? 'checked="checked"' : '' %> />
      <label class="todo-content"><%= text %></label>
      <span class="todo-destroy"></span>
    </div>
    <div class="edit">
      <input class="todo-input" type="text" value="<%= content %>" />
```

```
            </div>
        </div>
    </script>
```

Our `TodoView` can be modified to use Underscore templating as follows:

```
var TodoView = Backbone.View.extend({

  tagName: 'li',
  template: _.template($('#myTemplate').html()),

  initialize: function(options) {
    // ...
  },

  render: function() {
    this.$el.html(this.template(this.model.toJSON()));
    return this;
  },

  ...

});
```

So, what's going on here? We're first defining our template in a `<script>` tag with a custom script type (for example, `type=text/template`). As this isn't a script type any browser understands, it's simply ignored; however, referencing the script by an `id` attribute allows the template to be kept separate from other parts of the page.

In our view, we're the using the Underscore `_.template()` method to compile our template into a function that we can easily pass model data to later. In the line `this.model.toJSON()` we are simply returning a copy of the model's attributes for JSON stringification to the `template` method, creating a block of HTML that can now be appended to the DOM.

Note that, ideally, all of your template logic should exist outside of your specs, either in individual template files or embedded via `<script>` tags within your SpecRunner. This is generally more maintainable.

If you are working with much smaller templates and are not doing this, there is, however, a useful trick that can be applied to automatically create or extend templates in the Jasmine shared functional scope for each test.

By creating a new directory (say, *templates*) in the *spec* folder and including a new script file with the following contents into *SpecRunner.html*, we can manually add custom attributes representing smaller templates we wish to use:

```
beforeEach(function() {
  this.templates = _.extend(this.templates || {}, {
    todo: '<label class="todo-content">' +
            '<%= text %>' +
```

```
            '</label>'
    });
  });
```

To finish this off, we simply update our existing spec to reference the template when instantiating the `TodoView`:

```
describe('TodoView', function() {

  beforeEach(function() {
    ...
    this.view = new TodoView({
      model: this.model,
      template: this.templates.todo
    });
  });

  ...

});
```

The existing specs we've looked at would continue to pass using this approach, leaving us free to adjust the template with some additional conditional logic for todos with a status of done:

```
beforeEach(function() {
  this.templates = _.extend(this.templates || {}, {
    todo: '<label class="todo-content <%= done ? 'done' : '' %>"' +
          '<%= text %>' +
          '</label>'
  });
});
```

This will now also pass without any issues; however, as mentioned, this last approach probably only makes sense if you're working with smaller, highly dynamic templates.

Exercise

As an exercise, I recommend looking at the Jasmine Koans in *practicals\jasmine-koans* and trying to fix some of the purposefully failing tests it has to offer. This is an excellent way of learning how Jasmine specs and suites work, and working through the examples (without peeking back) will put your Backbone skills to the test too.

Further Reading

- "Testing Backbone Apps with SinonJS" (*http://bit.ly/13WgsG7*) by James Newbery
- "Jasmine Backbone.js Revisited" (*http://bit.ly/11hHphF*) by Chris Strom
- "Phantom.js and Backbone.js (and require.js)" (*http://bit.ly/ZmkeWt*) by Chris Strom

Summary

We have now covered how to write Jasmine tests for Backbone.js models, collections, and views. While testing routing can at times be desirable, some developers feel it can be optimal to leave this to third-party tools such as Selenium.

CHAPTER 14

QUnit

QUnit is a powerful JavaScript test suite written by jQuery team member Jörn Zaefferer (*http://bassistance.de/*) and used by many large open source projects (such as jQuery and Backbone.js) to test their code. It's capable of testing both standard JavaScript code in the browser and code on the server side (where supported environments include Rhino, V8, and SpiderMonkey). This makes it a robust solution for a large number of use cases.

Quite a few Backbone.js contributors feel that QUnit is a better introductory framework for testing if you don't wish to start off with Jasmine and BDD right away. As we'll see later on in this chapter, QUnit can also be combined with third-party solutions such as SinonJS to produce an even more powerful testing solution supporting spies and mocks, which some say is preferable over Jasmine.

My personal recommendation is that it's worth comparing both frameworks and opting for the solution that you feel the most comfortable with.

Getting Set Up

Luckily, getting QUnit set up is a fairly straightforward process that will take less than five minutes.

We first set up a testing environment composed of three files:

- An HTML *structure* for displaying test results
- The *qunit.js* file composing the testing framework
- The *qunit.css* file for styling test results

The latter two of these can be downloaded from the QUnit website (*http://qunitjs.com*).

If you would prefer, you can use a hosted version of the QUnit source files for testing purposes. The hosted URLs can be found at *https://github.com/jquery/qunit/*.

Sample HTML with QUnit-Compatible Markup

```html
<!DOCTYPE html>
<html>
<head>
    <title>QUnit Test Suite</title>

    <link rel="stylesheet" href="qunit.css">
    <script src="qunit.js"></script>

    <!-- Your application -->
    <script src="app.js"></script>

    <!-- Your tests -->
    <script src="tests.js"></script>
</head>
<body>
    <h1 id="qunit-header">QUnit Test Suite</h1>
    <h2 id="qunit-banner"></h2>
    <div id="qunit-testrunner-toolbar"></div>
    <h2 id="qunit-userAgent"></h2>
    <ol id="qunit-tests">test markup, hidden.</ol>
</body>
</html>
```

Let's go through the elements with QUnit mentioned in their ID. When QUnit is running:

- `qunit-header` shows the name of the test suite.
- `qunit-banner` shows up as red if a test fails and green if all tests pass.
- `qunit-testrunner-toolbar` contains additional options for configuring the display of tests.
- `qunit-userAgent` displays the `navigator.userAgent` property.
- `qunit-tests` is a container for our test results.

When running correctly, the preceding test runner looks as shown in Figure 14-1.

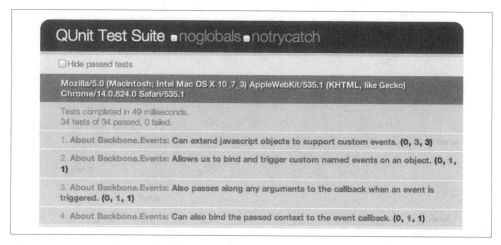

Figure 14-1. The QUnit test runner executing Backbone unit tests in the browser

The numbers of the form (a, b, c) after each test name correspond to a) failed asserts, b) passed asserts, and c) total asserts. Clicking on a test name expands it to display all of the assertions for that test case. Assertions in green have successfully passed (see Figure 14-2).

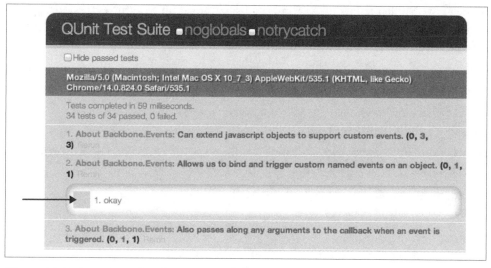

Figure 14-2. Assertions that have successfully passed are displayed with a green marker

If any tests fail, however, the test gets highlighted (and the QUnit banner at the top switches to red, as shown in Figure 14-3).

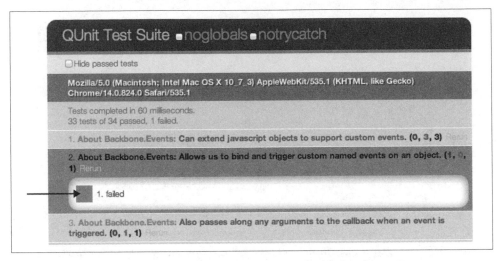

Figure 14-3. Failed tests in the QUnit test runner are highlighted in red

Assertions

QUnit supports a number of basic *assertions*, which are used in tests to verify that the result being returned by our code is what we expect. If an assertion fails, we know that a bug exists. Similar to Jasmine, QUnit can be used to easily test for regressions. Specifically, when a bug is found one can write an assertion to test the existence of the bug, write a patch, and then commit both. If subsequent changes to the code break the test, you'll know what was responsible and be able to address it more easily.

Some of the supported QUnit assertions we're going to look at first are:

ok (state, message)
:   Passes if the first argument is truthy

equal (actual, expected, message)
:   A simple comparison assertion with type coercion

notEqual (actual, expected, message)
:   The opposite of equal()

expect(amount)
:   The number of assertions expected to run within each test

strictEqual(actual, expected, message)
:   Offers a much stricter comparison than equal() and is considered the preferred method of checking equality, as it avoids stumbling on subtle coercion bugs

```
deepEqual( actual, expected, message )
```
Similar to `strictEqual`, comparing the contents (with ===) of the given objects, arrays, and primitives

Basic Test Case Using test(name, callback)

Creating new test cases with QUnit is relatively straightforward and can be done via `test()`, which constructs a test where the first argument is the `name` of the test to be displayed in our results and the second is a `callback` function containing all of our assertions. This is called as soon as QUnit is running.

```
var myString = 'Hello Backbone.js';

test( 'Our first QUnit test - asserting results', function(){

    // ok( boolean, message )
    ok( true, 'the test succeeds');
    ok( false, 'the test fails');

    // equal( actualValue, expectedValue, message )
    equal( myString, 'Hello Backbone.js', 'Expected value: Hello Backbone.js!');
});
```

What we're doing here is defining a variable with a specific value and then testing to ensure the value was what we expected it to be. We did so using the comparison assertion `equal()`, which expects its first argument to be a value being tested and the second argument to be the expected value. We also used `ok()`, which allows us to easily test against functions or variables that evaluate to Booleans.

 Optionally in our test case, we could have passed an expected value to `test()` defining the number of assertions we expect to run. This takes the form: `test( name, [expected], test )`; or by manually setting the expectation at the top of the test function, like so: `expect( 1 )`. I recommend you make a habit of always defining how many assertions you expect. More on this later.

Comparing the Actual Output of a Function Against the Expected Output

As testing a simple static variable is fairly trivial, we can take this further to test actual functions. In the following example, we test the output of a function that reverses a string to ensure that the output is correct using `equal()` and `notEqual()`:

```
function reverseString( str ){
    return str.split('').reverse().join('');
}
```

```
test( 'reverseString()', function() {
    expect( 5 );
    equal( reverseString('hello'), 'olleh', 'The value expected was olleh' );
    equal( reverseString('foobar'), 'raboof', 'The value expected was raboof' );
    equal( reverseString('world'), 'dlrow', 'The value expected was dlrow' );
    notEqual( reverseString('world'), 'dlroo', 'The value was expected to not
    be dlroo' );
    equal( reverseString('bubble'), 'double', 'The value expected was elbbub' );
})
```

Running these tests in the QUnit test runner (which you would see when your HTML test page was loaded), we would find that four of the assertions pass while the last one does not. The reason the test against 'double' fails is because it was purposefully written incorrectly. In your own projects, if a test fails to pass and your assertions are correct, you've probably just found a bug!

Adding Structure to Assertions

Housing all of our assertions in one test case can quickly become difficult to maintain, but luckily QUnit supports structuring blocks of assertions more cleanly. This can be done using module(), a method that allows us to easily group tests together. A typical approach to grouping might be keeping multiple tests for a specific method as part of the same group (module).

Basic QUnit Modules

```
module( 'Module One' );
test( 'first test', function() {} );
test( 'another test', function() {} );

module( 'Module Two' );
test( 'second test', function() {} );
test( 'another test', function() {} );

module( 'Module Three' );
test( 'third test', function() {} );
test( 'another test', function() {} );
```

We can take this further by introducing setup() and teardown() callbacks to our modules, where setup() is run before each test and teardown() is run after each test.

Using setup() and teardown()

```
module( 'Module One', {
    setup: function() {
        // run before
    },
    teardown: function() {
```

```
        // run after
    }
});

test('first test', function() {
    // run the first test
});
```

These callbacks can be used to define (or clear) any components we wish to instantiate for use in one or more of our tests. As we'll see shortly, this is ideal for defining new instances of views, collections, models, or routers from a project that we can then reference across multiple tests.

Using setup() and teardown() for Instantiation and Clean Up

```
// Define a simple model and collection modeling a store and
// list of stores

var Store = Backbone.Model.extend({});

var StoreList = Backbone.Collection.extend({
    model: Store,
    comparator: function( Store ) { return Store.get('name') }
});

// Define a group for our tests
module( 'StoreList sanity check', {
    setup: function() {
        this.list = new StoreList;
        this.list.add(new Store({ name: 'Costcutter' }));
        this.list.add(new Store({ name: 'Target' }));
        this.list.add(new Store({ name: 'Walmart' }));
        this.list.add(new Store({ name: 'Barnes & Noble' }));
    },
    teardown: function() {
        window.errors = null;
    }
});

// Test the order of items added
test( 'test ordering', function() {
    expect( 1 );
    var expected = ['Barnes & Noble', 'Costcutter', 'Target', 'Walmart'];
    var actual = this.list.pluck('name');
    deepEqual( actual, expected, 'is maintained by comparator' );
});
```

Here, a list of stores is created and stored on `setup()`. A `teardown()` callback is used to simply clear a list of errors we might be storing within the window scope, but is otherwise not needed.

Assertion Examples

Before we continue any further, let's review some more examples of how QUnit's various assertions can be correctly used when writing tests:

equal

> A comparison assertion. It passes if `actual == expected`.

```
test( 'equal', 2, function() {
  var actual = 6 - 5;
  equal( actual, true,  'passes as 1 == true' );
  equal( actual, 1,     'passes as 1 == 1' );
});
```

notEqual

> A comparison assertion. It passes if `actual != expected`.

```
test( 'notEqual', 2, function() {
  var actual = 6 - 5;
  notEqual( actual, false, 'passes as 1 != false' );
  notEqual( actual, 0,     'passes as 1 != 0' );
});
```

strictEqual

> A comparison assertion. It passes if `actual === expected`.

```
test( 'strictEqual', 2, function() {
  var actual = 6 - 5;
  strictEqual( actual, true, 'fails as 1 !== true' );
  strictEqual( actual, 1,    'passes as 1 === 1' );
});
```

notStrictEqual

> A comparison assertion. It passes if `actual !== expected`.

```
test('notStrictEqual', 2, function() {
  var actual = 6 - 5;
  notStrictEqual( actual, true,  'passes as 1 !== true' );
  notStrictEqual( actual, 1,     'fails as 1 === 1' );
});
```

deepEqual

> A recursive comparison assertion. Unlike `strictEqual()`, it works on objects, arrays, and primitives.

```
test('deepEqual', 4, function() {
  var actual = {q: 'foo', t: 'bar'};
  var el = $('div');
  var children = $('div').children();

  equal( actual, {q: 'foo', t: 'bar'},   'fails - objects are not equal
    using equal()' );
  deepEqual( actual, {q: 'foo', t: 'bar'},
```

```
      'passes - objects are equal' );
    equal( el, children, 'fails - jQuery objects are not the same' );
    deepEqual(el, children, 'fails - objects not equivalent' );

  });
```

notDeepEqual

A comparison assertion. This returns the opposite of deepEqual.

```
test('notDeepEqual', 2, function() {
  var actual = {q: 'foo', t: 'bar'};
  notEqual( actual, {q: 'foo', t: 'bar'},   'passes - objects are not equal' );
  notDeepEqual( actual, {q: 'foo', t: 'bar'},   'fails - objects are
    equivalent' );
});
```

raises

An assertion that tests if a callback throws any exceptions.

```
test('raises', 1, function() {
  raises(function() {
    throw new Error( 'Oh no! It`s an error!' );
  }, 'passes - an error was thrown inside our callback');
});
```

Fixtures

From time to time, we may need to write tests that modify the DOM. Managing the cleanup of such operations between tests can be a genuine pain, but thankfully QUnit has a solution to this problem in the form of the #qunit-fixture:

```
<!DOCTYPE html>
<html>
<head>
    <title>QUnit Test</title>
    <link rel="stylesheet" href="qunit.css">
    <script src="qunit.js"></script>
    <script src="app.js"></script>
    <script src="tests.js"></script>
</head>
<body>
    <h1 id="qunit-header">QUnit Test</h1>
    <h2 id="qunit-banner"></h2>
    <div id="qunit-testrunner-toolbar"></div>
    <h2 id="qunit-userAgent"></h2>
    <ol id="qunit-tests"></ol>
    <div id="qunit-fixture"></div>
</body>
</html>
```

We can either opt to place static markup in the fixture or just insert/append any DOM elements we may need to it. QUnit will automatically reset the innerHTML of the fixture after each test to its original value. In case you're using jQuery, it's useful to know that QUnit checks for its availability and will opt to use $(el).html() instead, which will clean up any jQuery event handlers too.

Fixtures Example

Now let's go through a more complete example of using fixtures. One thing that most of us are used to doing in jQuery is working with lists—they're often used to define the markup for menus, grids, and a number of other components. You may have used jQuery plug-ins before that manipulated a given list in a particular way, and it can be useful to test that the final (manipulated) output of the plug-in is what was expected.

For the purposes of our next example, we're going to use Ben Alman's $.enumerate() plug-in, which can prepend each item in a list by its index, optionally allowing us to set what the first number in the list is. The code snippet for the plug-in can be found here, followed by an example of the output it generates:

```
$.fn.enumerate = function( start ) {
    if ( typeof start !== 'undefined' ) {
        // Since `start` value was provided, enumerate and return
        // the initial jQuery object to allow chaining.

        return this.each(function(i){
            $(this).prepend( '<b>' + ( i + start ) + '</b> ' );
        });

    } else {
        // Since no `start` value was provided, function as a
        // getter, returning the appropriate value from the first
        // selected element.

        var val = this.eq( 0 ).children( 'b' ).eq( 0 ).text();
        return Number( val );
    }
};

/*
    <ul>
      <li>1. hello</li>
      <li>2. world</li>
      <li>3. i</li>
      <li>4. am</li>
      <li>5. foo</li>
    </ul>
*/
```

Let's now write some tests for the plug-in. First, we define the markup for a list containing some sample items inside our qunit-fixture element:

```
<div id="qunit-fixture">
    <ul>
        <li>hello</li>
        <li>world</li>
        <li>i</li>
        <li>am</li>
        <li>foo</li>
    </ul>
</div>
```

Next, we need to think about what should be tested. $.enumerate() supports a few different use cases, including:

No arguments passed
```
$(el).enumerate()
```

0 passed as an argument
```
$(el).enumerate(0)
```

1 passed as an argument
```
$(el).enumerate(1)
```

As the text value for each list item is of the form n. item-text and we require this only to test against the expected output, we can simply access the content using $(el).eq(index).text(). (For more information on .eq(), see *http://api.jquery.com/eq/*.)

Finally, here are our test cases:

```
module('jQuery#enumerate');

test( 'No arguments passed', 5, function() {
  var items = $('#qunit-fixture li').enumerate(); // 0
  equal( items.eq(0).text(), '0. hello', 'first item should have index 0' );
  equal( items.eq(1).text(), '1. world', 'second item should have index 1' );
  equal( items.eq(2).text(), '2. i', 'third item should have index 2' );
  equal( items.eq(3).text(), '3. am', 'fourth item should have index 3' );
  equal( items.eq(4).text(), '4. foo', 'fifth item should have index 4' );
});

test( '0 passed as an argument', 5, function() {
  var items = $('#qunit-fixture li').enumerate( 0 );
  equal( items.eq(0).text(), '0. hello', 'first item should have index 0' );
  equal( items.eq(1).text(), '1. world', 'second item should have index 1' );
  equal( items.eq(2).text(), '2. i', 'third item should have index 2' );
  equal( items.eq(3).text(), '3. am', 'fourth item should have index 3' );
  equal( items.eq(4).text(), '4. foo', 'fifth item should have index 4' );
});

test( '1 passed as an argument', 3, function() {
  var items = $('#qunit-fixture li').enumerate( 1 );
  equal( items.eq(0).text(), '1. hello', 'first item should have index 1' );
  equal( items.eq(1).text(), '2. world', 'second item should have index 2' );
  equal( items.eq(2).text(), '3. i', 'third item should have index 3' );
```

```
    equal( items.eq(3).text(), '4. am', 'fourth item should have index 4' );
    equal( items.eq(4).text(), '5. foo', 'fifth item should have index 5' );
});
```

Asynchronous Code

As with Jasmine, the effort required to run synchronous tests with QUnit is fairly minimal. That said, what about tests that require asynchronous callbacks (such as expensive
processes, Ajax requests, and so on)? When we're dealing with asynchronous code,
rather than letting QUnit control when the next test runs, we can tell it that we need it
to stop running and wait until it's OK to continue once again.

Remember: running asynchronous code without any special considerations can cause
incorrect assertions to appear in other tests, so we want to make sure we get it right.

Writing QUnit tests for asynchronous code is made possible via the start() and stop()
methods, which programmatically set the start and stop points during such tests. Here's
a simple example:

```
test('An async test', function(){
    stop();
    expect( 1 );
    $.ajax({
        url: '/test',
        dataType: 'json',
        success: function( data ){
            deepEqual(data, {
                topic: 'hello',
                message: 'hi there!''
            });
            ok(true, 'Asynchronous test passed!');
            start();
        }
    });
});
```

A jQuery $.ajax() request is used to connect to a test resource and assert that the data
returned is correct. deepEqual() is used here because it allows us to compare different
data types (for example, objects, arrays) and ensures that what is returned is exactly
what we're expecting. We know that our Ajax request is asynchronous, so we first call
stop(), then run the code making the request, and finally, at the very end of our callback,
inform QUnit that it is OK to continue running other tests.

Rather than including `stop()`, we can simply exclude it and substitute `test()` with `asyncTest()` if we prefer. This improves readability when you're dealing with a mixture of asynchronous and synchronous tests in your suite. While this setup should work fine for many use cases, there is no guarantee that the callback in our `$.ajax()` request will actually get called. To factor this into our tests, we can use `expect()` once again to define how many assertions we expect to see within our test. This is a healthy safety blanket, as it ensures that if a test completes with an insufficient number of assertions, we know something went wrong and can fix it.

CHAPTER 15

SinonJS

Similar to the section on testing Backbone.js apps using the Jasmine BDD framework, we're nearly ready to take what we've learned and write a number of QUnit tests for our Todo application.

Before we start, though, you may have noticed that QUnit doesn't support test spies. Test spies are functions that record arguments, exceptions, and return values for any of their calls. They're typically used to test callbacks and how functions may be used in the application being tested. In testing frameworks, spies usually are anonymous functions or wrappers around functions that already exist.

What Is SinonJS?

In order for us to substitute support for spies in QUnit, we will be taking advantage of a mocking framework called SinonJS (*http://sinonjs.org/*) by Christian Johansen. We will also be using the SinonJS-QUnit adapter (*http://sinonjs.org/qunit/*), which provides seamless integration with QUnit (meaning setup is minimal). SinonJS is completely test-framework–agnostic and should be easy to use with any testing framework, so it's ideal for our needs.

The framework supports three features we'll be taking advantage of for unit testing our application:

- Anonymous spies
- Spying on existing methods
- A rich inspection interface

Basic Spies

Using `this.spy()` without any arguments creates an anonymous spy. This is comparable to `jasmine.createSpy()`. We can observe basic usage of a SinonJS spy in the following example:

```
test('should call all subscribers for a message exactly once', function () {
    var message = getUniqueString();
    var spy = this.spy();

    PubSub.subscribe( message, spy );
    PubSub.publishSync( message, 'Hello World' );

    ok( spy.calledOnce, 'the subscriber was called once' );
});
```

Spying on Existing Functions

We can also use `this.spy()` to spy on existing functions (like jQuery's `$.ajax`) in the example that follows. When we are spying on a function that already exists, the function behaves normally, but we get access to data about its calls, which can be very useful for testing purposes.

```
test( 'should inspect the jQuery.getJSON usage of jQuery.ajax', function () {
    this.spy( jQuery, 'ajax' );

    jQuery.getJSON( '/todos/completed' );

    ok( jQuery.ajax.calledOnce );
    equals( jQuery.ajax.getCall(0).args[0].url, '/todos/completed' );
    equals( jQuery.ajax.getCall(0).args[0].dataType, 'json' );
});
```

Inspection Interface

SinonJS comes with a rich spy interface that allows us to test whether a spy was called with a specific argument, determine if it was called a specific number of times, and test against the values of arguments. You can find a complete list of features supported in the interface on SinonJS.org (*http://sinonjs.org/docs/*), but let's take a look at some examples demonstrating some of the most commonly used ones.

Matching arguments: Test that a spy was called with a specific set of arguments

```
test( 'Should call a subscriber with standard matching': function () {
    var spy = sinon.spy();

    PubSub.subscribe( 'message', spy );
    PubSub.publishSync( 'message', { id: 45 } );
```

```
        assertTrue( spy.calledWith( { id: 45 } ) );
});
```

Stricter argument matching: Test that a spy was called at least once with specific arguments and no others

```
test( 'Should call a subscriber with strict matching': function () {
    var spy = sinon.spy();

    PubSub.subscribe( 'message', spy );
    PubSub.publishSync( 'message', 'many', 'arguments' );
    PubSub.publishSync( 'message', 12, 34 );

    // This passes
    assertTrue( spy.calledWith('many') );

    // This however, fails
    assertTrue( spy.calledWithExactly( 'many' ) );
});
```

Testing call order: Test that a spy was called before or after another spy

```
test( 'Should call a subscriber and maintain call order': function () {
    var a = sinon.spy();
    var b = sinon.spy();

    PubSub.subscribe( 'message', a );
    PubSub.subscribe( 'event', b );

    PubSub.publishSync( 'message', { id: 45 } );
    PubSub.publishSync( 'event', [1, 2, 3] );

    assertTrue( a.calledBefore(b) );
    assertTrue( b.calledAfter(a) );
});
```

Match execution counts: Test that a spy was called a specific number of times

```
test( 'Should call a subscriber and check call counts', function () {
    var message = getUniqueString();
    var spy = this.spy();

    PubSub.subscribe( message, spy );
    PubSub.publishSync( message, 'some payload' );


    // Passes if spy was called once and only once.
    ok( spy.calledOnce ); // calledTwice and calledThrice are also supported

    // The number of recorded calls.
    equal( spy.callCount, 1 );

    // Directly checking the arguments of the call
```

```
        equals( spy.getCall(0).args[0], message );
    });
```

Stubs and Mocks

SinonJS also supports two other powerful features: *stubs* and *mocks*. Both stubs and mocks implement all of the features of the spy API, but have some added functionality.

Stubs

A stub allows us to replace any existing behavior for a specific method with something else. Stubs can be very useful for simulating exceptions and are most often used to write test cases when certain dependencies of your codebase may not yet be written.

Let us briefly re-explore our Backbone Todo application, which contained a Todo model and a `TodoList` collection. For the purpose of this walkthrough, we want to isolate our `TodoList` collection and fake the Todo model to test how adding new models might behave.

We can pretend that the models have yet to be written just to demonstrate how stubbing might be carried out. A shell collection containing only a reference to the model to be used might look like this:

```
var TodoList = Backbone.Collection.extend({
    model: Todo
});

// Let's assume our instance of this collection is
this.todoList;
```

Assuming our collection is instantiating new models itself, it's necessary for us to stub the model's constructor function for the test. We can do this by creating a simple stub as follows:

```
this.todoStub = sinon.stub( window, 'Todo' );
```

The preceding creates a stub of the `Todo` method on the `window` object. When stubbing a persistent object, we must restore it to its original state. We can do this in a `tear down()` as follows:

```
this.todoStub.restore();
```

After this, we need to alter what the constructor returns, which we can do efficiently using a plain `Backbone.Model` constructor. While this isn't a Todo model, it does still provide us an actual Backbone model.

```
setup: function() {
    this.model = new Backbone.Model({
        id: 2,
        title: 'Hello world'
```

```
    });
    this.todoStub.returns( this.model );
  });
```

The expectation here might be that this snippet would ensure our `TodoList` collection always instantiates a stubbed Todo model, but because a reference to the model in the collection is already present, we need to reset the `model` property of our collection as follows:

```
this.todoList.model = Todo;
```

The result of this is that when our `TodoList` collection instantiates new Todo models, it will return our plain Backbone model instance as desired. This allows us to write a test for the addition of new model literals as follows:

```
module( 'Should function when instantiated with model literals', {

  setup:function() {

    this.todoStub = sinon.stub(window, 'Todo');
    this.model = new Backbone.Model({
      id: 2,
      title: 'Hello world'
    });

    this.todoStub.returns(this.model);
    this.todos = new TodoList();

    // Let's reset the relationship to use a stub
    this.todos.model = Todo;

    // add a model
    this.todos.add({
      id: 2,
      title: 'Hello world'
    });
  },

  teardown: function() {
    this.todoStub.restore();
  }

});

test('should add a model', function() {
    equal( this.todos.length, 1 );
});

test('should find a model by id', function() {
    equal( this.todos.get(5).get('id'), 5 );
  });
});
```

Mocks

Mocks are effectively the same as stubs, but they mock a complete API and have some built-in expectations for how they should be used. The difference between a mock and a spy is that the expectations for mocks' use are predefined and the test will fail if any of these are not met.

Here's a snippet with sample usage of a mock based on PubSubJS. Here, we have a `clearTodo()` method as a callback and use mocks to verify its behavior.

```
test('should call all subscribers when exceptions', function () {
    var myAPI = { clearTodo: function () {} };

    var spy = this.spy();
    var mock = this.mock( myAPI );
    mock.expects( 'clearTodo' ).once().throws();

    PubSub.subscribe( 'message', myAPI.clearTodo );
    PubSub.subscribe( 'message', spy );
    PubSub.publishSync( 'message', undefined );

    mock.verify();
    ok( spy.calledOnce );
});
```

Exercise

We can now begin writing tests for our Todo application, which are listed and separated by component (for example, models, collections, and so on). It's useful to pay attention to the name of the test, the logic being tested, and most importantly the assertions being made, as this will give you some insight into how what we've learned can be applied to a complete application.

To get the most out of this section, I recommend looking at the QUnit Koans included in the *practicals/qunit-koans* folder—this is a port of the Backbone.js Jasmine Koans over to QUnit.

 In case you haven't had a chance to try out one of the Koans kits yet, they are a set of unit tests using a specific testing framework that both demonstrate how a set of tests for an application may be written, but also leave some tests unfilled so that you can complete them as an exercise.

Models

For our models, we want to at minimum test that:

- New instances can be created with the expected default values.
- Attributes can be set and retrieved correctly.
- Changes to state correctly fire off custom events where needed.
- Validation rules are correctly enforced.

```
module( 'About Backbone.Model');

test('Can be created with default values for its attributes.', function() {
    expect( 3 );

    var todo = new Todo();
    equal( todo.get('text'), '' );
    equal( todo.get('done'), false );
    equal( todo.get('order'), 0 );
});

test('Will set attributes on the model instance when created.', function() {
    expect( 1 );

    var todo = new Todo( { text: 'Get oil change for car.' } );
    equal( todo.get('text'), 'Get oil change for car.' );

});

test('Will call a custom initialize function on the model instance when
    created.', function() {
    expect( 1 );

    var toot = new Todo
        ({ text: 'Stop monkeys from throwing their own crap!' });
    equal( toot.get('text'),
        'Stop monkeys from throwing their own rainbows!' );
});

test('Fires a custom event when the state changes.', function() {
    expect( 1 );

    var spy = this.spy();
    var todo = new Todo();

    todo.on( 'change', spy );
    // Change the model state
    todo.set( { text: 'new text' } );

    ok( spy.calledOnce, 'A change event callback was correctly triggered' );
```

```
        });


    test('Can contain custom validation rules, and will trigger an invalid
        event on failed validation.', function() {
        expect( 3 );

        var errorCallback = this.spy();
        var todo = new Todo();

        todo.on('invalid', errorCallback);
        // Change the model state in such a way that validation will fail
        todo.set( { done: 'not a boolean' } );

        ok( errorCallback.called, 'A failed validation correctly triggered an
        error' );
        notEqual( errorCallback.getCall(0), undefined );
        equal( errorCallback.getCall(0).args[1], 'Todo.done must be a boolean
        value.' );

    });
```

Collections

For our collection we'll want to test that:

- The collection has a Todo model.
- Uses `localStorage` for syncing.
- That `done()`, `remaining()`, and `clear()` work as expected.
- The order for todos is numerically correct.

```
    describe('Test Collection', function() {

      beforeEach(function() {

        // Define new todos
        this.todoOne = new Todo;
        this.todoTwo = new Todo({
          title: "Buy some milk"
        });

        // Create a new collection of todos for testing
        return this.todos = new TodoList([this.todoOne, this.todoTwo]);
      });

      it('Has the Todo model', function() {
        return expect(this.todos.model).toBe(Todo);
      });

      it('Uses localStorage', function() {
```

```
    return expect(this.todos.localStorage).toEqual(new Store
    ('todos-backbone'));
  });

  describe('done', function() {
    return it('returns an array of the todos that are done', function() {
      this.todoTwo.done = true;
      return expect(this.todos.done()).toEqual([this.todoTwo]);
    });
  });

  describe('remaining', function() {
    return it('returns an array of the todos that are not done', function() {
      this.todoTwo.done = true;
      return expect(this.todos.remaining()).toEqual([this.todoOne]);
    });
  });

  describe('clear', function() {
    return it('destroys the current todo from localStorage', function() {
      expect(this.todos.models).toEqual([this.todoOne, this.todoTwo]);
      this.todos.clear(this.todoOne);
      return expect(this.todos.models).toEqual([this.todoTwo]);
    });
  });

  return describe('Order sets the order on todos ascending numerically',
    function() {
    it('defaults to one when there arent any items in the collection',
    function() {
      this.emptyTodos = new TodoApp.Collections.TodoList;
      return expect(this.emptyTodos.order()).toEqual(0);
    });

    return it('Increments the order by one each time', function() {
      expect(this.todos.order(this.todoOne)).toEqual(1);
      return expect(this.todos.order(this.todoTwo)).toEqual(2);
    });
  });
});

});
```

Views

For our views, we want to ensure:

- They are being correctly tied to a DOM element when created
- They can render, after which the DOM representation of the view should be visible
- They support wiring up view methods to DOM elements

One could also take this further and test that user interactions with the view correctly result in any models that need to be changed being updated correctly.

```
module( 'About Backbone.View', {
    setup: function() {
        $('body').append('<ul id="todoList"></ul>');
        this.todoView = new TodoView({ model: new Todo() });
    },
    teardown: function() {
        this.todoView.remove();
        $('#todoList').remove();
    }
});

test('Should be tied to a DOM element when created, based off the property
provided.', function() {
    expect( 1 );
    equal( this.todoView.el.tagName.toLowerCase(), 'li' );
});

test('Is backed by a model instance, which provides the data.', function() {
    expect( 2 );
    notEqual( this.todoView.model, undefined );
    equal( this.todoView.model.get('done'), false );
});

test('Can render, after which the DOM representation of the view will be
visible.', function() {
    this.todoView.render();

    // Append the DOM representation of the view to ul#todoList
    $('ul#todoList').append(this.todoView.el);

    // Check the number of li items rendered to the list
    equal($('#todoList').find('li').length, 1);
});

asyncTest('Can wire up view methods to DOM elements.', function() {
    expect( 2 );
    var viewElt;

    $('#todoList').append( this.todoView.render().el );

    setTimeout(function() {
        viewElt = $('#todoList li input.check').filter(':first');

        equal(viewElt.length > 0, true);

        // Ensure QUnit knows we can continue
        start();
    }, 1000, 'Expected DOM Elt to exist');
```

```
    // Trigger the view to toggle the 'done' status on an item or items
    $('#todoList li input.check').click();

    // Check the done status for the model is true
    equal( this.todoView.model.get('done'), true );
});
```

App

It can also be useful to write tests for any application bootstrap you may have in place. For the following module, our setup instantiates and appends to a TodoApp view, and we can test anything from local instances of views being correctly defined to application interactions correctly resulting in changes to instances of local collections.

```
module( 'About Backbone Applications' , {
    setup: function() {
        Backbone.localStorageDB = new Store('testTodos');
        $('#qunit-fixture').append('<div id="app"></div>');
        this.App = new TodoApp({ appendTo: $('#app') });
    },

    teardown: function() {
        this.App.todos.reset();
        $('#app').remove();
    }
});

test('Should bootstrap the application by initializing the Collection.',
function() {
    expect( 2 );

    // The todos collection should not be undefined
    notEqual( this.App.todos, undefined );

    // The initial length of our todos should however be zero
    equal( this.App.todos.length, 0 );
});

test( 'Should bind Collection events to View creation.' , function() {

    // Set the value of a brand new todo within the input box
    $('#new-todo').val( 'Buy some milk' );

    // Trigger the enter (return) key to be pressed inside #new-todo
    // causing the new item to be added to the todos collection
    $('#new-todo').trigger(new $.Event( 'keypress', { keyCode: 13 } ));

    // The length of our collection should now be 1
    equal( this.App.todos.length, 1 );
});
```

Further Reading and Resources

That's it for this section on testing applications with QUnit and SinonJS. I encourage you to try out the QUnit Backbone.js Koans (*https://github.com/addyosmani/backbone-koans-qunit*) and see if you can extend some of the examples. For further reading, consider looking at some of these additional resources:

- *Test-Driven JavaScript Development (book) (http://tddjs.com/)*
- *SinonJS/QUnit adapter (http://sinonjs.org/qunit/)*
- *Using Sinon.JS with QUnit (http://bit.ly/16tTGWl)*
- *Automating JavaScript Testing with QUnit (http://bit.ly/11YzmrQ)*
- *Unit Testing with QUnit (http://bit.ly/18v2dFc)*
- *Another QUnit/Backbone.js demo project (http://bit.ly/12s5cuK)*
- *SinonJS helpers for Backbone (http://bit.ly/17zHDF3)*

CHAPTER 16

Conclusions

I hope that you've found this introduction to Backbone.js of value. What you've hopefully learned is that while building a JavaScript-heavy application using nothing more than a DOM manipulation library (such as jQuery) is certainly a possible feat, it is difficult to build anything nontrivial without any formal structure in place. Your nested pile of jQuery callbacks and DOM elements is unlikely to scale and can be very difficult to maintain as your application grows.

The beauty of Backbone.js is its simplicity. It's very small given the functionality and flexibility it provides, which is evident if you begin to study the Backbone.js source. In the words of Jeremy Ashkenas: "The essential premise at the heart of Backbone has always been to try and discover the minimal set of data-structuring (Models and Collections) and user interface (Views and URLs) primitives that are useful when building web applications with JavaScript." It just helps you improve the structure of your applications, helping you better separate concerns. There isn't anything more to it than that.

Backbone offers models with key/value bindings and events, collections with an API of rich enumerable methods, declarative views with event handling, and a simple way to connect an existing API to your client-side application over a RESTful JSON interface. Use it, and you can abstract away data into sane models and your DOM manipulation into views, binding them together using nothing more than events.

Almost any developer working on JavaScript applications for a while will ultimately create a similar solution if that individual values architecture and maintainability. The alternative to using it or something similar is rolling your own—often a process that involves gluing together a diverse set of libraries that weren't built to work together. You might use jQuery BBQ for history management and Handlebars for templating, while writing abstracts for organizing and testing code by yourself.

Contrast this with Backbone, which has *literate (http://en.wikipedia.org/wiki/Liter ate_programming)* documentation (*http://backbonejs.org/docs/backbone.html*) of the source code, a thriving community of both users and hackers, and a large number of questions about it asked and answered daily on sites like Stack Overflow (*http://stacko verflow.com/search?q=backbone*). Rather than reinventing the wheel, you can reap the many advantages to structuring your application using a solution based on the collective knowledge and experience of an entire community.

In addition to helping provide sane structure to your applications, Backbone is highly extensible, supporting more custom architecture should you require more than what is prescribed out of the box. This is evident by the number of extensions and plug-ins that have been released for it over the past year, including some we have touched upon (such as MarionetteJS and Thorax).

These days, Backbone.js powers many complex web applications, ranging from the LinkedIn mobile app (*http://touch.www.linkedin.com/mobile.html*) to popular RSS readers such as NewsBlur (*http://newsblur.com*) through to social commentary widgets such as Disqus (*http://disqus.com/*). This small library of simple but sane abstractions has helped to create a new generation of rich web applications, and I and my collaborators hope that in time it can help you too.

If you're wondering whether it is worth using Backbone on a project, ask yourself whether what you are building is complex enough to merit using it. Are you hitting the limits of your ability to organize your code? Will your application have regular changes to what is displayed in the UI without a trip back to the server for new pages? Would you benefit from a separation of concerns? If so, a solution like Backbone may be able to help.

Google's Gmail is often cited as an example of a well-built single-page app. If you've used it, you might have noticed that it requests a large initial chunk, representing much of the JavaScript, CSS, and HTML most users will need, and everything extra needed after that occurs in the background. Gmail can easily switch between your inbox to your spam folder without having to rerender the whole page. Libraries like Backbone make it easier for web developers to create experiences like this.

That said, Backbone won't be able to help if you're planning to build something that isn't worth the learning curve associated with a library. If your application or site will still be using the server to do the heavy lifting of constructing and serving complete pages to the browser, you may find just using plain JavaScript or jQuery for simple effects or interactions to be more appropriate. Spend time assessing how suitable Backbone might be for you, and make the right choice on a per-project basis.

Backbone is neither difficult to learn nor use; however, the time and effort you spend learning how to structure applications using it will be well worth it. While reading this book will equip you with the fundamentals you need to understand the library, the best way to learn is to try building your own real-world applications. You will hopefully find that the end product is cleaner, better organized, and more maintainable code.

With that, I wish you the very best with your onward journey into the world of Backbone and will leave you with a quote from American writer Henry Miller (*http://en.wikipe dia.org/wiki/Henry_Miller*): "One's destination is never a place, but a new way of seeing things."

Further Learning

A Simple JavaScript MVC Implementation

A comprehensive discussion of Backbone's implementation is beyond the scope of this book. I can, however, present a simple MVC library—which we will call Cranium.js—that illustrates how frameworks such as Backbone implement the MVC pattern.

Like Backbone, we will rely on Underscore (*http://underscorejs.org*) for inheritance and templating.

Event System

At the heart of our JavaScript MVC implementation is an Event system (object) based on the publisher-subscriber pattern, which makes it possible for MVC components to communicate in an elegant, decoupled manner. Subscribers listen for specific events of interest and react when publishers broadcast these events.

Event is mixed into both the view and model components so that instances of either of these components can publish events of interest.

```
// cranium.js - Cranium.Events

var Cranium = Cranium || {};

// Set DOM selection utility
var $ = document.querySelector.bind(document) || this.jQuery || this.Zepto;

// Mix in to any object in order to provide it with custom events.
var Events = Cranium.Events = {
  // Keeps list of events and associated listeners
  channels: {},

  // Counter
  eventNumber: 0,
```

```
     // Announce events and passes data to the listeners;
     trigger: function (events, data) {
       for (var topic in Cranium.Events.channels){
         if (Cranium.Events.channels.hasOwnProperty(topic)) {
           if (topic.split("-")[0] == events){
             Cranium.Events.channels[topic](data) !== false ||
             delete Cranium.Events.channels[topic];
           }
         }
       }
     },
     // Registers an event type and its listener
     on: function (events, callback) {
       Cranium.Events.channels[events + --Cranium.Events.eventNumber] = callback;
     },
     // Unregisters an event type and its listener
     off: function(topic) {
       delete Cranium.Events.channels[topic];
     }
};
```

The Event system makes it possible for:

- A view to notify its subscribers of user interaction (such as clicks or input in a form), to update/rerender its presentation, etc.

- A model whose data has changed to notify its subscribers to update themselves (for example, view to rerender to show accurate/updated data) and so on.

Models

Models manage the (domain-specific) data for an application. They are concerned with neither the user interface nor presentation layers, but instead represent structured data that an application may require. When a model changes (such as when it is updated), it will typically notify its observers (subscribers) that a change has occurred so that they may react accordingly.

Let's see a simple implementation of the model:

```
// cranium.js - Cranium.Model

// Attributes represents data, model's properties.
// These are to be passed at Model instantiation.
// Also we are creating id for each Model instance
// so that it can identify itself (e.g., on chage
// announcements)
var Model = Cranium.Model = function (attributes) {
    this.id = _.uniqueId('model');
    this.attributes = attributes || {};
```

```
};

// Getter (accessor) method;
// returns named data item
Cranium.Model.prototype.get = function(attrName) {
    return this.attributes[attrName];
};

// Setter (mutator) method;
// Set/mix in into model mapped data (e.g.{name: "John"})
// and publishes the change event
Cranium.Model.prototype.set = function(attrs){
    if (_.isObject(attrs)) {
      _.extend(this.attributes, attrs);
      this.change(this.attributes);
    }
    return this;
};

// Returns clone of the Models data object
// (used for view template rendering)
Cranium.Model.prototype.toJSON = function(options) {
    return _.clone(this.attributes);
};

// Helper function that announces changes to the Model
// and passes the new data
Cranium.Model.prototype.change = function(attrs){
    this.trigger(this.id + 'update', attrs);
};

// Mix in Event system
_.extend(Cranium.Model.prototype, Cranium.Events);
```

Views

Views are a visual representation of models that present a filtered view of their current state. A view typically observes a model and is notified when the model changes, allowing the view to update itself accordingly. Design pattern literature commonly refers to views as *dumb*, given that their knowledge of models and controllers in an application is limited.

Let's explore views a little further using a simple JavaScript example:

```
// DOM View
var View = Cranium.View = function (options) {
  // Mix in options object (e.g., extending functionality)
  _.extend(this, options);
  this.id = _.uniqueId('view');
};
```

```
// Mix in Event system
_.extend(Cranium.View.prototype, Cranium.Events);
```

Controllers

Controllers are an intermediary between models and views and are classically responsible for two tasks:

- Updating the view when the model changes
- Updating the model when the user manipulates the view

```
// cranium.js - Cranium.Controller

// Controller tying together a model and view
var Controller = Cranium.Controller = function(options){
  // Mix in options object (e.g extending functionality)
  _.extend(this, options);
  this.id = _.uniqueId('controller');
  var parts, selector, eventType;

  // Parses Events object passed during the definition of the
  // controller and maps it to the defined method to handle it;
  if(this.events){
    _.each(this.events, function(method, eventName){
      parts = eventName.split('.');
      selector = parts[0];
      eventType = parts[1];
      $(selector)['on' + eventType] = this[method];
    }.bind(this));
  }
};
```

Practical Usage

Here is the HTML template for the primer that follows:

```
<!doctype html>
<html lang="en">
<head>
  <meta charset="utf-8">
  <title></title>
  <meta name="description" content="">
</head>
<body>
<div id="todo">
</div>
  <script type="text/template" class="todo-template">
    <div>
      <input id="todo_complete" type="checkbox" <%= completed %>>
      <%= title %>
    </div>
```

```
    </script>
    <script src="underscore-min.js"></script>
    <script src="cranium.js"></script>
    <script src="example.js"></script>
  </body>
  </html>
```

Cranium.js usage:

```javascript
// example.js - usage of Cranium MVC

// And todo instance
var todo1 = new Cranium.Model({
    title: "",
    completed: ""
});

console.log("First todo title - nothing set: " + todo1.get('title'));
todo1.set({title: "Do something"});
console.log("Its changed now: " + todo1.get('title'));
''
// View instance
var todoView = new Cranium.View({
  // DOM element selector
  el: '#todo',

  // Todo template; Underscore templating used
  template: _.template($('.todo-template').innerHTML),

  init: function (model) {
    this.render( model.toJSON() );

    this.on(model.id + 'update', this.render.bind(this));
  },
  render: function (data) {
    console.log("View about to render.");
    $(this.el).innerHTML = this.template( data );
  }
});

var todoController = new Cranium.Controller({
  // Specify the model to update
  model: todo1,

  // and the view to observe this model
  view:  todoView,

  events: {
    "#todo.click" : "toggleComplete"
  },

  // Initialize everything
  initialize: function () {
```

```
        this.view.init(this.model);
        return this;
    },
    // Toggles the value of the todo in the Model
    toggleComplete: function () {
        var completed = todoController.model.get('completed');
        console.log("Todo old 'completed' value?", completed);
        todoController.model.set({ completed: (!completed) ? 'checked': '' });
        console.log("Todo new 'completed' value?",
        todoController.model.get('completed'));
        return this;
    }
});


    // Let's start things off
    todoController.initialize();

    todo1.set({ title: "Due to this change Model will notify View and
    it will rerender"});
```

Samuel Clay, one of the authors of the first version of Backbone.js, says of Cranium.js: "Unsurprisingly, [it] looks a whole lot like the beginnings of Backbone. Views are dumb, so they get very little boilerplate and setup. Models are responsible for their attributes and announcing changes to those models."

I hope you've found this implementation helpful in explaining how you would go about writing your own library like Backbone from scratch, but more so that it encourages you to take advantage of mature existing solutions where possible but never be afraid to explore deeper down into what makes them tick.

MVP

Model-View-Presenter (MVP) is a derivative of the MVC design pattern that focuses on improving presentation logic. It originated at a company named Taligent (*http://en.wikipedia.org/wiki/Taligent*) in the early 1990s while the company was working on a model for a C++ CommonPoint environment. While both MVC and MVP target the separation of concerns across multiple components, there are some fundamental differences between them.

For the purposes of this summary, we will focus on the version of MVP most suitable for web-based architectures.

Models, Views, and Presenters

The P in MVP stands for *presenter*. It's a component that contains the user interface business logic for the view. Unlike MVC, invocations from the view are delegated to the presenter, which are decoupled from the view and instead talk to it through an interface. This allows for all kinds of useful things such as being able to mock views in unit tests.

The most common implementation of MVP is one that uses a *passive view* (a view that, for all intents and purposes, is dumb), containing little to no logic. MVP models are almost identical to MVC models and handle application data. The presenter acts as a mediator that talks to both the view and model; however, the view and model are isolated from each other. Presenters effectively bind models to views, a responsibility held by controllers in MVC. Presenters are at the heart of the MVP pattern, and as you can guess, incorporate the presentation logic behind views.

Solicited by a view, presenters perform any work having to do with user requests and pass data back to them. In this respect, they retrieve data, manipulate it, and determine how the data should be displayed in the view. In some implementations, the presenter also interacts with a service layer to persist data (models). Models may trigger events but it's the presenter's role to subscribe to them so that the presenter can update the view. In this passive architecture, we have no concept of direct data binding. Views expose setters that presenters can use to set data.

The benefit of this change from MVC is that it increases the testability of your application and provides a cleaner separation between the view and the model. This isn't without its costs, as the lack of data binding support in the pattern can often mean having to take care of this task separately.

Although a common implementation of a passive view (*http://bit.ly/132Ez3b*) is for the view to implement an interface, there are variations on it, including the use of events that can decouple the view from the presenter a little more. As we don't have the interface construct in JavaScript, we're using it more and more as a protocol than an explicit interface here. It's technically still an API, and it's probably fair for us to refer to it as an interface from that perspective.

There is also a supervising controller (*http://bit.ly/12s5PUZ*) variation of MVP, which is closer to the MVC and MVVM—Model-View-ViewModel (*http://bit.ly/12s5Lol*)—patterns, as it provides data binding from the model directly from the view. Key/value observing (KVO) plug-ins (such as Derick Bailey's `Backbone.ModelBinding` plug-in) introduce this idea of a supervising controller to Backbone.

MVP or MVC?

MVP is generally used most often in enterprise-level applications where it's necessary to reuse as much presentation logic as possible. Applications with very complex views and a great deal of user interaction may find that MVC doesn't quite fit the bill here, as solving this problem may mean heavily relying on multiple controllers. In MVP, all of this complex logic can be encapsulated in a presenter, which can simplify maintenance greatly.

Because MVP views are defined through an interface and the interface is technically the only point of contact between the system and the view (other than a presenter), this pattern also allows developers to write presentation logic without needing to wait for designers to produce layouts and graphics for the application.

Depending on the implementation, MVP may be more easy to automatically unit-test than MVC. The reason often cited for this is that the presenter can be used as a complete mock of the user interface and so it can be unit-tested independent of other components. In my experience, this really depends on the languages in which you are implementing MVP (there's quite a difference between opting for MVP for a JavaScript project over one for, say, ASP.NET).

At the end of the day, the underlying concerns you may have with MVC will likely hold true for MVP given that the differences between them are mainly semantic. As long as you are cleanly separating concerns into models, views, and controllers (or presenters), you should be achieving most of the same benefits regardless of the pattern you opt for.

MVC, MVP, and Backbone.js

There are very few, if any, architectural JavaScript frameworks that claim to implement the MVC or MVP patterns in their classical form, as many JavaScript developers don't view MVC and MVP as being mutually exclusive (we are actually more likely to see MVP strictly implemented when looking at web frameworks such as ASP.NET or GWT). This is because it's possible to have additional presenter/view logic in your application and yet still consider it a flavor of MVC.

Backbone contributor Irene Ros (*http://ireneros.com/*) subscribes to this way of thinking, as when she separates Backbone views out into their own distinct components, she needs something to actually assemble them for her. This could either be a controller route (such as a `Backbone.Router`) or a callback in response to data being fetched.

That said, some developers do feel that Backbone.js better fits the description of MVP than it does MVC . Their view is that:

- The presenter in MVP better describes the `Backbone.View` (the layer between view templates and the data bound to it) than a controller does.

- The model fits `Backbone.Model` (it isn't that different from the classical MVC model).

- The views best represent templates (such as Handlebars/Mustache markup templates).

A response to this could be that the view can also just be a view (as per MVC) because Backbone is flexible enough to let it be used for multiple purposes. The V in MVC and the P in MVP can both be accomplished by `Backbone.View` because they're able to achieve two purposes: both rendering atomic components and assembling those components rendered by other views.

We've also seen that in Backbone the responsibility of a controller is shared with both the Backbone.View and Backbone.Router, and in the following example we can actually see that aspects of that are certainly true.

Here, our Backbone TodoView uses the Observer pattern to subscribe to changes to a view's model in the line this.model.on('change',...). It also handles templating in the render() method, but unlike some other implementations, user interaction is also handled in the view (see events).

```javascript
// The DOM element for a todo item...
app.TodoView = Backbone.View.extend({

  //... is a list tag.
  tagName:  'li',

  // Pass the contents of the todo template through a templating
  // function, cache it for a single todo
  template: _.template( $('#item-template').html() ),

  // The DOM events specific to an item.
  events: {
    'click .toggle':  'togglecompleted'
  },

  // The TodoView listens for changes to its model, rerendering. Since there's
  // a one-to-one correspondence between a **Todo** and a **TodoView** in this
  // app, we set a direct reference on the model for convenience.
  initialize: function() {
    this.model.on( 'change', this.render, this );
    this.model.on( 'destroy', this.remove, this );
  },

  // Rerender the titles of the todo item.
  render: function() {
    this.$el.html( this.template( this.model.toJSON() ) );
    return this;
  },

  // Toggle the `"completed"` state of the model.
  togglecompleted: function() {
    this.model.toggle();
  },
});
```

Another (quite different) opinion is that Backbone more closely resembles Smalltalk-80 MVC (*http://bit.ly/151NYLr*), which we covered earlier.

As MarionetteJS author Derick Bailey has written (*http://bit.ly/131ML2y*), it's ultimately best not to force Backbone to fit any specific design patterns. Design patterns should be considered flexible guides to how applications may be structured, and in this respect, Backbone doesn't fit either MVC nor MVP perfectly. Instead, it borrows some of the best concepts from multiple architectural patterns and creates a flexible framework that just works well. Call it *the Backbone way*, MV*, or whatever helps reference its flavor of application architecture.

It *is*, however, worth understanding where and why these concepts originated, so I hope that my explanations of MVC and MVP have been of help. Most structural JavaScript frameworks will adopt their own take on classical patterns, either intentionally or by accident, but the important thing is that they help us develop applications that are organized, clean, and easy to maintain.

Namespacing

When learning how to use Backbone, you'll find that an important and commonly overlooked area by tutorials is *namespacing*. If you already have experience with namespacing in JavaScript, the following section will provide some advice on how to specifically apply concepts you know to Backbone; however, I will also be covering explanations for beginners to ensure that everyone is on the same page.

What Is Namespacing?

Namespacing is a way to avoid collisions with other objects or variables in the global namespace. Using namespacing reduces the potential of your code breaking because another script on the page is using the same variable names that you are. As a good citizen of the global namespace, you must do your best to minimize the possibility of your code breaking another developer's scripts.

JavaScript doesn't really have built-in support for namespaces like other languages, but it does have closures, which can be used to achieve a similar effect.

In this section we'll be taking a look at some examples of how you can namespace your models, views, routers, and other components. The patterns we'll be examining are:

- Single global variables
- Object literals
- Nested namespacing

Single global variables

One popular pattern for namespacing in JavaScript is opting for a single global variable as your primary object of reference. Here's a skeleton implementation of this, where we return an object with functions and properties:

```
var myApplication = (function(){
    function(){
      // ...
    },
    return {
      // ...
    }
})();
```

You've probably seen this technique before. A Backbone-specific example might look like this:

```
var myViews = (function(){
    return {
        TodoView: Backbone.View.extend({ .. }),
        TodosView: Backbone.View.extend({ .. }),
        AboutView: Backbone.View.extend({ .. });
        //etc.
    };
})();
```

Here we can return a set of views, but the same technique could return an entire collection of models, views, and routers depending on how you decide to structure your application. Although this works for certain situations, the biggest challenge with the single global variable pattern is ensuring that no one else has used the same global variable name as you have in the page.

One solution to this problem, as mentioned by Peter Michaux, is to use *prefix name-spacing*. It's a simple concept at heart, but the idea is that you select a common prefix name (in this example, myApplication_) and then define any methods, variables, or other objects after the prefix.

```
var myApplication_todoView = Backbone.View.extend({}),
    myApplication_todosView = Backbone.View.extend({});
```

This is effective from the perspective of trying to lower the chances of a particular variable existing in the global scope, but remember that a uniquely named object can have the same effect. This aside, the biggest issue with the pattern is that it can result in a large number of global objects once your application starts to grow.

For more on Peter's views about the single global variable pattern, read his excellent post on them (*http://bit.ly/18v4osf*).

There are several other variations on the single global variable pattern out in the wild; however, having reviewed quite a few, I felt the prefixing approach applied best to Backbone.

Object literals

Object literals have the advantage of not polluting the global namespace but assist in organizing code and parameters logically. They're beneficial if you wish to create easily readable structures that can be expanded to support deep nesting. Unlike simple global variables, object literals often also take into account tests for the existence of a variable by the same name, which helps reduce the chances of collision.

This example demonstrates two ways you can check to see if a namespace already exists before defining it. I commonly use option 2.

```
/* Doesn't check for existence of myApplication */
var myApplication = {};

/*
Does check for existence. If already defined, we use that instance.
Option 1:    if(!myApplication) myApplication = {};
Option 2:    var myApplication = myApplication || {};
We can then populate our object literal to support models, views, and collections
(or any data, really):
*/

var myApplication = {
    models : {},
    views : {
        pages : {}
    },
    collections : {}
};
```

You can also opt for adding properties directly to the namespace (such as your views, in the following example):

```
var myTodosViews = myTodosViews || {};
myTodosViews.todoView = Backbone.View.extend({});
myTodosViews.todosView = Backbone.View.extend({});
```

The benefit of this pattern is that you're able to easily encapsulate all of your models, views, routers, and so on in a way that clearly separates them and provides a solid foundation for extending your code.

This pattern has a number of benefits. It's often a good idea to decouple the default configuration for your application into a single area that can be easily modified without the need to search through your entire codebase just to alter it. Here's an example of a hypothetical object literal that stores application configuration settings:

```
var myConfig = {
  language: 'english',
  defaults: {
    enableDelegation: true,
    maxTodos: 40
  },
  theme: {
    skin: 'a',
    toolbars: {
      index: 'ui-navigation-toolbar',
      pages: 'ui-custom-toolbar'
    }
  }
}
```

Note that there are really only minor syntactical differences between the object literal pattern and a standard JSON data set. If, for any reason, you wish to use JSON for storing your configurations instead (for example, for simpler storage when sending to the backend), feel free to.

For more on the object literal pattern, I recommend reading Rebecca Murphey's excellent article on the topic (*http://bit.ly/13PCIO6*).

Nested namespacing

An extension of the object literal pattern is nested namespacing. It's another commonly used pattern that offers a lower risk of collision due to the fact that even if a top-level namespace already exists, it's unlikely the same nested children do. For example, Yahoo's YUI uses the nested object namespacing pattern extensively:

```
YAHOO.util.Dom.getElementsByClassName('test');
```

Even DocumentCloud (the creators of Backbone) uses the nested namespacing pattern in its main applications. A sample implementation of nested namespacing with Backbone may look like this:

```
var todoApp =  todoApp || {};

// perform similar check for nested children
todoApp.routers = todoApp.routers || {};
todoApp.model = todoApp.model || {};
todoApp.model.special = todoApp.model.special || {};

// routers
todoApp.routers.Workspace   = Backbone.Router.extend({});
todoApp.routers.TodoSearch = Backbone.Router.extend({});

// models
todoApp.model.Todo   = Backbone.Model.extend({});
todoApp.model.Notes = Backbone.Model.extend({});
```

```
// special models
todoApp.model.special.Admin = Backbone.Model.extend({});
```

This is readable, clearly organized, and a relatively safe way of namespacing your Backbone application. The only real caveat is that it requires your browser's JavaScript engine to first locate the `todoApp` object, then dig down until it gets to the function you're calling. However, developers such as Juriy Zaytsev (kangax) have tested and found the performance differences between single object namespacing and the nested approach to be quite negligible.

What Does DocumentCloud Use?

In case you were wondering, here is the original DocumentCloud (remember those guys who created Backbone?) workspace that uses namespacing in a necessary way. This approach makes sense, as the company's documents (and annotations and document lists) are embedded on third-party news sites.

```
// Provide top-level namespaces for our javascript.
(function() {
  window.dc = {};
  dc.controllers = {};
  dc.model = {};
  dc.app = {};
  dc.ui = {};
})();
```

As you can see, DocumentCloud opts for declaring a top-level namespace on the `window` called `dc`, a short-form name of the app, followed by nested namespaces for the controllers, models, UI, and other pieces of the application.

Recommendation

Of the preceding namespace patterns, the option that I prefer when writing Backbone applications is nested object namespacing with the object literal pattern.

Single global variables may work fine for applications that are relatively trivial. However, larger codebases requiring both namespaces and deep subnamespaces require a succinct solution that's both readable and scalable. I feel this pattern achieves both of these objectives and is a good choice for most Backbone development.

Backbone Dependency Details

The following sections provide insight into how Backbone uses jQuery/Zepto and Underscore.js.

DOM Manipulation

Although most developers won't need it, Backbone does support setting a custom DOM library to be used instead of these options. From the source:

```
// For Backbone's purposes, jQuery, Zepto, Ender, or My Library (kidding) owns
// the `$` variable.
 Backbone.$ = root.jQuery || root.Zepto || root.ender || root.$;
```

So, setting `Backbone.$ = myLibrary;` will allow you to use any custom DOM-manipulation library in place of the jQuery default.

Utilities

Underscore.js is heavily used in Backbone behind the scenes for everything from object extension to event binding. As the entire library is generally included, we get free access to a number of useful utilities we can use on collections, such as filtering `_.filter()`, sorting `_.sortBy()`, mapping `_.map()`, and so on.

From the source:

```
// Underscore methods that we want to implement on the Collection.
// 90% of the core usefulness of Backbone Collections is actually implemented
// right here:
var methods = ['forEach', 'each', 'map', 'collect', 'reduce', 'foldl',
'inject', 'reduceRight', 'foldr', 'find', 'detect', 'filter', 'select',
'reject', 'every', 'all', 'some', 'any', 'include', 'contains', 'invoke',
'max', 'min', 'toArray', 'size', 'first', 'head', 'take', 'initial', 'rest',
'tail', 'drop', 'last', 'without', 'indexOf', 'shuffle', 'lastIndexOf',
'isEmpty', 'chain'];

// Mix in each Underscore method as a proxy to `Collection#models`.
_.each(methods, function(method) {
    Collection.prototype[method] = function() {
        var args = slice.call(arguments);
        args.unshift(this.models);
        return _[method].apply(_, args);
    };
});
```

However, for a complete linked list of methods supported, see the official documentation (*http://bit.ly/13PCNkN*).

RESTful Persistence

We can sync models and collections in Backbone with the server using the `fetch`, `save`, and `destroy` methods. All of these methods delegate back to the `Backbone.sync` function, which actually wraps jQuery/Zepto's `$.ajax` function, calling GET, POST, and DELETE for the respective persistence methods on Backbone models.

From the source for *Backbone.sync*:

```
var methodMap = {
  'create': 'POST',
  'update': 'PUT',
  'patch':  'PATCH',
  'delete': 'DELETE',
  'read':   'GET'
};

Backbone.sync = function(method, model, options) {
    var type = methodMap[method];

    // ... Followed by lots of Backbone.js configuration, then..

    // Make the request, allowing the user to override any Ajax options.
    var xhr = options.xhr = Backbone.ajax(_.extend(params, options));
    model.trigger('request', model, xhr, options);
    return xhr;
```

Routing

Calls to `Backbone.History.start` rely on jQuery/Zepto binding `popState` or hash change event listeners back to the window object.

From the source for `Backbone.history.start`:

```
// Depending on whether we're using pushState or hashes, and whether
// 'onhashchange' is supported, determine how we check the URL state.
if (this._hasPushState) {
    Backbone.$(window)
        .on('popstate', this.checkUrl);
} else if (this._wantsHashChange && ('onhashchange' in window) && !oldIE) {
    Backbone.$(window)
        .on('hashchange', this.checkUrl);
} else if (this._wantsHashChange) {
    this._checkUrlInterval = setInterval(this.checkUrl, this.interval);
}
...
```

`Backbone.History.stop` similarly uses your DOM manipulation library to unbind these event listeners.

Backbone Versus Other Libraries and Frameworks

Backbone is just one of many different solutions available for structuring your application, and we're by no means advocating it as the be-all and end-all. It's served the contributors to this book well in building many simple and complex web applications, and I hope that it can serve you equally well. The answer to the question "Is Backbone better than X?" generally has a lot more to do with what kind of application you're building.

AngularJS and Ember.js are examples of powerful alternatives but differ from Backbone in that they are more opinionated. For some projects, this can be useful; for others, perhaps not. The important thing to remember is that there is no library or framework that's going to be the best solution for every use case, so it's important to learn about the tools at your disposal and decide which one is best on a project-by-project basis.

Choose the right tool for the right job. This is why I recommend spending some time doing a little due diligence. Consider productivity, ease of use, testability, community, and documentation. If you're looking for more concrete comparisons between frameworks, read:

- "Journey Through the JavaScript MVC Jungle" (*http://bit.ly/ZC3eL4*)
- "Rich JavaScript Applications—The Seven Frameworks" (*http://bit.ly/18v52pw*)

The authors behind Backbone.js, AngularJS, and Ember have also discussed some of the strengths and weaknesses of their solutions on Quora, StackOverflow, and so on:

- Jeremy Ashkenas on why Backbone (*http://bit.ly/ZC3gmm*)
- Tom Dale on Ember.js versus AngularJS (*http://b.qr.ae/10uU1Q7*)
- Brian Ford and Jeremy Ashkenas on Backbone versus Angular (discussion) (*http://bit.ly/162VGVD*)

The solution you opt for may need to support building nontrivial features and could end up being used to maintain the app for years to come, so think about things like:

What is the library/framework really capable of?
Spend time reviewing both the source code of the framework and official list of features to see how well they fit with your requirements. There will be projects that may require modifying or extending the underlying source, so make sure that if this might be the case, you've performed due diligence on the code. Has the framework been proven in production? Have developers actually built and deployed large applications with it that are publicly accessible? Backbone has a strong portfolio of these (SoundCloud, LinkedIn, Walmart), but not all frameworks do. Ember is used in a number of large apps, including the new version of ZenDesk. AngularJS has been used to build the YouTube app for PS3, among other places. It's not only important to know that a framework works in production, but also to be able to look at real-world code and be inspired by what can be built with it.

Is the framework mature?
I generally recommend that developers don't simply pick one and go with it. New projects often come with a lot of buzz surrounding their releases, but remember to

take care when selecting them for use on a production-level app. You don't want to risk the project being canned, going through major periods of refactoring, or other breaking changes that tend to be more carefully planned out when a framework is mature. Mature projects also tend to have more detailed documentation available, either as a part of their official or community-driven docs.

Is the framework flexible or opinionated?

Know what flavor you're after, because there are plenty of frameworks available that provide one or the other. Opinionated frameworks lock you into doing things in a specific way (theirs). By design they are limiting, but place less emphasis on developers having to figure out how things should work on their own. Have you really played with the framework?

Write a small application without using frameworks and then attempt to refactor your code with a framework to confirm whether it's easy to work with or not. As much as researching and reading up on code will influence your decision, it's equally important to write actual code using the framework to make sure you're comfortable with the concepts it enforces.

Does the framework have a comprehensive set of documentation?

Although demo applications can be useful for reference, you'll almost always find yourself consulting the official framework docs to find out what its API supports, how common tasks or components can be created with it, and what the gotchas worth noting are. Any framework worth its salt should have a detailed set of documentation that will help guide developers using it. Without this, you can find yourself heavily relying on IRC channels, groups, and self-discovery, which can be fine, but are often overly time-consuming when compared to a great set of docs provided upfront.

What is the total size of the framework, factoring in minification, gzipping, and any modular building that it supports?

What dependencies does the framework have? Frameworks tend to list only the total file size of the base library itself, not the sizes of the library's dependencies. This can mean the difference between opting for a library that initially looks quite small, but could be relatively large if it, say, depends on jQuery and other libraries.

Have you reviewed the community around the framework?

Is there an active community of project contributors and users who would be able to assist if you run into issues? Have enough developers been using the framework that there are existing reference applications, tutorials, and maybe even screencasts that you can use to learn more about it?

Resources

Books and Courses

- *Prosthetics and Orthotics* (*https://leanpub.com/building-backbone-plugins*)
- PeepCode: Backbone.js Basics (*https://peepcode.com/products/backbone-js*)
- Prosthetics and Orthotics—a recommended follow-up to this title (*https://lean pub.com/building-backbone-plugins*)
- *CodeSchool: Anatomy of Backbone* (*http://www.codeschool.com/courses/anatomy-of-backbonejs*)
- *Recipes with Backbone* (*http://recipeswithbackbone.com/*)
- *Backbone Patterns* (*http://ricostacruz.com/backbone-patterns/*)
- *Backbone on Rails* (*https://learn.thoughtbot.com/products/1-backbone-js-on-rails*)
- *Derick Bailey's Resources for Learning Backbone* (*http://lostechies.com/derickbailey*)
- *Learn Backbone.js Completely* (*http://javascriptissexy.com/learn-backbone-js-completely/*)
- *Backbone.js on Rails* (*https://learn.thoughtbot.com/products/1-backbone-js-on-rails*)

Extensions/Libraries

- MarionetteJS (*http://marionettejs.com/*)
- Backbone Layout Manager (*http://bit.ly/14MJw3n*)
- AuraJS (*http://bit.ly/13Wzr3k*)
- Thorax (*http://thoraxjs.org*)

- Lumbar (*http://bit.ly/13sFBUA*)
- Backbone Boilerplate (*http://bit.ly/YCoQs5*)
- Backbone Forms (*https://github.com/powmedia/backbone-forms*)
- Backbone-Nested (*http://afeld.github.com/backbone-nested/*)
- Backbone.Validation (*http://github.com/thedersen/backbone.validation*)
- Backbone.Offline (*https://github.com/Ask11/backbone.offline*)
- Backbone-relational (*https://github.com/PaulUithol/Backbone-relational*)
- Backgrid (*https://github.com/wyuenho/backgrid*)
- Backbone.ModelBinder (*http://bit.ly/14MJp7S*)
- Backbone Relational—for model relationships (*http://bit.ly/15FQOVY*)
- Backbone CouchDB (*http://bit.ly/YLix04*)
- Backbone.Validation—HTML5-inspired validations (*http://bit.ly/12P0JCu*)

Index

We'd like to hear your suggestions for improving our indexes. Send email to index@oreilly.com.

Todo List app (example), 88
Underscore functions for, 51
MVC, MVP, and Backbone.js, 326–328
simple JavaScript implementation of, 319–324
Smalltalk-80 MVC, 10
views in Backbone, 35–42
when to use JavaScript MV* framework, 3
MVP (Model-View-Presenter), 324
choosing between MVC and, 325
models, views, and presenters, 325
MVC, MVP, and Backbone.js, 326–328

N

name mapping, 197
namespaces
module scripts and, 179
namespacing, 328–332
defined, 328
DocumentCloud's use of, 332
nested, 331
object literals, 330
recommendation for, 332
single global variable, 329
navigate( ) method, routers, 65
navigation
jQuery Mobile, 243
jQuery Mobile delegating navigation to Backbone, 248
Netflix API
clientPager paginating results returned from, 214
requestPager requesting paginated results from, 210
NewsBlur, 316
noConflict mode for Backbone, 168
Node.js
installing, 106
lightweight web server, 226
using to create REST server, 106
using to handle pushState, 205
notDeepEqual( ) assertion, 297
notEqual( ) assertion, 296
notEqual( ) function, 293
notStrictEqual( ) assertion, 296
npm (node package manager)
installing, 106

O

object literals, 330
Observer pattern, 327
off method, 57
Olson, Lukas, 171
omit function
using with models in Backbone collections, 51
on( ) method, 56–59
on( ) method as event aggregator, 176
once( ) method
Backbone events, 46
online code editors, 28
OuterView object, 155
outside-in and pull-based (BDD), 266
overridden methods, calling, 169

P

pages in jQuery Mobile, 242
pagination, 207–223
Backbone.Paginator, 209
Backbone.Paginator.clientPager, 214–223
Backbone.Paginator.requestPager, 210–214
types encountered with client-side data, 208
pairs( ) function
using with models in Backbone collections, 52
parse( ) function, Backbone models, 119
passive views, 325
paths, custom, for RequireJS, 185
pattern language, semantics, 177
performance
jQuery Mobile, 258
PHP
Zend framework, 12
pick( ) function
using with models in Backbone collections, 51
pluck( ) function
using with collections, 50
plug-ins
Backbone plug-ins available from Bower package manager, 238
including in boilerplate module code, 235
POST requests
POST route for web server, 111
updating POST after adding keywords schema, 115

About the Author

Addy Osmani, a Developer Programs Engineer on the Chrome team at Google, has a passion for JavaScript application architecture. He's an engineer on the Yeoman team, has created popular projects like TodoMVC, and contributed to other open source projects such as Modernizr and jQuery. A prolific blogger (*http://addyosmani.com/blog*), Addy's articles are frequently featured in *JavaScript Weekly*, *Smashing Magazine*, and many other publications.

Colophon

The animal on the cover of *Developing Backbone.js Applications* is an Australasian snapper (*Pagrus auratus*), which is primarily found off the coast of Indonesia, China, the Philippines, Taiwan, New Zealand, Australia, and Japan. This fish goes by many names, depending on the region in which it's found, but it is a prized eating fish everywhere.

Australasian snapper spawn inshore and live in rocky areas and reefs. During spawning, they turn a metallic green, an indicator of highly concentrated acid building up in their scales. Their growth patterns vary based on region, but they can live up to 40 years.

The cover image is from Meyers Klein Lexicon. The cover font is Adobe ITC Garamond. The text font is Adobe Minion Pro; the heading font is Adobe Myriad Condensed; and the code font is Dalton Maag's Ubuntu Mono.

Have it your way.

Get even more for your money.